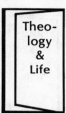

Theo-
logy
&
Life

THEOLOGY AND LIFE SERIES

Volume 5

The Bishop of Rome

J. M. R. Tillard, O.P.

Translated by John de Satgé

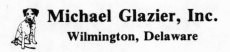
Michael Glazier, Inc.
Wilmington, Delaware

English translation of *L'Évêque de Rome* (©Éditions du Cerf 1982) first published in the United States of America by:

Michael Glazier, Inc.
1723 Delaware Avenue
Wilmington, Delaware 19806

English translation ©The Society for Promoting Christian Knowledge, London, England 1983.

ISBN: 0-89453-298-7
LC: 83-81507

Printed in the United States of America

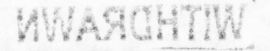

*Dedicated
to the Memory of
Paul VI*

Contents

Contents

Abbreviations

AAS	*Acta Apostolicae Sedis*
ACW	*Ancient Christian Writers*, Westminster (Maryland) and London
CD	*Christus Dominus*. Decree on the Pastoral Office of Bishops in the Church, Vatican II
CSEL	*Corpus Scriptorum Ecclesiasticorum Latinorum*, Vienna
DACL	*Dictionnaire d'archéologie chrétienne et de liturgie*, Paris
DC	*Documentation Catholique*, Paris
DS	*Denzinger-Schönmetzer*, Enchiridion Symbolorum, Freiburg
DTC	*Dictionnaire de théologie catholique*
ETL	*Ephemerides Theologicae Lovaniensis*, Louvain
JBL	*Journal of Biblical Literature*, Boston
JTS	*Journal of Theological Studies*, Oxford
LCC	*Library of Christian Classics*, London
LCD	*Lutherans and Catholics in Dialogue*, Minneapolis
LG	*Lumen Gentium*, Dogmatic Constitution on the Church, Vatican II
LTK	*Lexikon für Theologie und Kirche*, Freiburg
NRT	*Nouvelle Revue Théologique*, Louvain
NTS	*New Testament Studies*, Cambridge
PG	*Patrologia Graeca* (J. P. Migne), Paris
PL	*Patrologia Latina* (J. P. Migne), Paris
POC	*Proche-Orient Chrétien*, Beirut
RHE	*Revue d'Histoire écclesiastique*, Louvain
RSPT	*Revue des Sciences philosophiques et théologiques*, Paris
RSR	*Recherches de Science religieuse*, Paris
RT	*Revue Thomiste*, Paris–Toulouse
RTL	*Revue théologique de Louvain*, Ottignies-Louvain-le-Neuve
SC	*Sources Chrétiennes* series of texts, Paris
TWNT	*Theologisches Wörterbuch zum Neuen Testament*, Stuttgart
Mansi	J. Mansi, *Sacrorum conciliorum nova et amplissima collectio*, Arnhem and Leipzig, Welter 1927

Acknowledgements

Extracts from *Vatican II: Conciliar and Post-Conciliar Documents*, edited by Austin Flannery (1975), are reprinted by permission of Dominican Publications, Dublin, and Costello Publishing, New York.

Extracts from *Papal Primacy and the Universal Church (Lutherans and Catholics in Dialogue V)*, edited by Paul C. Empie and T. Austin Murphy, copyright 1974, are reprinted by permission of Augsburg Publishing House.

Extracts from essays by Stylianos Harkianos, originally published in *Concilium* 64 (1971), and by Hilaire Marot, originally published in *Concilium* 7 (1965), are reprinted by permission of T. & T. Clark.

Extracts from translations of ancient texts by S. L. Greenslade and C. C. Richardson, first published in the *Library of Christian Classics* Vols. I and V, are reprinted by permission of SCM Press.

The extract from *Peter in the New Testament*, edited by Raymond E. Brown, Karl P. Donfried and John Reumann (1974), is reprinted by permission of Geoffrey Chapman.

The extract from the declaration *Mysterium Ecclesiae* (1973) is from a translation by the National Catholic News Service, USA.

TRANSLATOR'S NOTE

My thanks are due to several friends who kindly helped with the translation or by establishing English references, notably Canon Roger Greenacre, Dom Alberic Stacpoole OSB, Canon Christopher Hill, the Reverend Geoffrey and Mrs Jill Pinnock and the Reverend Dr John McHugh; also to my daughter Judith who read the first, very rough, draft.

I have inserted a small number of explanatory notes in the text. These occur within parentheses and are followed by the abbreviation E.Tr.

JOHN DE SATGÉ

Preface

It has become difficult to write big books. Far from lightening the author's task, this fact has made it heavier. To treat the subject of the present work at proper depth would have needed twice the number of pages. We have had therefore to prune, to reduce, to summarize - to the point indeed where, on reading it through, we wonder whether we have allowed even the basic essentials to remain. Would it not have been well to keep in a long chapter on the nature of *episkope* in the Church and its ordination as a witness to the true nature of the Christian community? Have we perhaps gone too far in limiting historical evidence, especially in the matter of appeals to Rome? Does it not lack a well-documented account of the connection between the synodality of the churches and collegiality? Have we not left out too many bibliographical references which would have helped serious consideration?

We hope that these pages, born of long involvement in ecumenical work - Faith and Constitution, Anglican-Roman Catholic International Commission (ARCIC), Orthodox-Catholic Commission, Dialogue between Disciples of Christ and the Roman Catholic Church - and the fruit of many years teaching in the Faculty of Theology of the Dominican College of Ottawa, will nevertheless answer our purpose. That is in all humility to lay the foundations of that ecclesiology of communion which the present situation between the Churches calls for. We started with our book *Devant Dieu et pour le monde, le projet des religieux*, an examination of the part played by holiness in the life of the people of God. We hope to continue it in a book on the Eucharist now being completed. We here offer our reflections on *The Bishop of Rome* for the reason that, as the first chapter explains, several official ecumenical commissions have pronounced on the subject in a way which calls for deeper dogmatic study.

Other considerations also lend urgency to this book. A sense of unease is growing at the very heart of the Catholic community. The structures of collegiality and ministerial subsidiarity have not yet been set up with the clarity required by the fundamental insights of *Lumen Gentium*. Neither episcopal conferences nor the synods periodically meeting in Rome have yet acquired a status to match the Council's assertion about them. The situation is fluctuating and uncertain, and this at a time when the Churches and great ecclesial bodies separated from the see of Rome believe that the Spirit is impelling them towards restored communion. But these people do not wish to forgo that which connects them with deep seams in the Great Tradition of the undivided Church. In the words of one of the Anglican theologians most open to union with Rome, they would like a guarantee that 'the most positive fruits in the development of (their) Church, won at the price of much suffering and in the sincere intention of faithfulness to Jesus Christ, should not be devoured by centralism'. Outstanding among those fruits is respect for the laity and its role in the life of the Christian community, with recognition of the full responsibility of those ministers whom the Spirit himself has set at the head of the communities. It is just those fruits which are put at risk by the uncomfortable situation which has followed the euphoric years immediately after Vatican II.

Are we right in thinking, in spite of assertions that have been little tested, that the question of authority remains the great obstacle to unity? It would be a serious matter to avoid it by refusing to allow ourselves to be interrogated in depth by the questions which other people raise; and it would be specious to object, as has been done in circles where we have been surprised to hear it, that in attacking this problem we risk 'upsetting to no good purpose the delicate stability gained since Vatican II'. Do we or do we not allow the Spirit to lead us towards total transparency to the will of Christ?

If this book, limited as it is by the need for brevity, helps us to rethink this question in the light of the great rediscovery of all Christians around the Lord's Table, we shall have achieved our end.

J. M. R. TILLARD OP

1
The Pope . . .
More than a Pope?

The Pope...
More than a Pope?

The theological problem of the papacy stands out today as one of the most complex chapters in the doctrine of the Church. The threads of the skein are tangled. But it has become urgent to sort the matter out calmly and lucidly. The situation between the Churches demands it. In fact the question has a freshly sharpened edge both at the level of the Catholic Church, which other Churches call the Roman Catholic Church from its particular connection with the see of Rome, and at the ecumenical level.

A new ecumenical setting

The task is far from easy, as a few preliminary points will show. It is not possible nowadays to say what a pope is, without first distinguishing between several points of view. We have to make a distinction between the image of the papacy conveyed by the Great Tradition as a whole and that which the Catholic Church recognizes since Vatican II as the only one fully conformed to Christ's intention; between the way in which theologians conceive of exercising the primacy and that in which popular opinion understands it; between the function itself and the manner in which such and such a pope carries it out in his particular circumstances; between the pope exercising his ministry for the Catholic community as it has been since the schisms of East and West and the bishop of Rome exercising his 'primacy' at the heart of the restored communion of the Churches for which the Ecumenical Movement hopes and prepares. These understandings intersect, covering each other like tiles on a roof without overlapping completely. How, then, shall we gain a clear view?

Ecumenical research is currently making the matter even more complex, though in a different way from that suggested by a phrase such as 'the ecumenical dimensions of the Roman problem'. Dialogue between heads of Churches (Paul VI, Ramsey, Athenagoras) and between the officially appointed commissions have led groups outside the (Roman) Catholic Church to qualify that opposition to the papacy which their traditions had maintained since the breach with Rome, and which had in many cases occasioned the breach. The aggressiveness is dying down. This is indeed a considerable change for it amounts to a new theological factor which must be taken into account. Here are churches or ecclesial groupings actually coming to regard some exercise of primacy by the Roman see as 'normal', 'desirable', 'useful', or 'to some degree required'.

It is, of course, true that primacy conceived in these terms does not entirely agree with the way in which Rome understands it, especially since 1870. Should we then conclude that these wishes are bound to be futile? To do so would be to fail to take seriously the work of the Spirit of God beyond the limits of the Catholic Church. In that case a new question arises with urgent demands on the Catholic conscience: how far does the Second Vatican Council's fresh reading of the 1870 Definition allow us to welcome 'suggestions' from the other churches as a positive questioning to which the Spirit of Christ is no stranger? Should not the manner in which other churches 'receive' the definition of Vatican I, finalized by the Catholic Church alone, be taken into account, especially at a time when there is already an explicit will to find the way back to 'communion'? Does not the fact of this will towards unity create an entirely new condition of 'reception' of which ecclesiology must from now on take account? The undivided Church knew only of 'reception' by churches that wished to remain within the unity; perhaps now, after centuries of disunity, we should think in terms also of 'reception' by churches reaching out towards the reconstruction of unity. We have not yet got any theological assessment of the dogmatic implications of the *votum unitatis*, the will to, desire for and intention of unity.[1]

We already know the 'desires' of some of these Churches. In the case of the Orthodox Churches, there is as yet no report prepared by an officially authorized commission; the dialogue wanted by Paul VI began only in May–June 1980 after John Paul II's visit to Patriarch Demetrios. But in their exchange of letters and by their unequivocal signs of fellowship, Paul VI and Patriarch Athenagoras created a 'dialogue of charity' from which certain truths of great importance emerged.[2] Since more was at stake than a simple question of relationships between Rome and Constantinople, we must remind ourselves of their work.

To grasp the range of the new dogmatic climate brought in by Paul VI and Athenagoras, we need only remember the views of many Orthodox theologians on the subject. A particularly well informed expert had no hesitation in writing, in 1971,

. . . there are very many Orthodox, even among those best disposed towards the Catholic Church, who take the two definitions of 1870 as heresy in the strong sense: that is, as serious innovation in a matter of faith, contrary to Revelation and in particular contrary to the consensus of the Fathers. Catholic apologetic across the centuries has done its best to show that the definitions of Vatican I were in line with the teachings of Tradition. The Greek Fathers in particular were scrutinized closely for support. It must in honesty be recognized that supporting passages were weak and few. In any case they did not prove convincing to those for whom they were meant.[3]

This opinion is endorsed by an Orthodox theologian, less radical perhaps in his overall view but very definite in his estimate of Vatican I:

The question of whether the Roman primacy, formulated as it was at the First Vatican Council and also, unfortunately, at the Second, can have a place at all in . . . (Orthodox ecclesiology) . . . must be answered with an unqualified negative. This does not, however, mean rejecting the idea of a primacy within Orthodoxy. On the contrary, recognizing the ideas of synodality and collegiality leads directly towards recognizing one bishop as the first among the bishops, that is, to attribute the primacy to him; never, however, in the sense of 'supreme pontiff' but always as 'first among equals' . . . When the bishop of Rome understood his primacy in the sense of *primus inter pares*, he had the possibility of expressing a decisive opinion in questions of concern to the whole Church and of being respected by all; he was thus able to provide effectively a service essential to the whole Church. But as soon as he started to understand his own episcopal power as fundamentally different from the power of all other bishops, he forfeited the possibility of being in communion with Orthodoxy . . . When the pope bases his power on the Petrine succession and not on the common apostolic and episcopal succession, he cuts himself off not only from the communion of bishops but also from that of the whole Church . . . It is therefore not for constitutional and canonical reasons only that the synodical structure of the Church is so dear to the Orthodox; profoundly soteriological factors are involved. Both kinds of reason, always inter-related in Orthodox thought, combine to exclude categorically the Roman primacy of jurisdiction and infallibility.[4]

If, then, that section of the churches where, in the past, the Church of God expanded so rapidly and formulated its doctrine refuses now to accept this teaching, that refusal is not total. It concerns one way of exercising the primacy and the justification for it in Catholic tradition. The distinction is vital. And the *Tomos Agapes*, to give the title under which the correspondence between Paul VI and Athenagoras was published, throws fresh light on this distinction. The refusal is to be seen less as a covert locking of the door than of an opening towards a passionately desired communion.

It was in this spirit that Patriarch Athenagoras wrote to Paul VI on his election (via Metropolitan Maximos of Sardis) recalling that the Church of Rome is a 'sister Church', and is so 'in order to promote the spirit of unity in the Christian world and for the glory of the Name of our Lord Jesus Christ'.[5] Paul VI replied in a handwritten letter of great depth, and from that point an exchange of letters was to grow in number between Rome and Constantinople, now recognized explicitly as sister Churches.[6] A passage from the allocution to Paul VI delivered by Athenagoras's envoy on 16 February 1965 gives an excellent example of the tone adopted by Constantinople:

In due ecclesiastical form we first present ourselves to Your Holiness, the sovereign Bishop of the Old Rome, and we greet you

6

with a kiss in the Lord from your Eastern brother, Bishop of Constantinople, the New Rome. We have the honour to give you his patriarchal and fraternal letters, of which by the spoken word we have already become the interpreter. Your most blessed Holiness is the object of the most heartfelt brotherly sentiments from our most holy Patriarch, who prays for you fervently to the Lord.[7]

Later, when he met Paul VI at his palace, the Phanar, on 25 July 1967, the Patriarch of Constantinople replying to the Pope's address[8] did not hesitate to speak of 'the kiss of Old Rome bestowed on her younger sister' and of 'Peter's most holy successor'.[9] And in Rome, on 26 October 1967, he went so far as to declare that his brother, the bishop of Rome, is

> the bearer of apostolic grace and the successor to a shining company of holy and wise men who have shed lustre on this see which, by honour and rank, stands first in the living body of Christian churches dispersed throughout the world; and whose holiness, wisdom and valiant fight for the common faith of the undivided Church are a permanent asset and treasure for the entire Christian world.[10]

Later still, on 27 March 1971, he was to see in him 'the elder brother', 'the herald (*kerux*) and the eminent architect of the peace, the love and the unity of Christians and of the human race created in the image of God' within the Church militant.[11]

The wording of documents arising from such circumstances is not left to chance. It is true that Athenagoras did not speak in such a way as necessarily to commit all the Orthodox Churches, for the authority of an Oecumenical Patriarch does not include that right. But declarations of the kind we have cited carry special weight when they come from his mouth. Taken with the *Tomos Agapes* as a whole, they show a consistent line: whatever may be said about the assertions of Vatican I and their endorsement by Vatican II, and so about the Roman *doctrine* of the primacy, a certain praxis is still to be honoured and recognized today, for it perpetuates the role of the Roman see at the great moments of the undivided Church. Things are being said and done to show that, in spite of the rupture, the see of ancient Rome is still held to be 'the first by honour and rank in the living body of Christian churches dispersed throughout the world'.

The West itself has been split since the Reformation. But even here, churches meeting in an ecumenical spirit have been forced to reconsider from a new standpoint the predominant view, often more aggressive than reasoned, that the pope is a type of the Antichrist[12] and his primacy an unacceptable and usurped authority. Bilateral commissions officially representing their Churches have pursued the matter with results that have exceeded all hopes. Two examples must suffice: the joint declaration of the Lutheran-Roman Catholic Dialogue in the USA; and the Anglican-Roman Catholic International Commission (ARCIC) with its agreements made at Venice and later taken further at Windsor.

The Lutheran-Catholic declaration of 5 March 1974 is long and perhaps too academic, but it has the undeniable merit of expressing itself in plain language.[13] It opens by declaring:

> In these sessions we have . . . found common ground. There is a growing awareness among Lutherans of the necessity of a specific Ministry to serve the church's unity and universal mission, while Catholics increasingly see the need for a more nuanced understanding of the role of the papacy within the universal church. Lutherans and Catholics can now begin to envision possibilities of concord, and to hope for solutions to problems that have previously seemed insoluble. (Introd.)

It adds:

> The Reformers did not totally reject all aspects of the papal expression of the Petrine functions, but only what they regarded as its abuses. They hoped for a reform of the papacy precisely in order to preserve the unity of the church (No. 5).

But the situation nowadays is quite different:

> . . . the contemporary understanding of the New Testament and our knowledge of the processes at work in the history of the Church make possible a fresh approach to the structure and operations of the papacy. There is increasing agreement that the centralization of the Petrine function in a single person or office

8

results from a long process of development. Reflecting the many pressures of the centuries and the complexities of a worldwide church, the papal office can be seen both as a response to the guidance of the Spirit in the Christian community, and also as an institution which, in its human dimensions, is tarnished by frailty and even unfaithfulness. The Catholic members of this consultation see the institution of the papacy as developing from New Testament roots under the guidance of the Spirit. Without denying that God could have ordered the church differently, they believe that the papal form of the unifying is, in fact, God's gracious gift to his people. Lutheran theologians, although in the past chiefly critical of the structure and functioning of the papacy, can now recognize many of its positive contributions to the life of the church. Both groups can acknowledge that as the forms of the papacy have been adapted to changing historical settings in the past, it is possible that they will be modified to meet the needs of the church in the future more effectively (No. 21).

What modifications do they have in mind?

Perhaps this might involve a primacy in which the pope's service to unity in relation to the Lutheran Churches would be more pastoral than juridical. The one thing necessary, from the Lutheran point of view, is that the papal primacy be so structured that it clearly serve the gospel and the unity of the church of Christ, and that its exercise of power not subvert Christian freedom (No. 28).[14]

It comes as no surprise when this declaration ends by making specific proposals. The intention is to work towards joint recognition of a ministry of unity described as 'the Petrine function';

. . . Therefore we ask the Lutheran churches:
- if they are prepared to affirm with us that papal primacy, renewed in the light of the gospel, need not be a barrier to reconciliation;

- if they are able to acknowledge not only the legitimacy of the papal ministry in the service of the Roman Catholic communion but even the possibility and desirability of the papal Ministry, renewed under the gospel and committed to Christian freedom, in a larger communion which would include the Lutheran churches;

- if they are willing to open discussion regarding the concrete implications of such a primacy to them.

. . . Likewise we ask the Roman Catholic Church:

- if it is willing to open discussions on possible structures for reconciliation which would protect the legitimate traditions of the Lutheran communities and respect their spiritual heritage;

- if it is prepared to envisage the possibility of a reconciliation which would recognize the self-government of Lutheran Churches within a communion;

- if, in the expectation of a foreseeable reconciliation, it is ready to acknowledge the Lutheran Churches represented in our dialogue as sister churches which are already entitled to some measure of ecclesiastical communion (Nos. 32-3).

In explaining their position, Lutheran members of the Commission went so far as to say that in their eyes the hoped-for renewal of the papacy was for the good of their own churches. Lutheran teaching on the Church and the ministry constrained them to work towards it, they added. They considered it, moreover, one of the urgent needs of the day.[15]

When in 1980 the same Commission completed its reflections on the Petrine function by publishing a joint declaration on infallibility, its view remained unmodified:

For Lutherans, the developments of the last two decades have given a new outlook on the dogma of papal infallibility. Historical and linguistic studies on the meaning of the dogma, the emphasis since Vatican II on the collegial relationship of the pope and the bishops in theology and practice and the initiation of new styles of papal leadership by Pope John and Pope Paul can help Lutherans see that the pope is not an absolute monarch. The ministry of the bishop of Rome should be seen as a service under the authority of the Word of God. The doctrine of infallibility is an expression of confidence that the Spirit of God abides in his Church and guides it in the truth. This understanding should allay Lutheran fears that papal infallibility is a usurpation of the sovereign authority of Christ, and make it clear that this dogma is not the central doctrine of the Catholic Church and that it does not displace Christ from his redemptive and mediatorial role (No. 53).

10

More than that,

> Our Catholic partners have stimulated us to consider how vital it is
> for the Churches to speak, when occasion demands, with one voice
> in the world and how a universal teaching office such as that of the
> pope could exercise a Ministry of unity which is liberating and
> empowering rather than restrictive or repressive.[16]

There is no longer any question of the pope as the Antichrist![17]
The reference to the praxis of John XXIII and Paul VI, already
encountered in the *Tomos Agapes*, is significant. The doctrinal
positions of the Catholic tradition are judged and tested by the
manner in which those who have received the office implement
the Petrine ministry. A reading of the documents as a whole
shows clearly how the Lutherans have come to accept the
desirability[18] of the pope of Rome's ministry because they see
the need for the service to unity which he can bring. The service
to unity is thus not taken as one among the consequences of the
Roman primacy; it is the justification for that office. The
manner in which the primacy is exercised has therefore become
a decisive factor.

We turn now to the Anglican–Roman Catholic International
Commission. The Venice agreement of 1976, completed by its
sequel at Windsor in 1981, was cast in a very different style. A
sober document produced after six years of research, its conclusions are limited to those matters which in the past had
proved divisive. Other issues are not mentioned. Against that
background the significance of the passages following will be
seen:

> Although primacy and conciliarity are complementary elements of
> *episkope*, it has often happened that one has been emphasized at
> the expense of the other, even to the point of serious imbalance.
> When Churches have been separated from one another, this danger
> has been increased. The *koinonia* of the Churches requires that a
> power balance be preserved between the two, with the responsible
> participation of the whole people of God.
>
> If God's will for the unity in love and truth of the whole Christian
> community is to be fulfilled, this general pattern of the comple-
> mentary primatial and conciliar aspects of *episkope* serving the

11

koinonia of the Churches needs to be realized at the universal level. The only see which makes any claim to universal primacy and which has exercised and still exercises such *episkope* is the see of Rome, the city where Peter and Paul died.

It seems appropriate that, in any future union, a universal primacy such as has been described should be held by that see.

What we have written amounts to a consensus on authority in the Church and, in particular, on the basic principles of primacy. This consensus is of fundamental importance. While it does not wholly resolve all the problems associated with papal primacy, it provides us with a solid base for confronting them. It is when we move from these basic principles to particular claims of papal primacy that problems arise, the gravity of which will be variously judged (Nos. 22-4).

That was in 1976. By September 1981 the Commission had spent five years examining the problems mentioned - Catholic interpretation of the Petrine passages, primacy by divine right, universal immediate jurisdiction and infallibility - and was able to rejoice in the discovery that, though there were different emphases over infallibility, agreement was substantial. Once again, we should note, the primacy was explained as a 'service of unity' on a universal scale. But the history of the two traditions meant that from the start the Commission had to hold this service in tension with the conciliarity of the Churches. The *koinonia* which the Lord willed can only be realized in a manner in all respects consistent with the nature of the Church itself. This will involve the presence both of a universal primacy to ensure cohesion (and that, says the Report, can only come from the Roman see) and by a healthy conciliarity to guarantee the diversity which catholicity requires. If this makes it necessary for the Anglican Churches to recognize the papacy, it will be equally necessary for the Catholic Church to become more explicitly conciliar.

These, briefly sketched, are the 'wishes' of several great church groups who look for re-entry into communion with the (Roman) Catholic Church. They refuse to betray their own tradition while accepting the papacy. They mean, moreover, to keep many of the characteristics acquired since their breach with Rome, especially where those characteristics arose directly from the 'reforms' which their founders deemed necessary for a return to the true gospel. But they do not wish to make these characteristics the ground from which to mount an aggressive attack on all that the Catholic tradition has developed on its own since the separation. Their concern is rather to discover what these developments might contribute, within a reunited Church, to an exercise (praxis) of primacy which could satisfy the demands of the gospel. Did not the actions of the Reformers or the disputes of the East embody elements of the truth which in the heat of the day were jettisoned when it would have been better to welcome them?

In any case the circumstances are not the same as they were at the time of the several breaks. In the West especially, developments have been so considerable that a simple return to the situation as it was then is unthinkable. No longer may we divide the Christian world into two blocs, Eastern and Western. The East, itself carrying old, unhealed divisions like those which go back to the Monophysite quarrels as well as later separations such as the Old Believers in Russia, stands facing both the Roman Catholic and the Protestant groups. The worldwide missionary movement and, more recently, the rediscovery by the people of Asia and Africa of their cultural heritage has in any case made it impossible to characterize the Catholic Church as 'Latin'. Cultures as ancient and as rich as those of India and the Far East, for example, totally alien to Western schemes, and those of which the regions of Africa are so markedly becoming aware, should be seed-beds for the embodiment of the Word of God and its expression. Churches there being born are insisting on their own identity. The Catholic Church whose identity is expressed by communion with the see of Rome may no longer be simply equated with the Latin Church. The known impact of different cultures on the quality of social life as a whole shows that this diversification within the Catholic group must set up resonances in the relations between Rome and the other Churches of the Catholic communion. This in turn brings into question the status of episcopal conferences, on which important matter Catholic theology since Vatican II has been quite incoherent.

The Protestant group, for its part, exploded almost immediately into a vast number of different forms and traditions: some of them of great weight, such as the Lutheran, Reformed and Anglican traditions; others of lesser substance, but sometimes pointing up fundamental aspects of the life of faith as with the Methodists, the Disciples of Christ and the Kimbanguists. It is clear that, in the event of ecclesial communion being ecumenically restored, the voices of these groups could not be considered as secondary or as of negligible value. This would be true even if - perhaps especially if - they concern relations with the 'ministry of unity' exercised by the Roman see. One of the great merits of the Anglican-Roman Catholic dialogue is to have affirmed this unequivocally yet eirenically.

A question for the Roman Catholic tradition

What should be the reaction of the (Roman) Catholic Church to the changed attitudes of the Eastern Churches and of many groups deriving from the Reformation? It must be one of joy and thanksgiving in the first place, as we recognize the Spirit of God at work in these developments. But such thanksgiving would be false if it amounted to nothing beyond pious phrases spoken from convention rather than conviction. It should inspire some activity leading towards further communion. By itself it is not enough. If today's situation makes unthinkable any simple return to the state of affairs before the breach, and if the Catholic Church genuinely desires unity, then that Church must realize that she herself is being questioned and being called upon if necessary to modify some of her attitudes. Let it be said at once that this is not a matter of bestowing paternalistically some margin of autonomy upon the other groups, some juridical independence, some liturgical initiative, in return for entering into full communion. The Catholic Church must ask herself whether her own way of understanding the primacy does not need to be reviewed, especially in so far as it has developed in isolation, its balance unchecked by the Eastern tradition or by critical voices insisting on a return to the purity of the gospel.

Two basic dogmatic principles are involved. The first is tied to the phrase in *Lumen Gentium* 8: *subsistit in*. The course of events leading to this choice of words is well known, but their significance has not been properly grasped. At one and the same moment the Catholic community affirms that in her resides the unique Church of God in all that is needed for her fullness – sacramental, institutional and spiritual – and also recognizes that this Church can exist outside her own boundaries, although without that fullness. The grace of God is at work there too. It is therefore important to take with all seriousness what ecclesial groups beyond the Catholic frontiers say when they declare their will to recover universal *koinonia*, especially when the particular wishes of different groups coincide. Why should we not assess intuitions about the Church which originate outside our own frontiers as sympathetically and positively as Vatican II assessed the values of holiness, the sacramental life, respect for the Word and the missionary zeal to be found in the same groups? This is all the more important since, as has already been pointed out, the intuition in question bears especially on the way in which primacy should be exercised within the restored *koinonia*. Those who ask these questions, being led by the Spirit of God in their search for unity, have no intention but the good of the one and only Church of God which subsists in the Catholic community but which exists also at the universal level broken in pieces, and which the Spirit wishes to lead back into complete communion. The Catholic Church, secure in holding from God a particular responsibility which is increasingly recognized by others, should, in the process leading up to this reconciled communion, re-read the declarations of Vatican I and Vatican II in the light of the new situation. But if the Church is to be guaranteed the Spirit's help in this re-reading, she must undertake to heed the voice of those who, like her, and sometimes more painfully, yearn after unity.

Furthermore – and this brings us to the second dogmatic point – the new reading which we are considering is needed in respect of those solemn declarations which the Catholic Church made with the Spirit's guarantee, but which the other ecclesial groups were unable to 'receive'; notably the Eastern Churches whose ecclesial status has never been questioned. Since the Church of God 'subsists' in the Catholic community welded into the communion of the Roman see, the decisions of this body taken in due form are decisions of the Church and must be regarded as such. If that is not the case, *subsistit in* is an empty phrase and Vatican II's discussions of it a farce. All the same they are decisions of the Church *as* she subsists within that state of violence and abnormality which has been hers since the Great Schism between East and West, soon to be followed by the divisions within the West itself. If we take seriously the implications of the ecumenical movement, we are bound to add that the state of 'subsistence' of the Church of God in the Catholic community is a state of expectation. We dare to say, in the strength of that hope which the Spirit brings, that it is a provisional state. The ministry of Paul VI, taking its stand on the work of the Second Vatican Council, showed the extent of the Catholic Church's refusal to come to terms with this 'provisional' state, this condition of waiting.

For the 'provisional' to become 'definitive' in the sense of the great definitions of the undivided Church - Nicaea, Constantinople, Chalcedon - the content of the teaching must be 'received' by the whole body of Churches, in an act which would remake the universal *koinonia*. But this reception will not come about without changes in shades of meaning, in emphasis or balance, changes which themselves belong to the dynamics of this reception. Until this ecumenical seal has been affixed, solemn definitions of general councils of the Catholic Church and of the bishop of Rome will be without definitive ecumenical significance, especially those in which the East has not agreed. In such areas the truth is still in process of declaring itself.

All this shows up clearly the confusion caused by our use of the term 'ecumenical council'. Catholic tradition has followed Robert Bellarmine in taking as ecumenical all those councils received by the Roman see. On that reckoning they number twenty-one. John XXIII, and Paul VI at the start of his occupation of the Roman see, adopted this numbering.[19] It would, however, be more accurate to reserve the title 'ecumenical' for the seven councils of the undivided Church.[20] Besides returning to the Great Tradition, this usage would avoid giving the impression of an irritating ecclesiological self-sufficiency. It has not been possible to speak strictly of ecumenical councils since

Christianity split into two blocs, Eastern and Western, both having origins rooted in the apostolic tradition, both centred on the Eucharist and episcopate – which remained true of much of the post-Reformation West – both grounded in the faith of the Fathers.[21] The drama of the Church divided and torn lies precisely here. Paul VI opened the matter discreetly in his letter for the seventh centenary of the Second Council of Lyons, itself concerned with reconciliation between East and West: 'This Council of Lyons is counted as the sixth of the general synods held in the West.'[22] The Councils of Trent, Vatican I and Vatican II could well be described in similar terms. Although acknowledged by that portion of the Christian world in which the Church of God subsists with everything needed for its fullness, they are not in practice acknowledged by the Church with that fullness. Their decisions are marked by a limit in ecumenical quality.

Proposals or hopes put forward on the grounds of their wish to recover universal *koinonia*, by Christian communities separated from Rome, should therefore stimulate the Catholic Church to ask herself how far the truth of dogmatic definitions guaranteed by the Spirit encloses the whole truth. It is not a question of denying her own doctrinal statements but of setting beside them the positions taken by other partners, especially those who are admitted to be sister churches,[23] who care as much as she does about faithfulness to Christ and his Spirit. Why should she fear a confrontation of this kind, if she believes that the Spirit is at work in the movement impelling Christendom towards unity today and if she is confident also of the same Spirit at work in her own 'infallible judgements'? The irreformability proclaimed by Vatican I imposes no such fear.

Awareness of the abnormal situation of the Church of God by that group in which she subsists in all essentials, that is, by the Catholic community, should thus lead that Church to think no longer only of herself, but to widen her horizons now that it is a question of bringing the Church back to the state of unity which God wishes. It has been noticed[24] how tactfully Paul VI opened up a way ahead in a speech he made to the Secretariat for Christian Unity on 28 April 1967:

The Pope, as we well know, is undoubtedly the gravest obstacle in the path of ecumenism. What shall we say? Should we refer once more to titles which justify our mission? Should we once more attempt to present it in its exact terms such as it is really intended to be – the indispensable principle of truth, charity, and unity? A pastoral mission of guidance, of service and of brotherhood . . .[25]

Those are not the exact terms in which Vatican I, followed by Vatican II, defined the papal function. Yet the controlling insight of the 1870 definition may be found there, in no way compromised. It has to some extent been re-read in the light of Eastern thought such as shines through the *Tomos Agapes.*

A definition of the papacy marked by a particular historical context

One preliminary question with far-reaching consequences must be asked within the Catholic tradition itself before any ecumenical re-reading of the Catholic definition of the primacy becomes possible. Is not the pope in fact 'more than a pope' in ordinary Catholic attitudes? It is a highly sensitive question and it must be tackled dispassionately.

The climate of ultramontane opinion which accompanied and to some extent brought about the definition of pontifical primacy in 1870 has marked the Catholic understanding of the papacy as deeply as if the two were to be identified. Catholic outlook, at the level even of spontaneous reactions from several episcopates, has come to look upon the pope with religious or simply emotional attitudes which sometimes obscure the essential characteristics of the bishop of Rome's function. Vatican II has hardly touched Catholic sentiment at this point. The rank and file thirst for a papacy that will satisfy their taste for 'marvels'. An ancient spring that knows neither theological criticism nor enlightened pastoral care lies hidden in devotion and popular spirituality, waiting for a pretext to break out. When, for instance, the pope was unable to attend a congress at Lourdes on the theme of the Eucharist, interest in the subject declined to the point where the enormous attendance expected – 'a sign which cannot lie of the revival of faith in the sacrament of the bread broken for a new world' it had been called – dwindled disquietingly. That perhaps was 'the sign which cannot lie'! Or again, when the bishops of a region allowed their attention to wander, an official leaflet of Catholic instruction in Canada carried the definition of the pope as 'successor to God'.[26] A slip, perhaps, but another 'sign which cannot lie'. After the pope had visited the Philippines, a lay catechist was asked why the visit was so important to him. 'Because', he told the television camera crew, 'the pope is the person on whose word the whole life of the Church depends.' A clumsy phrase, no doubt, but again, 'a sign which cannot lie'. The present Catholic vision of the papacy magnifies the office. It makes the pope 'more than a pope'.

The pope of whom the Fathers of Vatican I could hardly help thinking possessed, it is true, a personality which lent itself to such excesses. Without descending to the attacks of a prosecuting counsel of dubious taste,[27] we must recognize that Giovanni Maria Mastaï-Ferretti, Pope Pius IX (1846–78), was a very complex person.[28]

He was emotional, his theological studies had been perfunctory, he was always supported more by an intense Marian piety than by any deep grasp of dogmatic issues and he often spoke from the heart without listening to the voices of reason.[29] It was indeed said of Pius IX that he relied above all on the charm which he radiated[30] and the sympathy which his misfortunes brought him to impress a new face upon the papacy. All this took place in a political climate where the rank-and-file Christian people, bewildered, felt 'a need to make immediately visible the presence of God in the midst of their troubles'.[31] For many believers of the time he became a symbol compounded from his winning ways, his obvious and easy piety, his charming gestures,[32] his noble bearing, like a disarmed monarch, and his contact with the pilgrims whom the railway brought to Rome. He seemed to be, as it were, a reliable magnetic pole, 'a refuge at once profoundly human and doggedly faithful' when the Christian ideal was under judgement, a point of stability and hope at the moment when so many civil societies were breaking up. His purpose of 'restoring' Catholic life by grouping round himself 'all the living forces of Catholicism to react against the mounting wave of anti-Christian liberalism'[33] found a spontaneous echo. It is no falsification of history to say that his personality was in such close harmony with the circumstances in which he was working that to many he was the man of the situation, of that particular situation. So deeply was the definition of 1870 marked by this fact that it was 'as much the triumph of a man as of a doctrine; it was the exaltation of the pope at the same time as that of the papacy'.[34] A clear-headed ultramontane declared with some embarrassment: 'The person of Pius IX somehow gives too much strength to the cause of Rome.'[35] The ideal of the papacy was thus defined around the image of a pope 'super-pope', as was the 'devotion to the pope' which developed. The life of the Catholic Church ever since has been deeply disturbed by it.

The personality of Pius IX interacted with ultramontanism to the point of osmosis. Ultramontanism may be defined as the tendency to concentrate all church authority in 'the centre of the Church', which means Rome. Everything should come from the head, that is to say, the pope. This explains why Gallicanism appeared as the symbol of the enemy to be knocked down and such men as Febronius, Eybel, Tamburini and Passaglia, whom Vatican I was to attack, as 'dangerous thinkers'.[36] They made relative not so much the importance of Rome as the absolute quality of her overall control. Wherever the links with the centre are no longer those of strict dependence, 'thought risks being led astray' as it sinks into liberalism. The Church is conceived of as a pyramid where even thought comes down 'from the top'. The encyclical *Quanta Cura* and, above all, the condemnation of eighty propositions in the *Syllabus* may be taken as the ultramontane charter. The ultramontane temper, it is interesting to note, is always marked by fear of intellectual freedom in the Church. Now it provided the cocoon within which the definition of papal primacy could slowly develop. It will thus be enlightening to review briefly some of its most distinguishing characteristics.

All the characteristics of ultramontanism come to the same point, whether they concern the relation of the Church to civil society or her own internal life. It is of first importance to see the pope as the authority which the universe needs to save it from disintegration by the destructive forces assailing it. The views of Joseph de Maistre and De Bonald are well known. J. de Maistre's letter to M. Blacas deserves quotation:

> No public morals or national character without religion, no European religion without Christianity, no Christianity without Catholicism, no Catholicism without the pope, no pope without the supremacy which belongs to him.[37]

Lammenais was to take up the same refrain, but this time as a way of salvation for liberalism itself, now vitiated by anarchy: 'Without pope no Church; without Church no Christianity; without Christianity no society; so that the life of European nations has its source, its only source, in the power of the pontiff.'[38] Since the temporal power of the pope is threatened, let us strengthen his spiritual power. But is it possible to look upon the pope's spiritual power in this way without overstepping the specific limits of the papal function?

The true limits of the papal function were similarly exceeded in the sphere of internal church life. There was Dom Guéranger, abbot of Solesmes, with his campaign for the suppression of local rites in favour of the Roman liturgy as the one for the whole Church. By doing whatever the pope does, Catholics everywhere will be united in 'the mystery of the liturgy'. Referring matters to Rome was encouraged wherever need arose:[39] by laymen, by priests unhappy with their bishop, by bishops unhappy with their colleagues, by religious unhappy with their superiors and by superiors looking for support against those who were subject to them. Resting one's case on support from 'the head of the Church', or from one of the congregations, became the final answer. The canonists set themselves to justify this policy by showing that 'the head of the Church' had a duty to show himself present everywhere to his people and that his responsibilities included bringing the variety of local customs and special rules into healthy conformity with the views and ways of the Roman Church, mistress of all the other Churches. This passed into catechetical teaching.[40] The Catholic press, especially the Jesuit *La Civiltà cattolica* and Louis Veuillot's

L'Univers, devoted body and soul to the ultramontane cause, disseminated everything that came out of Rome, creating the impression that, to be reliable, Christian thought and Christian judgement of events must spring from 'the rock which is the head of the Church'. At the level of theology, the influence of the Roman College and the Roman theology[41] was to carry all before it. The College moulded the professors charged with spreading throughout the seminaries, as willed by the Council of Trent, the teaching of those who advised 'the head of the Church' and who were to be associated with drafting the Vatican I texts. Any moves to open the Christian mind towards modern thought were distrusted as much as any emphasis on the proper authority of local churches, which explains the choice of matters to be condemned and books to be placed on the Index. The definition of the dogma of the Immaculate Conception in 1854 came as a 'providential' argument reinforcing the view that there was only one Supreme Doctor to whom all other teachers can but submit.[42]

What was to be the attitude when those others were the bishops? A sensitive and subtle Sulpician priest, adviser to the Bishop of Sens, told in his *Journal de mon voyage et de mon séjour à Rome* of a Roman prelate who declared: 'I am very happy that the bishops are coming to Rome, for they will see that the pope is everything and the bishops nothing.'[43] This is in line with the ultramontane doctrine of the Church: bishops are relegated to a subordinate level, for everything centres on 'the head of the Church'. Bishops are at most the organs for transmitting the thoughts and decisions of the head and any pretensions of their own cause irritation at Rome. In England the convert Manning went so far as to assert that the pope is infallible 'apart from the bishops', which from his pen means more or less 'whatever may be the opinion of the bishops'.[44] The columns of *L'Univers* instantly cry 'Gallicanism!' of anyone who dares to prefer the opinions of a bishop to that of someone 'close to the head of the Church'.[45] At another level it is easy to see that after the collapse of the Catholic monarchies, national episcopates have nothing like such high cards to play as Rome when it comes to defending certain interests against the new government. In much the same way, the little Christian communities coming into being through the overseas missions have only Rome to look to, to become aware of what it means to belong to the Catholic Church; for without strong, firm authority the Church would fall apart.[46] 'The head of the Church' was thus seen as God's providential answer to the needs of the Church. But the bishops saw their function devalued, placed as it were in brackets. The Church now became 'the society of the faithful governed by the pope'. As the Abbé Icard subtly put it, 'They think they will glorify and exalt the head of the Church by separating him from all the other shepherds.'[47] This 'head of the Church' has in practice become 'more than a pope'.

It needed the conjunction of ultramontane theory and the Mastaï pope's personal fascination to point up the extravagance of the situation and its dangers. What had until then been confined to more intellectual circles now moved out into the soul of the people. A mark so deeply engraved can hardly be effaced. It engendered a devotion to the pope of which Dom Cuthbert Butler did not hesitate to say, after citing examples,[48] that it sometimes borders on blasphemy; but Manning saw nothing to revise, *L'Univers* acclaimed it and *La Civiltà cattolica* joined in the chorus. Let the reader decide. 'When the pope meditates, it is God who thinks in him,' the second paper declared.[49] Butler instanced hymns where *Deus* had been replaced by *Pius*.[50] The famous doctrine of the three white bearers of Christ - Mary, the Host and the Pope - now came in with expanding Marian devotion. In 1862, for example, Mgr Pie

being with Count Lafond at the Château de Nozet in the Nièvre, where he consecrated an altar, said this about the pope and Rome to this generous friend of them both: 'After the real presence of Jesus Christ in the sacrament of the Eucharist, nothing can make us feel and touch more closely the Saviour's person than the sight of his Vicar on earth. Speaking personally, I have never climbed the steps which lead to the place of his throne without gasping from that emotion made up of fear, respect and love which one experiences on approaching the Tabernacle.'[51]

Opponents of this view were naturally not slow to mention

historical episodes showing that the papal whiteness was far from immaculate. The names of Sixtus IV and his nephews, of Alexander VI and his children spring to mind. And how is it possible to speak without qualification of 'the vice-God of mankind'[52] when one remembers Julius II, whom Guillaume Budé called 'the bloodstained chief of the gladiators', while Duplessis-Mornay was scandalized to see him 'desert the throne of St Peter to sleep in a guard-room, and God knows how fine the mitres, crosses and croziers looked as they fluttered over the battlefields'.[53] Would the papacy have changed its nature, ceasing to be exercised by men of human weakness? At some point the problem of 'the heretical pope' discussed in Tradition would have to be raised.[54] Ultramontanism was silent over the posthumous condemnation of Pope Honorius by the Third Council of Constantinople in 681, a condemnation confirmed by Leo II. The *Decretum* of Gratian (40.6) allows that the pope may be judged if he comes to 'deviate in the faith'. It is thus impossible to say without qualification, as Lamennais did to Lacordaire and Montalembert when he received the encyclical *Mirari Vos* (1832) in Munich, 'God has spoken and it remains only to say: *Fiat voluntas tua.*'[55] Nor could one write, as did Veuillot's friend du Lac, that even in questions where religion and politics mingle, we should 'follow the rule laid down by the representative of Jesus Christ upon earth, . . . the Sovereign Pontiff'.[56] But the ultramontane temper does not allow such distinctions. It is stubbornly unable to grasp that any impassioned exaltation of the pope, buttressed by polemic, using phrases uncritically, raising him almost to divinity – 'he is Peter and he has the Word'[57] – runs the risk of compromising the cause of God himself, as Cuthbert Butler finely put it. But anyone who dared to raise some major objection was taken to be depraved.[58]

Such was the ultramontane climate, with Pius IX reigning over the Church at the moment when the political power of the Papal States crumbled, when on 18 July 1870 the First Vatican Council promulgated the constitution *Pastor Aeternus*. The bishop of Grenoble had noted in 1867: 'The great idea running through the pontificate of Pius IX is to profit from the extraordinary combination of circumstances which gave him the events of present-day Europe as a weapon to crush the final remains of Gallicanism.'[59] Comments made by the leading lights of the majority at the Council show that this had indeed been the dominant purpose. As the jubilant Mgr Pie put it: 'From now on it is a matter of faith that there is only one sovereign power in the Church, and that that sovereignty resides completely in the Vicar of Jesus Christ.'[60] The reporter of the schema on infallibility declared that the *modus* of Mgr Dupanloup, who wanted to insert as a condition of infallibility that the pope should be supported by the witness of the Churches (*innixus testimoniis ecclesiarum*) was rejected for fear that it maintained the substance of Gallicanism. The majority 'therefore emphasized the meaning of the disputed phrases; and, in face of threats from within and without, the Church nevertheless affirmed her constitution.'[61] The Council, once summoned, was to be the Council of the papal power, as much in matters of obedience to discipline as over the interpretation of doctrine. And this 'papal power' was considered absolute in those circles which looked towards Rome. Before his dramatic change of views, Lamennais in 1830 addressed the pope yet to be elected in these words from his famous article in *L'Avenir*: 'Our faith salutes you in advance; in advance we bring before your feet the homage of unlimited submission and an inalienable love.'[62] And at the election of Leo XIII, Mgr Pie wrote to his people: '*Habemus papam* . . . a pope, that is a father; a pope, that is an infallible teacher. If the need should arise, if doubtful matters gain ground beyond the possibility of settlement by existing definitions and the ordinary teaching of the *magisterium*, the pope who is the living rule of faith will speak from the height of his throne, and the matter will be settled. The submission of our spirit will match the filial affection of our heart.'[63] These two quotations convey perfectly the spirit which bathed the Council.

'Pastor Aeternus': a subtle document interpreted by an ultramontane outlook

It is not necessary to go over the fascinating story of the constitution *Pastor Aeternus*. The 'minority', whose part was of leading importance, saw to it that the first drafts, prepared by ultramontane Jesuits from the College of Rome, were purged of their excesses. The 'majority' were obliged to make finer distinctions and several of the clarifications brought by Mgr Zinelli in the name of the Deputation of the Faith allowed for a more flexible interpretation of the doctrine than a Manning, a Mgr Pie and, above all, Pius IX himself, would have have wished. It proved necessary to concede several points to the minority, yet without involving 'the slightest weakness' over the fundamental issue. When all its words are weighed in the light of the discussions which took place,[64] the constitution emerges as the charter of a firmly ultramontane view of the Church, but one more moderate than many had hoped for and one which, through its silence on certain issues and its occasional imprecision, is not without openings for further discussion.

We shall return to the text, but for the present concentrate on three important points. The constitution sees the ministry of the one it calls the Roman pontiff as a service towards the unity of the whole people of God (*DS* 3050); and claims to understand it in the light of 'the ancient and constant faith of the universal Church' (*DS* 3052), expressed in the witness of 'the acts of ecumenical councils and the holy canons' (*DS* 3059), lived out in 'the continuous practice of the Church' and transmitted in the declarations made by ecumenical councils, 'especially those where East and West met in the unity of faith and love' (*DS* 3065). It is thus a matter of power, *potestas*, but power in relation to a service, a function (*munus*). And its purpose is 'that the episcopate may be one and undivided and that, thanks to the close and mutual unity of the priests, the whole number of believers should be kept in unity of faith and communion' (*DS* 3051). Moreover the constitution speaks of the Roman *church* and its primacy as that which carries and explains the primacy of the Roman pontiff. 'It is towards the Roman church, on account of its superior origin, that it has always been necessary for every Church, that is, for the faithful from everywhere, to turn in order that they should be made one body only in that holy see from which flow all the rights of the venerable communion' (*DS* 3057). 'The Roman church, by the Lord's disposition, possesses over all others a primacy of ordinary power, and this power of jurisdiction of the Roman pontiff, truly episcopal, is immediate' (*DS* 3057, 3060). It is astonishing that the implications of this progression from the Roman church to the Roman pontiff have not been investigated. Anyhow, the infallibility which the Roman pontiff enjoys under certain circumstances and conditions is the one which Christ provided for his Church (see *DS* 3074).

This shade of moderation becomes increasingly evident the more one studies the discussions surrounding Vatican I. But it is matched by very serious limitations and grave consequences. The most serious – and, it must be said, the one most explicitly desired by the majority – is the lack of any precise statement about the rights of the episcopate to match those claimed for the Roman pontiff. Mgr Pie's already quoted claim, 'There is only one sovereign power in the Church and . . . that sovereignty resides completely in the vicar of Jesus Christ', is nearly synonymous with the assertion that there is only one head in the Church of God and that he alone holds all power from God. There is nothing to forbid a Catholic who reads the constitution without being able to interpret some of its phrases from the tone of the debates from supposing that Manning's 'apart from the bishops' can be applied to the whole area of the Roman pontiff's jurisdiction as well as his authority in doctrine as an adequate expression of papal power.

One precious paragraph, however, enables us at least to reopen the problem despite the abstract language used.

This power of the sovereign pontiff in no way obstructs the ordinary and immediate power of episcopal jurisdiction, by which the bishops, established by the Holy Spirit (Acts 20.28) as successors to the Apostles, feed and govern as true pastors the flock committed to each one. On the contrary, this power is asserted, strengthened and vindicated by the supreme and universal pastor, as Gregory the Great says: 'My honour is the honour of the universal church. My honour is the solid strength of my brothers (in the episcopal dignity). Then am I truly honoured, when honour is not denied to each one to whom it is due' (*DS* 3061).

One would like to know how, in practice, the power of the

Roman pontiff is to promote rather than stifle that of the other bishops.

Besides, almost nothing is said about the practical limits to the power (*potestas*) and jurisdiction of 'the head of the Church' in relation to the episcopate, which is the other side of the same problem. This again is not due to neglect but to the deliberate intention of the Deputation of the Faith. With Pius IX himself, the Deputation were afraid of anything that might expose the power of the head of the Church to encroachment from the bishops. Its members were inflexibly set against any discussion of criteria for establishing limits to the exercise of primacy. Nevertheless there are two openings to explore. The first is the statement often made during the discussions that the pope's function and the power needed for it exist *ad aedificationem Ecclesiae non ad destructionem*,[65] for the building-up of the Church, not its destruction. This implies that everything which works against the building-up of the Church as Christ willed it and along the ways attested by living Tradition must be contrary to the truth of the papal function, so that power thus deployed is being improperly used. The other point of entry is, once again, a remark by Mgr Zinelli: 'A plenary and supreme authority was conferred on Peter and his successors in the Church, plenary in the sense that it could be limited not by any greater human power but only by natural and divine law.'[66] The principle of limitation for the plenary authority of the Roman pontiff was thus admitted, its criteria being the two laws which Vatican I took to be fundamental - compare the discussions surrounding the constitution *Dei Filius* - natural law and divine law. But again, one would like to know the actual areas where these limits come into play. The Council did not delay over it.

The constitution *Pastor Aeternus*, we are therefore persuaded, lends itself to a moderate interpretation when the finer points in the discussions surrounding it are taken into account, marginally though these are represented in the text itself. But from the end of the Council itself the document was 'received' and commented on as an ultramontane triumph, extremist sentiments being once more read into it. It was that party's victory.[67] From that time on, any teaching which did not honour the supreme power of 'the head of the Church' in absolute terms would carry the stigma of error; in the eyes of the average Catholic, it would be a distortion of the Council's meaning.

Maximizing interpretations of *Pastor Aeternus* were to be sustained and given currency in the 'Roman theology' which now imposed itself as the dominant school of thought. This type of thought is in fact 'a well-defined style of understanding Vatican I.'[68] Its very distinctive interpretation is presented and accepted as 'the Church's opinion'. Priests were educated to this school of thought, generally taught by professors who had graduated from Rome. It was to be the mould in which 'the Catholic awareness' was formed until Vatican II. For those who were thus nourished by a teaching which blurred all finer distinctions, the Church had a 'head' described in terms which made him 'more than a pope'. The distinctive characteristics were not simply those of their own time, which would have been unavoidable, but those of a definite trend. Examples supporting this statement are easily found.

For a quick grasp of the Church's thought at a particular time, nothing is more typical or important than the material provided for catechetical instruction. The following extracts, chosen from many, may speak for themselves:

Q. Describe the earlier and the present constitution of the Church.

A. To begin with, the Apostles were equal among themselves and had only one head, Jesus Christ. But before leaving the world, Jesus wished to provide a vicar or substitute for himself. He chose St Peter, declared his intention of making him the foundation of the Church, promised him the keys of the Kingdom of Heaven and charged him to feed and govern the whole flock, both pastors and people. These measures completed the constitution of the Church.

We see there a hierarchy thus established: at the summit, Peter, who is the supreme head; below, the Apostles who administer and govern with the help of assistants chosen from among the first disciples; and finally, the mass of the faithful who hear and obey.

The hierarchical constitution today is identically the same. We have at the top our holy father the Pope, vicar of Christ, successor to St Peter, the visible head of the whole Church, the father and teacher of all Christians.

Below stand the Bishops, successors to the Apostles, charged with the spiritual rule of the dioceses, under the authority of our holy father the Pope. They are helped by the Parish Priests and the other Priests, who are fellow-workers with the Bishops and who work, under their authority, for the salvation of souls: some, like the parish priests, at the head of a parish; the others - chaplains, curates etc. - are their assistants.[69]

The following assertions echo this view of the pope as the 'substitute' for Christ, which justifies the supreme place accorded to him:

The Pope is the vicar of Jesus Christ. He has the same mission as Jesus Christ, the same power, the same destiny: to instruct, sanctify, do good, . . . and to suffer.[70]

Q. Who is St Peter's successor?

A. Our Holy Father the Pope is St Peter's successor. He occupies the place of Jesus Christ on earth.[71]

Q. Who is the visible head of the Church?

A. It is our Holy Father the Pope, the bishop of Rome, who is the *vicar of Jesus Christ* and the *visible head* of the Church. The word Pope comes from a Greek word meaning 'Father'.

The *vicar* of Jesus Christ means the representative of Jesus Christ, the person who *holds on earth the place* of Jesus Christ.

The Pope is the *visible* head, that is to say, the head whom one can see.[72]

Pope: successor of God, pastor of all the faithful and the one sent to ensure the common good of the universal Church and the good of each of the churches.[73]

Q. What is a bishop?

A. A bishop is a priest specially consecrated in order to occupy among us the place of Our Holy Father the Pope.

Q. What is Our Holy Father the Pope?

A. Our Holy Father the Pope is the visible head of all those who are baptized . . .

30

Q. Who gave the Pope and the bishops the power to confirm?

A. It was Our Lord Jesus Christ who, while He was on earth, gave the Pope and the bishops the power to confirm.[74]

Consider finally this pearl, with its triumphant vision of the Pontiff-King:

> The pope expresses his sovereignty through the court which surrounds him. The papal court exhibits the same organization and the same customs as you would find at the courts of secular sovereigns. The pope has about six hundred soldiers to guard his residence . . . As a sovereign, the pope mints money, confers decorations, has a white and yellow flag, ambassadors (legates, apostolic nuncios) to every nation, etc. Those who are shocked by this pomp, remembering that Jesus Christ was not surrounded by a similar court, forget that the pope does not represent Jesus Christ pursued by his enemies, shamed and humiliated on the cross, but the divine Saviour *gloriously raised* to the heavens. Besides, the pope, by reason of his position, is frequently in contact with sovereigns and their ambassadors: he must therefore take account of their customs if he is not to compromise himself and his ministry.[75]

The list of passages like this, written between 1900 and 1980, could be extended almost endlessly. We could call upon extracts from 'sermons', but we will repeat only the main themes. The exaltation of the pope and the view that bishops are consecrated 'to occupy among us the place of our Holy Father the Pope' proclaim the triumph of ultramontanism. For all the careful distinctions, Vatican I has virtually consecrated this view.

We do not exaggerate when we add that an ultramontane vision of the papacy is to be found even in more enlightened Catholicism. Here are some indications of it. In 1920 Mgr Alfred Baudrillart, a member of the French Academy and Rector of the Institut Catholique in Paris, introduced Benedict XV as 'God's representative on earth'.[76] In 1956, an outstanding canonist, well abreast of the research into the doctrine of the Church made in the years preceding Vatican II, could still write:

We should not be surprised, as we said again recently, to see the pope gradually taking on the mission which the bishops have previously exercised in their dioceses, for it would not be to the good of the Church or the world if different and perhaps contradictory positions were upheld in each and every bishopric. If, in a world which is becoming one, the Church wishes to remain one, the papacy must speak, must speak often and must direct everything. That is why this twentieth century is becoming a new dawn in the Church, the dawn of a universal world, of an international society. And as the national states disappear, the bishoprics will lose their sovereignty, leaving to Peter and his successors the general management of the whole Catholic movement, of all Catholic activity, of all apostolic work.[77]

At the time when John XXIII announced the opening of Vatican II, the Rome correspondent of the newspaper *La Croix* expressed in these words a question which arose spontaneously for Catholic journalists:

Is an ecumenical council still needed after the dogma of the pope's infallibility? Other journalists have had the same reaction. And I have read that even some theologians formerly believed that the era of ecumenical councils was quite past. Why bring to Rome two thousand patriarchs, archbishops, bishops and superiors-general of religious orders to accomplish what the head of the Church can do on his own? Why, if I may express myself frankly, this general state of commotion, this loss of time, indeed this waste of energy, this futile expense?[78]

And even Karl Rahner, in a note added to a study of the episcopate published after the opening of the Council (in 1964) but doubtless written earlier, still echoed a maximizing view of the papacy.[79]

Another sign of this inflated ultramontanism, so different from the vastly more prudent and sober tone of *Pastor Aeternus*, is a particular conception of the ordinary magisterium of the Roman pontiff. This may be seen in the way every judgement which comes from Rome is implicitly canonized, whether it be dogmatic, theological or spiritual. Before the influence of Vatican II made itself felt, the starting-point of theological reflection in many theological faculties and seminaries was 'the teaching of the magisterium', which was then illustrated from Scripture, Tradition and reason. The views of anyone not on the same wavelength as 'the centre of Christianity' were systematically ignored, indeed considered suspect; theological light could only shine from 'on high'. What is more, even though *Pastor Aeternus* had set out quite explicitly the circumstances and conditions needed for a 'judgement' of the pope to be deemed infallible, it was usual to attach to encyclicals, whose numbers increased greatly from the pontificate of Gregory XVI (died 1846), a weight very little less than that of documents guaranteed by the Holy Spirit. Besides, the charism of a theologian was unable to function except as a delegate of the magisterium (the *missio canonica*), and its chief purpose was to justify and support magisterial assertions. Once Rome had spoken, even in a manner not technically solemn, any controversy must be extinguished. In the encyclical *Humani Generis* (1950), Pius XII himself wrote: 'When the Roman pontiffs go out of their way to pronounce on some subject which has hitherto been controverted, it must be clear to everybody that, in the mind and intentions of the pontiffs concerned, this subject can no longer be regarded as a matter of free debate among theologians.' For it is not 'to be supposed that a position advanced in an encyclical does not, *ipso facto*, claim assent' on the grounds that 'the popes do not exercise their teaching authority to the full' (*DS* 3884-6; Eng. trans. *False Trends in Modern Teaching* (CTS 1959), 20). For many Christians, a papal encyclical by definition carries more weight than the declarations of an episcopal conference. All truth should be sought from 'on high'. The Church of God contains only one teacher whom one 'ought' to trust even when he is talking informally to pilgrims.[80] But does not this make that teacher 'more than a pope'?

As for bishops, the average Catholic considers them of secondary importance, as the examples have shown; except, perhaps, when the aura of the cardinalate lends them something of the Roman authority. After Mgr Pie was made cardinal, the clergy of Poitiers declared: 'Pope Paul II said that for conducting ordinary business the sovereign pontiff could, if necessary, make do with the light of human wisdom; for the choice of bishops he needed angelic light; but for the election of a cardinal, nothing less than divine light was necessary.'[81] Vatican I would never have passed such a phrase, but the idea it embodies is widespread. But cardinals, several of whom are genuine residential bishops, are not the only ones to be rated above bishops in Catholic sentiment. The apostolic nuncio, a simple titular bishop without a real see, has in some places prevailed over the heads of the local episcopate as being 'the Holy Father's representative'. How many files, how many complaints of religious communities against their bishop, how many denunciations issuing from zealous but unenlightened priests have found the diplomatic bag to be the route to a positive response from 'on high' . . .

The way in which *Pastor Aeternus* has been received in the life of the Church gives what may be a typical example of the influence which the habit and temper of the time can have on the actual effect made by a carefully weighed document. A theological vision has been injected into the conciliar text and, in Catholic understanding, has become indistinguishable from the doctrine which is there defined.

Vatican II:
a new reading in a new context, with fragile results

When the Second Vatican Council opened in 1962, Roman Catholic theologians who did not endorse the 'Roman theology' had become aware of an imbalance in the doctrine of the Church as it was held by the dominant school of thought, which had received a boost during the pontificate of Pius XII (1939-58). They had become interested in the traditions of other churches, notably the Eastern Orthodox,[82] and they had themselves been nourished in the renewal of patristic and liturgical studies. Among matters studied afresh was the theology surrounding the episcopate. The mere announcement of a council which would be open to other Christian traditions was enough to provoke serious study on what councils meant and on the relationship between the pope and the other bishops. In a climate of opinion which was no longer Gallican (Vatican I had won that battle!) but which, like it or not, was becoming increasingly ecumenical, the centring of everything on Rome had, with the 'vision' underpinning it, become a problem. A genuinely functioning episcopal ministry was clearly required.[83]

Watched from the beginning by a worried 'minority' (successors of those who had formed the victorious 'majority' at Vatican I), Vatican II in no way changed the letter of *Pastor Aeternus*.[84] A good example occurs in the introduction to the Decree on the Pastoral Office of Bishops, *Christus Dominus*, which was drafted after *Lumen Gentium*. It would have rejoiced the hearts of the 1870 Deputation of the Faith.

> In this Church of Christ the Roman pontiff, as the successor of Peter, to whom Christ entrusted the care of his sheep and lambs, has been granted by God supreme, immediate and universal power in the care of souls. As pastor of all the faithful, his mission is to promote the common good of the universal Church and the particular good of all the churches. He is therefore endowed with the primacy of ordinary power over all the churches (*CD* 2.1).[85]

A first glance might suggest that there was no change, especially since theology has not freed Roman Catholic 'tradition' from a crushing scruple which has already been referred to. It bears on the infallibility which attaches to dogmatic declarations when they are given a new reading by a body carrying the same authority as the one which promulgated them. The hard-pressed minority of Vatican II demanded that 'nothing be changed even of the letter of Vatican I'.

What *Lumen Gentium* has done is to set this repeat of Vatican I within a new perspective. The vision which controls its teaching on the Church is no longer that of the ultramontane majority of 1870, but that of the more balanced and lucid elements in the minority of Vatican I. In other words, the minority of Vatican I has become the majority of Vatican II and vice versa. We may therefore say that at Vatican II *Pastor Aeternus* was 'received' in the dogmatic sense by the minority of Vatican I after nearly a century of deepening study and fresh thought. The importance of this new reception in a new climate is too little recognized: Vatican I and Vatican II together form a dialectical unity in which one should be interpreted by the other.

Where Vatican I sees the Church in its earthly form starting from its 'head', the bishop of Rome, Vatican II sees it starting from the bishops as 'successors of the apostles' (*LG* 18, 20, 22, 23, 24, etc.), and who, taken together as a whole, comprise the foundation of the universal Church (*LG* 19). By divine institution, the bishops are indeed the 'heads' of the Church who 'direct the house of the living God' (*LG* 18), its shepherds (*LG* 20), its pontiffs (*LG* 21), the 'acme of the sacred ministry' (*LG* 21). All this comes to them through the sacrament of episcopal consecration. At an even deeper level, the bishops are the authentic *vicarii et legati Christi* for the government of the churches (*LG* 27). Vatican II is thus entirely clear: the fullness of that ministry which builds, guides and leads the whole Church belongs to the body of bishops as such, following in the wake of the mission entrusted to the apostles as a group (*LG* 20, 21).

Lumen Gentium sets the *officium* of what it still calls 'the Roman pontiff' firmly within this shared mission, treating it indeed as a function of that mission. In this context it takes up the main passages in the early paragraphs of *Pastor Aeternus*:

> Jesus Christ, the eternal pastor, set up the holy Church by entrusting the apostles with their mission as he himself had been sent by the Father . . . He willed that their successors, the bishops namely, should be the shepherds in his Church until the end of the world. In order that the episcopate itself, however, might be one and undivided he put Peter at the head of the other disciples, and in him he set up a lasting and visible source and foundation of the unity both of faith and of communion (*LG* 18, Flannery p. 370).

But the constitution proposes also to

> proclaim publicly and enunciate clearly the doctrine concerning bishops, successors of the apostles, who together with Peter's successor, the Vicar of Christ and the visible head of the whole Church, direct the house of the living God (ibid.).

The scheme no longer has the shape of a pyramid. The line no longer travels from the pope to the bishops, with the weight on the former at the expense of the latter; but from the bishops to the pope. A series of balancing statements, which made the new minority grind their teeth, kept in the forefront of debate the fact that Christ had built his Church not on Peter only but on the apostles with Peter at their head. It is an essential distinction. With great clarity the Council presents the Church in terms of its nature and apostolic origins; the Roman pontiff's function is seen to lie within that apostolicity, of which it is indeed one of the guarantees, but which extends beyond the function. The content of Vatican I is assumed and in no way explained away. But it has been restored to its traditional context, which had offended ultramontanism, and this has changed its emphasis completely. Thus one may no longer say with complete accuracy that the pope is *the* vicar of Christ; *Lumen Gentium* 27 obliges us to say that all the bishops are truly *vicarii et legati Christi*. A pope who was exclusively vicar of Christ would be more than a pope. Nor may one say any longer that he is *the* (visible) head of the Church; *Lumen Gentium* 18 reminds us that all the bishops by virtue of divine institution *domum Dei viventis regunt*. A pope who was *the* head would be more than a pope. The picture is no longer that of a perfect hierarchical society copied exactly from a civil monarchy.

The shift in emphasis by which one now understands the pope's function by looking at the bishops and not the other way round ties in with a more profound development without which the real issue at stake would not appear. It concerns the movement from an ecclesiology starting with the idea of the universal Church divided into portions called dioceses, to an ecclesiology which understands the Church as the communion of all the local churches: the universal Church arises from the communion of churches. In the area of our special concern, this is the great new insight of Vatican II compared with Vatican I.

While, therefore, accepting the position on the primacy of the Roman pontiff established by *Pastor Aeternus*, we may enclose it within a vision of the Church which implies a very different understanding of the primatial function from that which ultramontanism preferred. Two passages from Vatican II are especially important. The local churches

. . . are in fact, in their own localities, the new people called by God, in the power of the Holy Spirit and as the result of full conviction . . . In them the faithful are gathered together through the preaching of the Gospel of Christ, and the mystery of the Lord's Supper is celebrated 'so that, by means of the flesh and blood of the Lord the whole brotherhood of the Body may be welded together.' In each altar community, under the sacred minis-try of the bishop, a manifest symbol is to be seen of that charity and 'unity of the mystical body, without which there can be no salvation.' In these communities . . . Christ is present through whose power and influence the One, Holy, Catholic and Apostolic Church is constituted. For 'the sharing in the body and blood of Christ has no other effect than to accomplish our transformation into what we receive' (*LG* 26, Flannery p. 381).

A diocese . . . loyal to its pastor and formed by him into one community in the Holy Spirit through the Gospel and the Eucharist . . . constitutes one particular church in which the one, holy, catholic and apostolic Church of Christ is truly present and active (*CD* 11, Flannery p. 569.)

This means that the Church of God, seen in its universality, is the *communion* of local or particular churches. The universal Church is not to be identified as a vast whole, divided into portions each one of which is imperfect on its own. It is born from the *koinonia*, in each of which, through its celebration of a true Eucharist, *vere inest et operatur Una Sancta Catholica et Apostolica Christi Ecclesia*.

The ecclesiology of the Church as a communion of local churches entrusted to the *episkope* of bishops in communion with each other should be considered in close connection with another major theme of *Lumen Gentium*: the fact that episcopal authority and its juridical institution is founded on a sacrament – the episcopate. The full weight of this assertion from *Lumen Gentium* needs to be brought to bear on the theology of the papacy. For it is clear that whatever is founded upon a sacra-ment must have priority within the Church of God: the Church comes about by faith and sacraments and all its essential marks are to be found within the osmosis of faith and sacraments. To deny this would be to forsake the Great Tradition, that of the Church still undivided which takes precedence over the divided Churches. For the election of a pope has never been reckoned a sacrament. What is more, neither the election nor the enthronement of a pope conveys any 'indelible character'; when a pope resigns he simply ceases to be pope.

For *Lumen Gentium* the episcopate itself is a sacrament. In view of its function, indeed, the power of hierarchy in the Church can only derive from the sacrament, not from some distinct *ordo jurisdictionis* with its source in the pope. The episcopate is an essential tool for the construction of the Church. If 'the individual bishops are the visible source and foundation (*visibile principium et fundamentum*) of unity in their own particular churches, which are constituted after the model of the universal Church; it is in these and formed out of them that the one and unique Catholic Church exists' (*LG* 23, Flannery p. 376), then everything which they need for the discharge of their office comes to them in their sacramental ordination. If it were otherwise, the Catholic Church could not be formed out of these local (or particular) churches, for its constituent principles belong to the realm of the Spirit and the sacraments. In other words, putting the supreme pontiff above the bishops in a sort of pseudo-sacramental halo which makes him transcend the episcopal order in 'dignity'[86] makes him beyond all doubt something *more than* and *different from a pope*. Worse still, it would put the Church of God in a totally false relationship with the mystery of the sacraments, thus affecting its own true nature.

At this deep level, the *receptio* of Vatican I by Vatican II amounts to a re-reading of the former which exemplifies 'dogmatic development' along a different line from that which, since Newman, has been regarded as normal, and which many of the Vatican I fathers accepted.[87] The difference lies in the idea of development not by the addition of new truths but by clarification.

The mission and power of the papacy should therefore be understood as inseparable from those of the college of bishops. We should think of the government of the Church as a dynamic tension within a single mission, that of the episcopal college as such (obviously including the head, but a head which is only a head with its body); and of a single power, which the sacrament gives, for the pope carries out his office on the basis of the power which was given him when he was consecrated bishop. Since indeed the universal Church is to be found within the local church, the mission and power of each bishop responsible for a local church must by its nature include a dimension of 'solicitude for the universal Church'. This is not some external addition to the bishop's pastoral responsibility within his diocese (*LG* 23). It is formally the same solicitude which becomes fully explicit in the case of the bishop of Rome – we shall see how and why in the next chapter. Approaching it from the other end, we may say that since the local church opens out into the universal Church, the mission and power of the bishop with particular responsibility for catholicity (the bishop of Rome) are bound from their very nature to have an impact at the local level also. Hence the parallel assertions concerning a college of bishops who, in union with their head, the bishop of Rome, 'have supreme and full authority over the universal Church'; and a head who 'by reason of his office . . . has full, supreme and universal power over the whole Church' (*LG* 22). The order of these adjectives is hardly fortuitous ('power' and 'authority' both render the Latin *potestas* – E. Tr.). Moreover the bishops said, spelling out a matter which Vatican I had recognized thanks to prodding from the minority:

> The pastoral charge, that is, the permanent and daily care of the sheep, is entrusted to them fully (*plene*) nor are they to be regarded as vicars of the Roman Pontiff; for they exercise the power which they possess in their own right and are called in the truest sense of the term prelates of the people whom they govern. Consequently their authority, far from being damaged by the supreme and universal power, is much rather defended, upheld and strengthened by it . . . (*LG* 27, Flannery p. 383).

The papacy is rooted in the episcopate. For the bishop of Rome, as for all the bishops, everything derives from one and the same sacrament (episcopacy), from one and the same mission to build and to keep the Church in communion, from one and the same power given for the sake of this mission. But this power operates in different ways according to the office which each member receives within the college. In the case of the bishop of Rome, the dimension of *sollicitudo universalis* is extended to a special degree, though always remaining within the sacramental grace of the episcopate.

Such then is the place of the papacy according to Vatican II. It belongs to the episcopal ministry and must not be severed from its roots there. A dialectical tension exists at the heart of this ministry possessed by all the bishops with the bishop of Rome at the head of the college, and must be maintained: a tension between the local or particular pole and the universal pole; between the pole of plurality and the pole of unity whose interplay is the stuff of communion. This is what allows *Ecclesia catholica* to be present in *ecclesia localis* and *Ecclesia catholica* (*universalis*) to be built from the communion of the *ecclesiae locales*. For one of these poles to take over the other is impossible. So is the idea that the power needed by one of the poles should spring from the power of the other – as if, for instance, the power of local bishops, whether on their own or together, originated in the bishop of Rome, or vice versa. It would deny the sacramental equality of the two powers. If it indeed happened, plurality would slip slowly into division and unity into more or less despotic centralization.

But *Lumen Gentium* never settled the difficult question of the boundaries in practice between the authority and power of the bishop of Rome and that of the other bishops: whether because of the 'minority's' influence, or from having too little time for its theology to ripen,[88] or too little time generally, or from fear of provoking average Catholic opinion. The only guideline issuing from the Council on this point is that in July 1964 the assembled Fathers refused an amendment which Paul VI wanted. He wished to end *Lumen Gentium* 22 with a note to say that the Roman pontiff ought certainly to take account of the collegial power of the bishops, but that he himself owed account to God alone, *uni Domino divinctus*.[89] The Commission replied: 'The Roman pontiff is bound to abide by Revelation itself, the basic structure of the Church, the sacraments, the definitions of the first Councils, etc. It is impossible to list them all'.[90] Another indication occurs in the famous *nota praevia* or preliminary note of explanation which the Theological Commission supplied for a guide to interpreting *Lumen Gentium*'s teaching on collegiality. The pope was to take his decisions *intuitu boni Ecclesiae*, in consideration of the welfare of the Church. This phrase includes all that the first paragraphs of *Lumen Gentium* chapter 3 expound from revealed data concerning the mission of the apostolic College, the place of the local church and the college of bishops in the fundamental structure of the Church, and the sacraments, especially the Eucharist and the episcopate, all in accordance with the tradition of the first councils. It is the Theological Commission's answer refusing Paul VI's amendment. To do otherwise would be to act *non ad aedificationem sed ad destructionem Ecclesiae*. And Vatican I laid heavy emphasis on the Roman pontiff's duty to keep his ministry *ad aedificationem*.[91]

Vatican II thus gave no firm juridical norm, no canonically formulated limit which would make it quite clear how far the pope's powers extended. Balanced teaching on the matter is to be gathered from the teaching as a whole. Such theological optimism makes for an uncomfortable situation and one fraught with peril, as we shall see. In the final analysis Vatican II, like *Pastor Aeternus*, puts its trust in the activity of the Spirit present in the Church as well as in the personal judgement of the Roman pontiff. The *sensus fidelium* here comes into play, understood as a *conspiratio* of the faithful and the bishops.[92] It must be taken seriously but without stimulating the old ultramontane reflexes. Moreover, the notion of the Church's indefectibility is involved, which Catholic tradition has never taken seriously enough, tending to supplant it by that of infallibility. If it should happen that the Roman pontiff oversteps the limits which his specific office of maintaining the Church in communion imposes on his actions, the bishops and laity, nudged by the Spirit, will know how to react: assuming, of course, that they really know what are the mission and nature of the primacy.

Uneasiness, however, returns. The old ultramontane outlook and the popular instruction to which it gave rise have never disappeared, so that Vatican II's lack of clarity over practical relationships between the power of the college of bishops and that of the Roman pontiff leads to a shaky situation. A critical and dispassionate study of the institutions set up to embody Vatican II so that it genuinely enters into the lives of the people of God shows that in this matter we are not yet free from the ecclesiological attitudes of recent centuries. The fundamental point at issue is the balance of power between the bishop of Rome and the other bishops in the episcopal college. Because Vatican II was not clear, theology since has reflected the misgivings already mentioned about rethinking the troublesome points of Vatican I in the light of the new Council; we find ourselves facing the kind of uncertainty which inclines many people to cling to the past.

That observation holds good at several levels. They all show a tendency to preserve what is called the 'solitude' of the universal primate such as Vatican I wished for: his position above the communion of the other bishops, his 'being set apart', his 'transcendence', to revive an ultramontane term. New institutions have indeed been added, but without the corrections to the old one which would bring the two into harmony. There is no need to assume bad faith and it would be odious to sniff out some political plot against Vatican II. The reason is to be found in the imprecise nature of current theology, making it a source of hesitations which encourage the status quo.

A good example is the confusion over the standing of the synod of Bishops.[93] To begin with, at the time when the idea of the synod was being born and taking shape, it was understood to express not only the communion of the bishops but in some ways also collegiality itself.[94] The Decree on the Pastoral Charge of Bishops made of the synod a 'testimony to the participation of all the bishops in hierarchical communion in the care of the universal Church' (*CD* 5). The Secretary of the conciliar commission responsible went so far as to write:

> This synod is not strictly speaking an organ of the college of bishops, qualified to carry on in the name of the College business of a collegiate nature . . . Nevertheless this synod, made up of bishops chosen from the universal episcopate, is the manifest sign of the care which all the bishops have for the entire Church and of their responsibility towards the universal Church.[95]

And at the opening of the 1969 synod, Paul VI declared: 'Remembering that the episcopate is the true successor to the apostles and that they for their part formed a particular group, chosen and willed by Christ, it has seemed a happy thing to take up once more the concept and the term collegiality, applying it to the order of bishops.'[96]

Several episcopates saw in the synod the chance of better contact with the Roman centre, and especially some degree of sharing in the making of decisions. But it did not work out. First of all, the synod is tangled up in badly thought out procedures and so has not so far been able to function in such a way that its decisions were totally protected from pressure. But even if this point were corrected, which is both possible and desirable, a difficult ecclesiological problem would remain. The synod only exists in order to let the Roman pontiff know its opinion. It is not able to address the Church directly so as to express, in communion with the pope but not simply preparing the pope's own decision, the judgement of the universal episcopate on the matters at issue. Its conclusions are addressed to the pope and it is for him to decide if they should be published, and how. It is true that in certain cases the pontiff may give the synod the right to decide, but only by way of concession or permission. The synod of 1974, on evangelization, succeeded in producing a noteworthy document for Paul VI, but it was not without a sense of frustration among the bishops. There is a basic incompatibility between the ways of a monarchy, which the title Roman pontiff suggests, and the wishes of a synodical assembly. The former works within a closed circuit and leans on a court which does not readily put up with the crystallization of opinions which might well encroach on its own preserves. The latter by contrast wishes to be continually attentive to the *sensus fidelium* even if the end result is not as solid as a firm, clear declaration. Recent Roman synods have done no more than set the customs of a monarchy alongside the procedures of an assembly without being able to co-ordinate them.

The same difficulty is found in episcopal conferences. Little by little they have seen themselves granted fairly wide powers of discretion.[97] Only a few areas are exempted. But has this 'received' authority the strength implied by a full recognition of collegiality, articulated with Rome and referring to her but not dominated by her? This is yet another case of choosing 'either . . . or' instead of 'both . . . and' because it is so hard to reconcile the two things. Favours are still granted because dependence on Rome seems the more certain way and is in any case so deeply engrained.

Putting it briefly, one has the impression that the new institutions responsible for translating Vatican II into the dynamics of church life have not so far succeeded in jointing together the *munus* of the Roman pontiff with the *munus* of the whole college of bishops; or the freedom of the Roman pontiff, claimed so firmly by Vatican I though not without ultramontane overtones, with the demands of collegiality which Vatican II reasserted, but too vaguely; or the privilege of the Roman pontiff, so deeply engraved on the Roman Catholic consciousness by ultramontane mystique, and the rights of the college of bishops claimed throughout history but still under suspicion for Gallican leanings. Concern for safety has made us continue to revolve round a monarchical view without realizing that expressions of collegiality become something more than a means of serving the primacy. In so doing we turn our backs on Vatican II. Putting collegiality at the service of the pope's power reverts to making him 'more than a pope'. Primacy in the Great Tradition is at the service of collegiality, not the other way round. It is a serious problem, for it perpetuates a hesitation and an ambiguity which could slowly lead on to wither the fruits of Vatican II.

Has not this process, indeed, already begun? Here are a few examples. It can happen that we make fewer distinctions with regard to papal power since Vatican II than did Vatican I itself.[98] Vatican I said that 'the Lord willed that there should be in his Church a principle of unity, that is, an element qualified of itself and capable for ever of preserving the unity of faith and communion and keeping the Church from heresy and schism', the 'successor of Peter'. This is how that text from Vatican I is understood a century later, after it had been re-read by Vatican II; it occurs in a working paper for the 1969 synod: 'Peter's successor, having authority over the whole people of God, is instituted as the visible principle of the co-ordination and direction of every activity of the Church (*principium visibile*

coordinationis et moderationis totius activitatis Ecclesiae).
Now:

> Let us compare the views of Vatican I with this document which is
> supposed to be inspired by *Pastor Aeternus* via *Lumen Gentium*. It
> is one thing to be a principle effective in safeguarding the unity of
> faith and communion in order to avoid schisms and heresies, but
> quite another to co-ordinate and direct every activity of the Church.
> The working paper for the 1969 synod emphasizes the central-
> ization and bends the meaning which Vatican I gave to *principium*.[99]

And this, we would add, in a document prepared for a synod
whose agenda included the proper relationship between 'the
Roman centre' and the local churches. But at Rome, in the
circles where the working paper was drawn up, they felt it
necessary to take in hand those episcopal conferences, for some
of them were 'keeping their distance' from central authority
and thus 'asserting themselves'. The reply was once more to
make the pope 'more than a pope'.

Another example is afforded by the policy of 'concessions'.
Vatican II's Decree on the Pastoral Office of Bishops in the
Church says: 'Bishops . . . enjoy as of right in the dioceses
assigned to them all ordinary, special and immediate power
which is necessary for the exercise of their pastoral office, but
always without prejudice to the power which the Roman pontiff
possesses, *by virtue of his office*, of reserving certain matters to
himself or to some other authority' (*CD* 8). This power is
indeed given to them by the sacrament of episcopal ordination
itself, and so by the Holy Spirit. Yet the actual practice seems to
be carried out in the spirit of the *Motu Proprio 'Pastorale
Munus'* of 3 December 1963.[100] According to this document
the Roman pontiff *concedes* to the bishops and episcopal conferences the *powers* and *privileges* (which they already have
through the sacrament). And some of the rights 'granted' by
the sacrament are, as it were, 'withdrawn' by virtue of the
Roman pontiff's power to do so *intuitu boni Ecclesiae*. The
sacramental is thus restricted in favour of the canonical. Once
again it is thought better for safety's sake or from fear of 'a
certain disorder' for the Roman pontiff to have the privilege
over against his brother bishops of 'conceding' juridically at his

pleasure (in fact restoring to them) that which they certainly need to remain true bishops, but bishops now in complete dependence. Once more, for all the grace of sacramental episcopacy, the ineradicable ultramontane attitude has meant another fall into the temptation of making the pope 'more than a pope' - and the bishops correspondingly less than bishops.

One last case must be cited. The very important paragraph 22 of *Lumen Gentium* declares after long discussion that a Christian becomes a member of the episcopal college *by virtue* of sacramental consecration (*vi consecrationis*) and taking into account hierarchical communion (*communione*) with the head of the college (the pope). The meaning of the passage is clear.[101] Hierarchical communion is not a cause but simply a condition (otherwise the Orthodox would not be true bishops). Yet Cardinal Journet, in an article on collegiality contributed to *Nova et Vetera* with all the weight of his reputation behind it, interprets the paragraph in a way which will be authoritative in the eyes of many, and which hardens the meaning:

> Bishops enter the episcopal college:
> *a* initially by episcopal consecration, which confers on them an indelible qualification;
> *b* fully by the arrival of a canonical or juridical decision, issuing from the supreme authority, and from which the result for the consecrated subject will be his hierarchical communion.

G. Thils, who cites this text, justly observes:

> This analysis . . . reduces to an *initium* that which Christ brings about sacramentally, and raises to a *fullness* that which is added at a juridical level by hierarchical authority. A ruling of this kind respects neither the text nor the spirit of Vatican II. The analysis betrays the sense of the document.[102]

Having said that authors who write like that after the Second Vatican Council ignore 'no doubt unconsciously' the distinctions so carefully introduced by *Lumen Gentium*, he adds: 'But this unconscious activity always works in favour of pontifical power.'

This judgement is correct. Many indications lead us to make it our own. Other examples which we cannot stop to analyse confirm its justice: such as the calling of a plenary assembly of the college of cardinals in November 1979, when no attempt had been made since Vatican II to place this college in relation to the authority of the college of bishops. We are forced to make a realistic assessment. In spite of Vatican II's new reading of Vatican I, the post-conciliar Church has not yet provided itself with institutions that will enable it to adapt itself to the ecclesiology of communion, whose foundations *Lumen Gentium* laid without securing them deeply enough. The question raised by the post-conciliar institutions is fundamentally one for dogmatics and must be treated as such before it can be considered canonically; at present, these institutions are following the trend of Catholicism since Vatican I by sliding 'unconsciously' in the direction of pontifical power. We should not attempt to revise or correct Vatican II, but dig into it deeply enough to discover how the two plenary powers of *Lumen Gentium* 22, the Roman pontiff and the college of bishops, may be jointed and tied in together in unity.

The task is hardly easy. Catholic theology on this point is still in its stammering infancy, a fact which worries those other ecclesial groups in dialogue with Rome with a view to organic unity. Moreover, it should not be forgotten that a new code of canon law is in preparation. Will it be able to come up satisfactorily at this crucial point? Will those who are drafting it also tend unconsciously to favour pontifical power? Will they make the Roman pontiff (unless they have the happy idea of changing this title to *bishop of Rome*) into the pope or into more than a pope? Putting it in other terms, will the expected legislation, which will last a long time, be founded on the fact that the Roman pontiff exercises his *sollicitudo omnium ecclesiarum* from within the communion of bishops and in an essential relationship with that communion, or will it tend to leave him in his solitude? Will it make him the *primus* of a college of bishops or the sovereign pontiff who has bishops under him? Looking at the matter from the other end, will it take careful account of the fact that every bishop of a local church is by that very fact a bishop *for* the universal Church (*LG* 23) and has therefore, as from the Holy Spirit, the right to execute that responsibility in other ways than simply when he is consulted? In a word, the file on the dogmatic theology of the papacy is not closed. One of its most complex chapters has still to be written.

This chapter cannot be written by the Catholic Church alone. It will take shape only in so far as that Church sets herself to listen to the other Christian communities who are eager to reconstruct with her the unity of the Body of Christ, notably those whom she continues to regard as sister churches. Only in this way will the ultramontane temptation be overcome, for its roots are strong.

The two Vatican Councils have not yet been 'received' by these other Christians; they are councils celebrated by the Catholic Church alone, general councils strictly speaking, duly called, presided over and their findings promulgated by the Roman pontiff. Moreover, in spite of vague desires and initiatives,[103] these other Christians were not summoned to Vatican I. Their presence as observers at the Second Vatican Council represented a considerable thaw in the situation, though not enough to have extended the ecumenicity in the strict sense of the Council in question. But if – as Vatican II asserts and we believe – the Catholic Church is that in which the Church of God *subsists* with all essential elements (although she 'exists' also outside her frontiers), the official declarations which Rome holds to be guaranteed by the Spirit may not be refused. It is in this sense that Vatican I calls them *irreformabiles*. It is necessary, we said, to 're-read' them in the new light shed by the ecumenical will to 'remake unity'. This will respect their irreformable quality, for it is not a matter of denying them but of opening out their truth.

The maximizing view of the papacy conveyed here by the expression 'the pope has become more than a pope' is not unconnected with the fact that in the West he who is known as the Roman pontiff possesses three distinct primacies. As bishop of Rome – his real title, as we shall see – he holds a 'regional' primacy, a patriarchal primacy (as patriarch of the West) and an 'apostolic' primacy, special and unique in the heart of the universal episcopal college. Little by little these three primacies, each by nature very different from the others, have come to be embraced as one. The demands they severally carry have been first mingled then confused. It is clear that current ecumenical research has it in mind to disentangle the apostolic primacy from this confused situation. We must recall the broad outlines of what this involves.[104]

The roots of a certain attitude

In the days of the undivided Church, before the breach with the East – the Photian Schism around 890, the excommunication of Michael Cerularius in 1054, the aggravation by Innocent III's decision to appoint bishops for the Eastern sees, including Constantinople after that town was sacked in 1204 – the bishop of Rome was universally regarded as patriarch of the West. The title was not just one of honour. Canon 34 of the Apostolic Canons and canon 6 of the Ecumenical Council of Nicaea show that the sees were grouped together regionally from an early date. Each regional group of bishops had a 'first' (*protos*) put at its head who was invested with the 'power' required by his office.[105] The Council of Nicaea recognized that such a *protos* was by already ancient custom to be found at Alexandria, Antioch and Rome. The evidence shows that the 'power' was founded on the privileges (*presbeia*) not of the person but of the church. Alexandria, Antioch and Rome exchanged letters of communion through their *protos*.

Within this communion of churches and their primates, Rome held a special position. She stood out from the others increasingly:

> This means that the bishop of Rome holds an *administrative* office for the churches of Italy (and of the West generally) *but not for the Church as a whole*; for that she has a primacy as a direction finder and as a touchstone of unity.
>
> It is also true to say that the primates of Alexandria and Antioch are regional primates, while the bishop of Rome holds a regional primacy and in addition a primacy *of quite a different type* in relation to the Church as a whole.[106]

The state of affairs is well described in the following passage:

> An outline of three zones may already be seen, considered in relation to Rome, operating at the double level of 'provincial' and

'patriarchal', but its features will not be fully clear before the later part of the fourth century. In the third century the first zone may be seen, centred around Rome. The remainder of the West forms the second zone, tied to its centre with links of varying closeness: Africa, firmly structured around Carthage, had special links with Rome because of the existing Rome–Carthage connection; Spain and Gaul, where the organization of the Church was little developed and the links with Rome were partly those of evangelization (Spain in the second century, Gaul in the third). Finally there was the East which owed nothing of its origins to Rome and where Alexandria and Antioch tend to exercise a very different sort of predominance, though not without analogy with that of Rome in the West.

It is also important to notice, regarding the Roman primacy, that throughout the Ante-Nicene period Rome was recognized as a centre to which doctrinal questions might be referred. Towards the middle of the third century her bishop claimed 'the succession to Peter', but other churches saw the Roman prerogatives in a different light. Ignatius, for instance, speaks of Rome's 'presidency of love'; Irenaeus of the *potentior principalitas* (that of having been founded by Peter and Paul); and Cyprian of the *Ecclesia principalis*, but none of these corresponds exactly to Petrine succession as that had in all probability already come to be understood at Rome. Certain disagreements with Rome – from Asia in 190 about the date of Easter, from Africa and Cappadocia in 256 on the question of heretical baptism – point the same way. But this primacy was, at Rome as elsewhere, perfectly compatible with different levels of regional organization within the universal Church, and these were to be formally sanctioned by the whole Church at the first Ecumenical Council.

The germ of this twofold organization, metropolitan and supra-metropolitan, went back to the apostolic period and was effectively canonized at Nicaea (325), which may thus be seen as the logical outcome of a uniform development.[107]

Acting sometimes under pressure of circumstances, sometimes profiting from favourable situations, the church of Rome was to combine into a single embrace her regional primacy, her patriarchal primacy and her distinctive 'apostolic' responsibility within the communion of churches.[108] During the first thousand years the powers of the Eastern patriarchates were not understood to be a way of sharing in the papal government. Even less did they seem to be privileges which Rome had 'conceded'. They were, rather, an expression of episcopal jurisdiction itself. They translated into practice 'the awareness that the college of bishops, united with Rome, regulates its own affairs in a given area.'[109] The day would indeed come when Rome referred to these powers as privileges conceded and renewed. Boniface VIII did not hesitate to declare that the Holy See had itself set up primacies and patriarchates, metropolitanates and episcopal sees. The Roman see came to consider that even those sees outside her patriarchal zone, for which indeed she held responsibility of another kind, fell within her absolute control. It was her place to allow them their margin of autonomy. The primacy with regard to the Church as a whole thus came to take on colours which changed its true nature. Rome's wish to become *Mater et Magistra* of the whole of the West spilled over into the particular function (*munus*) which the bishop of Rome has in relation to the Church as a whole.[110] Much more was claimed for this function than really belongs to it when it is considered strictly for what it is.

We should therefore distinguish between the authority which properly belongs to the specific function (*munus*) of the bishop of Rome within the universal communion of churches and the claims produced by confusion between the several primacies enjoyed by the Roman see. An excellent way to grasp the difference is to contrast the attitude of Gregory the Great (590-604) with that of Gregory VII, pope five hundred years later (1073-85). This is how Gregory the Great replied to the patriarch of Alexandria who had addressed him as 'universal bishop':

Your Beatitude . . . speaks to me, saying 'as you have commanded'. I must ask you not to use such words in speaking of me, for I know what I am and what you are. In rank you are my brothers, in manner of life my fathers. I have therefore not given orders but have simply done my best to indicate what I think useful. But I have the impression that your Beatitude has not taken care to remember what I had hoped to establish in your memory. For I said that you ought not to address me in that fashion, nor ought you so to address anyone else. And here at the head of your letter I find the proud title of universal pope, which I have refused. I pray your most beloved Holiness not to do it again, because what is exaggeratedly attributed to another is taken away from you. It is not in words that I would find my greatness, but in manner of life. And I do not consider that to be an honour which, as I know, undermines the honour of my brothers. My honour is the honour of the universal Church. My honour is the solid strength of my brothers. Then am I truly honoured, when honour is not denied to each one to whom it is due. If your Holiness calls me universal pope, you deny to yourself that which you attribute in a universal sense to me. Let that not be so. Away with those words which inflate vanity and wound charity.[111]

Gregory's prestige certainly overflowed the boundaries of his Latin patriarchate. It fell to his lot to send directives to the Eastern bishops, to take initiatives such as the mission to the heathen as when he sent Augustine to preach to the Angles. But he still had respect for proper independence; he refused to impose one universal Roman ritual and he insisted that the Church should adopt the cultures of peoples evangelized.[112] He speaks the language of respect and fraternal love.

The other Gregory, the holy monk Hildebrand, who sincerely wished to effect the moral reform of the Church by tightening the links with Rome, speaks only in terms of 'papal prerogatives'.[113] We must try to assess it. In his *Dictatus Papae* he proclaimed:

1   The Roman church was founded by the Lord alone.

2   Only the Roman pontiff deserves to be called universal.

3   Only he can depose or absolve bishops.

4   In a Council, his legate can give orders to all bishops even if he is himself of lower rank and he alone is empowered to pronounce a sentence of deposition.

5   The pope may depose those who do not attend.

6   It is forbidden to remain under the same roof as one whom he has excommunicated.

7   He alone may, as circumstances require, establish new laws, organize the admission of new peoples (*novas plebes congregare*), change a collegiate church into an abbey, divide a wealthy bishopric, unite poor bishoprics.

8   He alone may use the imperial insignia.

9   The pope is the only man whose feet all princes are bound to kiss.

10   He is the only man whose name is pronounced in all the churches.

11   His name is unique in the world.

12   He may depose emperors.

13   He may, should need arise, translate a bishop from one see to another.

14   He may at will ordain a cleric of any church.

15   He whom he has ordained may govern another church, but he may not fight; he may not receive a higher grade of orders from another bishop.

16   No synod may be called General except on his instruction.

17   No canonical text exists outside his authority.

18   His sentence may not be varied by anyone and he may by himself vary those given by everyone.

19   He may not be judged by anyone.

20   No one may condemn a decision of the Holy See.

21   Important cases from every church must be referred to him.

22   The Roman Church has never erred and, as Scripture shows, can never err.

23   The Roman pontiff, if canonically ordained, undoubtedly becomes holy by the merits of St Peter, according to the belief of St Ennodius bishop of Pavia in agreement with that of many of the Fathers, as may be seen from the Decree of the blessed pope Symmachus.

24   On his order and with his authorization, subjects are permitted to sue.

25   He may depose and absolve bishops outside any synodal assembly.

26   He who is not with the Roman Church is not to be deemed a Catholic.

27   The pope may release subjects from an oath of fidelity made to those who are unjust.[114]

What a change of climate! From now on, the vocabulary is one of power. He who speaks thus from Rome is Roman pontiff indeed. This language is the more serious in that it may well have been in part provoked by the aggressive attitude of Constantinople.[115] Rome is affirming her claims. Her bishop goes on to accord himself the outward marks of sovereignty, taking the tiara.[116] However noble the intended aim of liberty over against the princes, a slope had been dug which half a century after Gregory VII's death would lead St Bernard, himself a defender of papal theocracy,[117] to write to Eugene III in about 1148:

> I do not know that one would have seen Peter in procession tricked out with jewels or silks, or sheltered beneath a golden canopy, or riding astride a white mount, or with an escort of soldiers or surrounded by a boisterous retinue of servants . . . Tolerate, then, as a concession to our time, this splendour which makes you successor to Constantine, but take care you do not come to hold it as your due.[118]

Soon we come to Boniface VIII (1294-1303) and his bull *Unam Sanctam* which was evoked, as we know, by his struggle with Philip the Fair. No longer was the Holy See's lordship over the world subject to any limit. The Church has received from God the two swords and it is she who has delegated the secular sword to the State. The *plenitudo potestatis* of the Roman pontiff was absolute. Now appears the claim which reaches the heart of our problem: *subesse Romano Pontifici omni humanae creaturae declaramus, dicimus, diffinimus omnino esse de necessitate salutis* (DS 875): 'We declare, state and define that it is absolutely necessary to salvation for every human creature to be subject to the Roman pontiff.' If the Greeks or others refuse this submission, that very fact proclaims them *se de ovibus Christi non esse* (DS 872): 'to be no part of Christ's sheep'. But we must quote the full text, published on 18 November 1302:

> We are obliged by the faith and hold – and we do firmly believe and sincerely confess – that there is one Holy Catholic and Apostolic Church, and that outside this Church there is neither salvation nor remission of sins, as the spouse proclaims in the Song, 'One is my dove, one is my perfect one, the only one from her mother, preferred before her that bore her.' (Song of Sol. 6.9)
>
> She represents the one mystical Body of which Christ is the head, God being the head of Christ. In this Church there is 'one Lord, one faith, one baptism'. (Eph. 4.5) At the time of the flood there was one ark of Noah, symbolizing the one Church; this was completed in one cubit (Gen. 6.16), and had one, namely Noah, as helmsman and captain; outside which all things on earth, we read, were destroyed. We venerate her, the only one, as the Lord said through his prophet: 'Deliver, O God, my soul from the sword, and my only one from the foot of the dog!' (Ps. 21.21) For he prayed at the same time for the soul, that is to say, for himself, the head, and for the body, since he called the body his only one, that is, the Church, because of the unity between the Church and her spouse, in the faith, in the sacraments and in love. She is the seamless robe (John 19.23) of the Saviour, not torn but taken by lot. This is why this Church, the one and only, has only one body and one head – not two heads, like a monster – namely Christ, and Christ's vicar is Peter, and Peter's successor, for the Lord said to Peter himself, 'Feed my sheep.' (John 21.17) 'My sheep' he said in general, not these or those sheep; wherefore he is understood to have committed them all to him. Therefore if the Greeks or others say that they were not committed to Peter and his successors, they necessarily confess that they are not of Christ's sheep, for the Lord says in John, 'There is one fold and one shepherd.' (John 10.16)
>
> And we learn from the words of the gospel that in this Church and in her power are two swords, the spiritual and the temporal. For when the apostles said 'Behold, here' (that is, in the Church, since it was the apostles who spoke) 'are two swords' – the Lord did not reply, 'It is too much', but 'It is enough.' (Luke 22,38) Truly he who denies that the temporal sword is in the power of Peter, misunderstands the words of the Lord, 'Put up thy sword into the

sheath.' (John 18.11) Both are in the power of the Church, the spiritual sword and the material. But the latter is to be used for the Church, the former by her; the former by the priest, the latter by kings and captains but at the will and by the permission of the priest. The one sword, then, should be under the other, and temporal authority subject to spiritual . . . The Truth attests that the spiritual power can establish the earthly power and can judge it if it is not good . . . If, therefore, the earthly power err, it shall be judged by the spiritual power; and if a lesser power err, it shall be judged by a greater. But if the supreme power err, it can be judged only by God, not by man; for the testimony of the apostle is: 'The spiritual man judgeth all things, yet he himself is judged of no man' (1 Cor. 2.15). For this authority, although given to a man and exercised by a man, is not human, but rather divine, given at God's mouth to Peter and established on a rock for him and his successors in him whom he confessed, the Lord saying to Peter himself, 'Whatsoever thou shalt bind . . .' (Matt. 16.19) Whoever therefore resists this power thus ordained of God, 'resists the ordinance of God' (Rom. 13.2), unless like Manes he imagines that there are two beginnings (*principia*); an opinion which we judge false and heretical for, according to Moses, it was not in the beginnings (*in principiis*) but 'in the beginning (*in principio*) God created the heaven and the earth' (Gen. 1.1).

Furthermore we declare, state, define and pronounce that it is altogether necessary to salvation for every human creature to be subject to the Roman pontiff (*DS* 870-75).

So the Church and indeed the whole design of God, is riveted to the papacy, dependent upon it, concentrated on it. Apart from God himself, nothing can escape the *plenitudo potestatis* of Christ's vicar. Everything has been entrusted to Peter and his successor (*DS* 870). The *plenitudo* allows no exceptions and no concessions.[119]

It did not take long to articulate a theory accounting for the absolute *plenitudo* which had developed. Its fullest expression occurs in the writings of Augustine Trionfo, often called Augustine of Ancona, an Augustinian hermit who died in 1328.[120] He asserted that the Roman pontiff enjoyed the only 'power' which came *a Deo immediate*. From this he deduced that all power (*potestas, jurisdictio*) flowed from the pope, both within the Church and, except in so far as immediate execution was concerned, within civil society also. The pontiff was therefore subject to no control; he possessed supreme power in matters of doctrine and so of determining what was to be believed: *determinare quae sunt fidei*; he was the author of positive law, with divine law and natural law alone outside his control; his power reached even the unbaptized; the emperor, like all earthly sovereigns, was *minister papae*; 'universal justice' derived from this power, which extended even to the saints in heaven and the souls in purgatory, hell and limbo alone remaining outside its scope. In fact,

> This papal power does not extend only to all Christians, but even to pagans and Jews, to the extent of the demands made by the chief concerns of divine law. (Q. 22-4, pp. 136-9) In one sense it reaches to the Church Triumphant, since the canonization of saints derives from the pope; though here he enjoys only relative infallibility: *secundum allegata et probata sibi*. (Q. 14, a.4, p. 98) The Church Suffering is certainly included; for the dead being still *viatores*, on their journey, remain *de foro papae*. (Q. 29, a.4, p. 178) It is for the pope therefore to distribute the prayers of the Church among them and in theory there is nothing to stop him emptying the whole of purgatory. But here he must pay special attention to the *clavis discretionis et scientiae* as well as the *clavis potentiae*. (Q. 30, a.5, p. 185; Q. 32, a.3, p. 194) As for hell and the limbos (Q. 33-4), they are quite outside his province.[121]

How could one avoid supposing that a Roman pontiff, endowed with *plenitudo potestatis* of such exalted dimensions, was more than a pope?

It was not long, either, before popular, unsophisticated art, that important witness to general Christian feeling, came to represent God the Father in the likeness of the Roman pontiff; this is found even in missals. Thus a fifteenth-century French missal now in the museum at Cluny shows him crowned with a tiara and seated on the papal throne. It was perhaps less grossly misguided to give the pope the title 'vicar of God', *vicarius Dei*, but its dogmatic implications were no less dangerous. It left a deposit in the thought of Innocent III (died 1216), who said that the pope 'stands mid-way between God and man, . . . less than God but more than man'.[122] Innocent IV (died 1254) used the title to extend his power beyond the limits of the faithful and the great theorists of papal power, John de Torquemada (died 1468) and Robert Bellarmine (died 1621) found it the most useful term for a general outline of papal power.[123] The cardinals Colonna in a note dated 10 May 1297 on the deposition and translation of bishops, declared this to be reserved to the pope on the grounds that *quodammodo Deus est, id est Dei vicarius* (in some way he is God, that is to say, he is God's vicar).[124] John André (died 1348) explains: in his office the pope *non est homo sed Dei vicarius*, he is no mere man but God's vicar.[125] Alvarez Pelayo (died 1349) was even more precise: *non est homo simpliciter sed Deus, id est vicarius Dei*, he is *quodammodo* God, in some way God, *quasi Deus in terris est* (as it were God on earth).[126] The canonist Beldus de Ubaldis repeats this teaching at the same period[127] and it is echoed a few decades later by Louis du Pont.[128] The famous Panormitanus (Nicolas de Tudeschi, died 1445), while making some finer distinctions,[129] did not hesitate to write that we must think of God himself being at work in what the pope does as vicar of God.[130] His thought is indeed more flexible than his words. But those words are uttered.

The ultramontane expressions met in our survey can thus claim a long pedigree. They have been smoothed by the usage of centuries, which explains why it is so hard to rid the Catholic mind of them. They form part of an ethos which has confused the several levels of authority properly belonging to the bishops of Rome, resulting in an interplay of claims sometimes provoked by unclear historical situations, sometimes thought necessary to restore the Church to the purity of the gospel, sometimes fed by an appetite for power. It is hard to sort it out. But the facts remain. Expressions like 'the pope is the vicar of God' or 'the pope is God's successor', carefully avoided by Vatican I, still reappear after Vatican II.[131] It cannot be denied that in Catholic attitudes generally, as much as possible is made of the pope.

We have travelled far from the time when Leo the Great

(440-61) called himself modestly 'the vicar of Peter' and even then was careful to add, 'the blessed apostle Peter does not cease from presiding over his see (of Rome)'.[132] Even earlier this had been how Siricius, who died in 399, saw it.[133] The popes of the fifth and sixth centuries thought of themselves simply as 'holding the place' of Peter, perpetuating within the communion of bishops the 'once for all' of Peter's apostolate. In the eleventh and twelfth centuries 'vicar of Peter', 'vicar of Peter and Paul', and 'vicar of the apostolic see' still remained the ordinary titles.[134] They were no mere figures of speech from the pen of Gregory VII.[135] But soon after, thanks especially to Innocent III, 'vicar of Christ' became the preferred expression, which changed the fine traditional meaning of that phrase.[136] The Roman pontiff had now in effect begun to say, 'although successor to the Prince of the Apostles, we are not his vicar nor that of any man or apostle, but we are the vicar of Jesus Christ himself'.[137]

The title has now received a plenary juridical meaning which it already had alongside its sacramental meaning, but the juridical has now taken clear precedence over the sacramental. It means that a superior authority has devolved powers upon his representative for the duration of his own absence. This authority is Christ's. Augustine Trionfo defined it thus in 1324: '*Papa succedit Petro in personali administratione . . . , Christo autem succedit in officio et in universali iurisdictione.*' (Summa XIX, 4) '*Papa est nomen iurisdictionis.*' In this situation the pope owes his power not to the title of bishop of Rome and to the apostolic see, but directly as *caput Ecclesiae* to the title of vicar of Christ: according to Augustine, he might well not be bishop of Rome . . .

This is clearly a distortion and was criticized as such even at the time. It was not the teaching of Vatican I which, in citing the speech made to the Council of Ephesus by the legate Philip and then the Decree of Florence, speaks of the primacy of jurisdiction delivered to Peter and since him '*Suis successoribus episcopis sanctae Romanae sedis*' (*DS* 3056 and 3059), indeed of the *Ecclesia Romana* (*DS* 3060).[138]

From the rending of the Church to the will for unity

During the time when this vision of the papacy was taking more solid shape in the West, even before the reign of Gregory VII, the drift which for several centuries had taken the East further from the West led to a total break. The *episcopus Ecclesiae Catholicae*, which had been understood in earlier centuries as *Ecclesia Catholica Urbis Romae*, the bishop of the local church at Rome which had stayed faithful to the apostolic faith[139] – this bishop now considered himself to be a universal bishop with the entire Church for his diocese; and at the very moment when a large part of that Church had severed all links with him.

Michael Cerularius was patriarch of Constantinople from 1043 to 1058. His opposite number during the long dispute with Rome was the legate of Leo IX (who died in 1054), Cardinal Humbert de Moyenmoutier, a man whose reforming ideas were influential but whose character lacked moderation. His mind being closed to the just requests of the East, he had no hesitation in describing as a 'synagogue of Satan' any church which refused certain of the Roman demands. On occasions he decided questions more by abuse than by sweet reason. He it was who, on 16 July 1054, marched into the church of Sancta Sophia at Constantinople with his retinue, during the solemn liturgy, deposited on the altar a sentence of excommunication against the patriarch and marched out, shaking the dust from his shoes. Indeed,

> the bull of excommunication was a very curious production, bearing more clearly than any previous documents the stamp of Cardinal Humbert: vehemence bordering on violence and insult, a display of dubious historical learning and accusations which could not always be verified.[140]

On 7 December 1965, the bishop of Rome, Paul VI, and the patriarch of Constantinople, Athenagoras, lifted this excommunication.[141] The gesture was rich in symbolic meaning, as both parties to it, always on the watch for gestures of ecumenical significance, would have wished. It has to do with both Rome and the East.

The Eastern Church turns towards her Western 'sister' in

order to give that communion between them, never wholly broken, the fullness which the Lord intended. The Western Church undertakes to adopt an attitude towards her Eastern 'sister', an attitude which is sisterly but also just, in respecting both the long history of the latter (which has generated its own rights) and, above all, the true nature of communion between churches. But Roman maximizing views of the papacy, further inflated after the schism by the *Dictatus Papae* of Gregory VII and the bull *Unam Sanctam* of Boniface VIII, have in spite of certain nuances of Vatican I and the clarifications of Vatican II, continued to mark the Western Catholic view of the papacy down to our own times. They will therefore have to form a main topic for discussion within the new relations which it is hoped to establish. The Roman pontiff[142] must no longer be 'more than a pope'.[143]

A similar desire for unity within the West itself, torn apart since the Reformation, also brings with it the same anxieties and the same questions over the exercise of Roman power. The problem is no longer to know if there should be a pope. What is now asked of the (Roman) Catholic Church is to show what the pope is when he is not more than a pope. It may be that the declaration *Mysterium Ecclesiae* (1973) opens a way ahead:

> . . . it must first be observed that the meaning of the pronounce-
> ments of faith depends partly on the expressive power of the
> language used at a certain point of time and in particular circum-
> stances. Moreover, it sometimes happens that some dogmatic
> truth is first expressed incompletely (but not falsely), and at a later
> date, when considered in a broader context of faith or human
> knowledge, it receives a fuller and more perfect expression. In
> addition, when the Church makes new pronouncements, she intends
> to confirm or clarify what is in some way contained in Sacred
> Scripture or in previous expressions of Tradition. But at the same
> time she usually has the intention of solving certain questions or
> removing certain errors. All these things have to be taken into
> account in order that these pronouncements may be properly
> interpreted. Finally, even though the truths which the Church
> intends to teach through her dogmatic formulas are distinct from
> the changeable conceptions of a given epoch and can be expressed

without them, nevertheless, it can sometimes happen that these truths may be enunciated by the Sacred Magisterium in terms that bear the traces of such conceptions.

In view of the above, it must be stated that the dogmatic formulas of the Church's Magisterium were from the very beginning suitable for communicating revealed truth, and that as they are, they remain for ever suitable for communicating this truth to those who interpret them correctly. It does not follow, however, that every one of these formulas has always been (suitable for communicating truth) or will always be so to the same extent. For this reason theologians seek to define exactly the intention of teaching proper to the various formulas, and in carrying out this work they are of considerable assistance to the living Magisterium of the Church, to which they remain subordinated. For this reason also it often happens that ancient dogmatic formulas and others closely connected with them remain living and fruitful in the habitual usage of the Church, but with suitable expository and explanatory additions that maintain and clarify their original meaning. In addition, it has sometimes happened that in this habitual usage of the Church certain of these formulas gave way to new expressions which, proposed and approved by the Sacred Magisterium, presented more clearly or more completely the same meaning.[144]

2
The Pope: Bishop of Rome

The Pope:
Bishop of Rome

What then is the pope when he is only the pope? To find the answer demands method. Nothing would be more unfortunate than to set off aimlessly on a quest as important as this, both for its subject and in view of the ecumenical climate we have described. We could easily go round in circles.

These considerations make it important to understand *Pastor Aeternus* in the way that Vatican II received it, in the light of the Great Tradition. On one hand belief that the Holy Spirit is at work in the Church makes it almost impossible to separate Vatican I from Vatican II. On the other hand, the assertion that the Church of God subsists in the Catholic Church but not so as to be confined within her makes us refuse any solution which proposes to 'forget Vatican I' (*sic*). For the very name of an ecumenical search for *communion* in the truth of the faith demands that we must be honest.[1] Even though it be true, as the declaration *Mysterium Ecclesiae* of 24 June 1973 insists, that dogmatic formulas of the (Roman) Catholic Church are able to give only an incomplete answer, calling for a deeper understanding in a wider context before reaching a more complete and perfect expression;[2] and although it sometimes needs a long time for the actual formulas to stand out clearly from meanings they have taken on from their immediate context and from the historical moment of their formulation;[3] they are nevertheless not false. The task must therefore be to open them out, not to deny them. We have earlier expressed our belief that the solemn affirmations of the two Vatican Councils are among those which need 'ecumenical interpretation' to bring them to that degree of purity from distorting factors and of fullness of meaning which will be sealed only when they are 'received' by the whole body of Churches rooted in the apostolic tradition.

Taking our stand within the (Roman) Catholic tradition, then, we will try to project on to *Pastor Aeternus* the light of Tradition, especially as it was in the period of the Church known as undivided, when, despite ancient conflicts and schisms, the East as such and the West as such were not yet separated. The Fathers of Vatican I had indeed claimed to carry forward this 'ancient and constant faith of the universal Church' (*DS* 3052) rooted in the period 'when East met with West in the unity of faith and love' (*DS* 3065). For this is the normative period.[4] We shall naturally take account of the way in which other ecclesial traditions read the literature of the period. And we shall not forget how the (Roman) Catholic Church has, especially since the breach with the East and the Reformation schisms, given herself a type of primacy related to the conditions of her life then and not to that earlier 'communion of all the Churches' which had been shattered by schism.

From the primacy of the Church of Rome to that of her bishop

We noted earlier that the constitution *Pastor Aeternus* of Vatican I speaks of the apostolic see and of the Roman church in its central chapter (*DS* 3059, 3060, 3062, 3063) and in other places where it lays down the status of the Roman pontiff (*DS* 3056, 3057, 3066, 3067, 3069-71). In one of these key paragraphs the pope's power of jurisdiction even seems to depend on the supremacy of the Roman church among all the churches: 'We teach and declare that the Roman church has by the Lord's arrangement a primacy of ordinary power over all the other churches and that this power of jurisdiction of the Roman pontiff, truly episcopal, is immediate' (*DS* 3060). The same relationship between the see or seat (*cathedra, sedes*) and the bishop who occupies it breaks through again when the latter is deemed infallible when he speaks *ex cathedra*, from his seat (*DS* 3074, 3071). Moreover, the text makes it clear that it is the infallibility of the entire Church which is exercised by the one who speaks 'from this seat' (*DS* 3074).

It is of course important not to isolate and stress exaggeratedly the dependence in *Pastor Aeternus* of the bishop of Rome on the place of his church, his see, his *cathedra* (which is the heart of his cathedral). The same Vatican I document includes statements which ratify the reverse relationship. The dependence must, however, at least be recalled. It bears witness to roots which go down deep into the tradition of the undivided Church. For there at least the primacy which Rome was recognized to hold was tied in the first place not to the person of the bishop but to the particular significance which the local church at Rome had among the local churches.[5]

The importance of the see itself (*sedes*) and its precedence over the bishop who occupies it (the *sedens*[6]) must always be remembered. It is in a way the dignity of the *sedes* which colours the *sedens* rather than the other way round. Once it has been founded the local church precedes its bishop, even though it would not exist without him. The episcopal see is contained within the church. And throughout the first centuries it was also the local church who chose the occupant of the see, even though it was the bishops of neighbouring sees who would ordain him once the local church had vouched for the faith and other qualities of the man chosen.

Early in the third century the *Apostolic Tradition*, following no doubt an already ancient practice, laid down: 'Let the bishop be ordained being in all things without fault, chosen by the people. And when he has been found acceptable to all . . . let the bishops lay hands on him' (ch. 2). This was aimed at something more than democratic procedures, a matter which would not have concerned the people of that time. It belongs to the understanding of the Church along the lines we have recalled. The same comment applies to Leo the Great when in the fifth century he echoed this law so vigorously.[7] And in the East, where the discipline developed into 'a sort of co-option decided at the level of the college of bishops',[8] ecclesiastical law as far as the fourth-century texts never denied the local church 'the right to take part in the choice of its bishop'.[9] The local church itself in its communion of clergy and laity comes first and is as a whole the guardian of apostolicity. The bishops follow each other on the *sedes*. As he takes his place on the *cathedra* after the occupants of neighbouring sees have laid hands on him with the prayers of the community, each new bishop becomes the bearer of his see's tradition, charged to receive it, to defend it, to make it grow and to guard it within the communion of all the churches. This applies also to the relation between the Church of Rome and its bishop. If he has certain prerogatives within the college of bishops, he has them because of the eminence of his see.

Events following the death of Fabian, bishop of Rome, in January 250 provide an interesting example. The emperor Decius tried to prevent the election of a successor. During the long interval before Cornelius was elected in the spring of 251, a group of 'confessors of the faith' and of the Roman clergy took over the running of the Roman church.[10] They even sent four letters to Cyprian and the clergy of Carthage, at that time in the grip of a serious crisis: Novatian was one of the authors. So even when 'the see is empty, priests and faithful continue to be concerned with events beyond the sea and the mountains: they reckon to make it known',[11] Harnack did not fail to comment:

> What makes this Church so great is that she knows her duty in a more universal way and carries it out with more assurance than do the other churches . . . The college of priests and deacons feels and speaks as a bishop; for it is not upon the bishops only, or at least not in one particular way, that the incomparable authority of Rome rests; but on her origins and history, on the faith and the love, on the sincerity and the devotion of the entire *Ecclesia Romana*. The documents relating to the period of the vacancy in the see provide one of the most illuminating pages in the story of how her primacy developed.[12]

Although deprived of her bishop, the local church of Rome never supposed that this paradoxical situation excused her from her duties.

A passage from Tertullian's *De praescriptione*, about AD 200, also bears witness to the authority which attached to the local church of Rome:

> Run through the apostolic churches, where the very thrones of the apostles preside to this day over their districts, where the authentic letters of the apostles are still recited, bringing the voice and face of

each one of them to mind. If Achaea is nearest to you, you have Corinth. If you are not far from Macedonia, you have Philippi and Thessalonica. If you can go to Asia, you have Ephesus. If you are close to Italy, you have Rome, the nearest authority for us also. How fortunate is that church upon which the apostles poured their whole teaching together with their blood, where Peter suffered like his Lord, where Paul was crowned with John's death (the Baptist), where the apostle John, after he had been immersed in boiling oil without harm, was banished to an island.

Let us see what she learned, what she taught, what bond of friendship she had with the churches of Africa. She knows one Lord God, Creator of the universe, and Jesus Christ, born of the Virgin Mary, Son of God the Creator, and the resurrection of the flesh; she unites the Law and the Prophets with the writings of the evangelists and apostles; from that source she drinks her faith, and that faith she seals with water, clothes with the Holy Spirit, feeds with the Eucharist, encourages to martyrdom; and against that teaching she receives no one.[13]

It is the teaching by the word and the witness, rooted in the great apostolic tradition, which confers upon the churches that authority and prestige which sheds lustre on those whom the Spirit places at their head. The distinctive authority of the bishop of Rome thus derives from that of his church, from the apostolic throne (*sedes*) from which he presides. His primacy in the college of bishops is given him through the privilege of his apostolic see.[14] Is not the church of Rome, in the very ancient words of Ignatius of Antioch, 'the church which presides in love'?[15]

The constitution *Pastor Aeternus* relates its teaching specifically to the great ecumenical councils of the undivided Church (*DS* 3065). Here also the connection between episcopal sees and bishops is along the line we have described. The sixth canon of Nicaea (325) connects the power of the bishops of certain sees, among them Rome, with the prerogatives (*presbeia*) of the churches in question:

Let the ancient customs prevail which are in Egypt and Libya and Pentapolis, according to which the bishop of Alexandria has authority (*exousia*) over all these places. For this is also customary

71

to the bishop of Rome. In like manner in Antioch and in the other provinces (*eparchiais*), the privileges (*presbeia*) are to be preserved to the churches. But this is clearly to be understood that if anyone be made a bishop without the consent of the metropolitan, the great synod declares that he shall not be a bishop.[16]

The Nicene Fathers thus recognized the prerogatives of the sees of Alexandria and Antioch which support the authority and power of their bishops. The case of Rome is alluded to in a parenthesis only.[17] Latin translators who try to read into it 'an elliptical definition of primacy' probably overstrain the original idea.[18] One could no doubt simply conclude that 'the example of the great Western church reinforces ancient ecclesiastical traditions'.[19] Moreover, it is clear that the three sees accorded a special place in the organization of the Church are not simply the three capitals of the then world. They are also 'the three sees for which Eusebius throughout his *Ecclesiastical History* consistently supplies the succession of bishops going back to the apostles'.[20] Would their bishops have been accorded such great power (*exousia*) if these churches had not been of apostolic foundation?[21]

Theodoret of Cyrrhus showed the same understanding when he wrote to the pope Leo asking for justice to be done him in the backwash which followed the Council of Ephesus – where the influence of Pope Celestine had certainly been 'less discreet than that of Sylvester at Nicaea':[22]

He praises the faith of the city of Rome and recalls the words of the apostle Paul. (Rom. 1.8) He grounds the pre-eminence of the see of the bishop of Rome on the fact that this city is the capital of the Empire, but also because it is the site of the tombs of the apostles Peter and Paul, and so ultimately on its apostolic origins.[23]

At the Council of Chalcedon in 451, the legates of Bishop Leo of Rome themselves base his universal authority on the precedence of the Church of Rome within the universal Church.

From the start of the first session, Paschasinus, the pope's legate, calls Leo

'the pope [the Greek says simply *episkopos*] of the city of Rome which is the head of all the Churches' . . . If the city of Rome – that is, the Church of that city – is the head of all the other particular Churches, the same should be said of the bishop of that city. It is a short step from 'head of all the Churches' to 'bishop of all the Churches'. In fact the legates refer to the bishop of Rome as 'archbishop of all the Churches', which is found in the Greek version of the Acts at the start of the fourth session, while the Latin translation says 'pope of the universal Church'. The variant translation shows that no importance was attached to the difference between 'universal Church' and 'all the churches'.[24]

The Third Council of Constantinople in 681 'received' the letter of Pope Agatho, who described himself as 'bishop of the holy, catholic and apostolic Church of the city of Rome'.[25] Now among the factors which worked in favour of this reception, apart from the harmony of its contents with the witness of the blessed Peter, was the fact that it came from 'the very holy archbishop of the first apostolic see of ancient Rome'.[26] Moreover, the Acts of this Council were to be sent to the five patriarchal sees, with Rome at the head of the list:

> to the apostolic see of the blessed prince of the apostles, Peter, that is, to the most holy and blessed patriarch Agatho, the most holy pope of ancient Rome; to the see of the most holy, catholic and apostolic, the great Church of Constantinople, that is, to George, the most holy and most blessed patriarch . . .[27]

It is to be noted that in both cases the bishop of Rome is styled only in connection with the quality of his see and its duties, as would be any bishop of an important see. And when, after Agatho's death before the end of the Council, Leo II took on the condemnation of Pope Honorius who had been declared heretical, he used a formula which reveals the same point of view: Honorius 'had not brought lustre to that apostolic Church (of Rome) by means of the apostolic tradition'.[28] For, as a bishop, he who presided on the *cathedra* of Rome could not be seen apart from his relationship to his see and so to his local church.[29] His prerogatives and responsibilities alike are those of the church whose servant, minister and representative he is.

The documents just cited show that the East allowed a special authority to the bishop of Rome which Rome herself claimed, especially in the person of Leo the Great.[30] The terms of this authority, expressed in precise, carefully chosen language, must not be pressed too far. Its roots are set firmly in the primacy of this church among the others. It is the primacy of the first see (*prima sedes*), the primacy of that apostolic church which possessed what Irenaeus called the most powerful origin (*potentior principalitas*), which was reflected on to the one who occupied its chair (the *sedens*).[31]

The local church of the 'City', founded by the apostles Peter and Paul

What is the source of that primacy of the local church at Rome within the communion of all the churches? How should we explain the cluster of privileges (*presbeia*) which make up her particular authority? These are questions which anyone who reflects deeply upon the evidence of tradition must ask.

It may perhaps cause surprise that Jerusalem is not the most important see in Christendom and that the church which guards the 'trophies' of the Lord himself, the cross and the tomb, should not hold the office of *potentior principalitas*. It is even more surprising to find that Canon 7 of Nicaea accords that church only one primacy of honour, that which belongs to her from being the place of departure for the newborn faith.[32] At the first Council of Constantinople in 381, the famous Canon 3 gave standing to an accomplished fact by recognizing in Constantinople, the New Rome, a primacy of honour second only to that of the Old Rome.[33] Not until the Council of Chalcedon in 451 did Jerusalem acquire an authentic jurisdiction over the three Palestines. But she remained in the fifth and lowest place in what became the pentarchy, by which the Church was divided into five great patriarchates.[34] A century later, the *Novellae* of Justinian established permanently this order of precedence with the Church of Rome at the head, its bishop finding himself styled 'the first of all the priests'.[35]

The hierarchy of the Churches was thus determined in relation not to the story of Jesus, but to the apostolic mission and witness. It derives from the apostolicity of the Church. Its great centres are therefore not the holy places of the Lord's life, ministry and Passion, but those points on the map of the world where in the power of the Spirit the gospel of God took root in order to spread out among all the peoples of the world. The local church at Rome is first among the churches because the martyrdom of Peter and Paul there made it the supreme place of apostolic witness, not because it was established before the others. It is certainly true that the fact that Rome was the city, the capital, was not without influence on the directions in which the gospel spread. It may even be that this was the determining fact up to the time that the two apostles arrived there. Until Leo the Great refused to accept Canon 28 of Chalcedon, which made the importance of a see depend too heavily on the political importance of a city (in this case, Constantinople), the parallel between the administrative position of cities and the privileges (*presbeia*) of churches went without saying.[36] It was not surprising; the reverse would have been astonishing. Nevertheless, the geographical importance is, as it were, relativized by that of the apostolic witness which 'those whom the Lord had sent' brought to the place.

Irenaeus of Lyons (about 180) undoubtedly gives the clearest and most important statement of the unparalleled claim to apostolicity, and so the outstanding authority, of the local church of Rome:

> Anyone who wishes to discern the truth may see in every Church in the whole world the Apostolic tradition clear and manifest. We can enumerate those who were appointed as bishops in the churches by the Apostles and their successors to our own day, who never knew and never taught anything resembling their foolish doctrine . . . But (as it would be very long in a book of this kind to enumerate the episcopal lists in all the churches) by pointing out the apostolic tradition and faith announced to mankind, which has been brought down to our time by successions of bishops, in the greatest, most ancient and well-known church, founded and established by the two most glorious apostles, Peter and Paul, at Rome, we can confound all who in any other way, either for self-pleasing or for vainglory, or by blindness or perversity, hold unauthorized meetings.

It is with this church, on account of her more powerful origin (*propter potentiorem principalitatem*) that it is necessary that every church should agree, that is, the faithful from all sides; (this church) where that which is the tradition from the apostles has been preserved always by those who are from all parts.

The blessed apostles after founding and building up the church entrusted the office of bishop to Linus. Paul speaks of this Linus in his letter to Timothy. Anacletus followed him. After him, in the third place after the apostles the episcopate came to Clement, who not only saw the apostles but spoke with them; he had their preaching ringing in his ears and Tradition before his eyes. He was not alone in this, for there were still many left at the time who had been instructed by the apostles. When Clement was bishop a great dissension arose among the brethren in Corinth, and the church in Rome sent a powerful letter to the Corinthians urging them to restore peace, renewing their faith and announcing to them the faith that they had lately received from the apostles. This was to the effect that there is one God almighty, Maker of heaven and earth, Creator of man, who brought in the flood, called Abraham, led his people out of the land of Egypt, appointed the Law, sent the Prophets, and has prepared fire for the devil and his angels.[37]

The local church at Rome thus owes her greatness and her particular place to her link with 'the most glorious apostles Peter and Paul'. That is the source of her 'most powerful origin', *potentior principalitas*.[38] But if Peter and Paul are called 'most glorious', it can only be a reference to their martyrdom at Rome.[39] For Irenaeus, the death within her boundaries of Peter and Paul means that God has signed the church of Rome with the greatest and most powerful, most authentically apostolic seal.

To see how well the thought of Irenaeus harmonizes with the Tradition that it transmits, we may recall certain items included in that Tradition. About the year 95 Clement of Rome wrote this about the two apostles in his letter to the Corinthians, which Irenaeus knew:[40]

Peter, who by reason of wicked jealousy, not only once or twice but frequently endured suffering and thus, bearing his witness, went to the glorious place which he merited. By reason of rivalry and contention Paul showed how to win the prize for patient endurance. Seven times he was in chains; he was exiled, stoned, became a herald (of the gospel) in East and West, and won the noble renown which his faith merited. To the whole world he taught righteousness, and reaching the limits of the West he bore his witness before rulers. And so, released from this world, he was taken up into the holy place and became the greatest example of patient suffering.[41]

To this 'witness' has since been added 'a great multitude of the elect who by reason of jealousy were the victims of many outrages and tortures and who became outstanding examples among us'.[42] The martyrdom of the two apostles is seen both as the beginning and as the pattern of witness to Christ in face of 'jealousy'.

In the same period Ignatius of Antioch wrote to the church of Rome, and he also associated the two apostles Peter and Paul, inseparable from each other, with the destiny of the church 'which presides in love'. He was thinking of their martyrdom:

I plead with you, do not do me an unseasonable kindness. Let me be fodder for wild beasts - that is how I can get to God. I am God's wheat and I am being ground by the teeth of wild beasts to make a pure loaf for Christ. I would rather that you fawn on the beasts so that they may be my tomb and no scrap of my body be left. Thus, when I have fallen asleep, I shall be burden to no one. Then I shall be a real disciple of Jesus Christ when the world sees my body no more. Pray Christ for me that I may become God's sacrifice. I do not give you orders like Peter and Paul. They were apostles: I am a convict. They were at liberty: I am still a slave. But if I suffer, I shall be emancipated by Jesus Christ; and united with him, I shall rise to freedom. Even now as a prisoner, I am learning to forgo my own wishes.[43]

Peter and Paul are still associated together in a letter which Dionysius of Corinth wrote to Soter, bishop of Rome, around 170. Dionysius certainly wanted to emphasize that Rome was not the only church founded by the apostles. But he put it in a way which 'recognizes that the church at Rome carries more weight than that of Corinth',[44] and he does not separate the two apostles in their part at the beginnings of the Roman community. Eusebius of Caesarea transcribed this letter:

> And that they were martyred both on the same occasion, Dionysius, bishop of the Corinthians, proves in the following manner:
> 'In these ways you also, by such an admonition, have united the planting that came from Peter and Paul, of both the Romans and the Corinthians. For indeed both planted also in our Corinth, and likewise taught us; and likewise they taught together also in Italy, and were martyred on the same occasion.'
> These quotations I have made, in order to accredit still further the facts of the history.[45]

We have already quoted Tertullian of Carthage who, at about the same period as Irenaeus, spoke of the Roman church as the fortunate church 'upon which the apostles poured their whole teaching together with their blood'.[46] In about AD 255 the bishop of Caesarea, Firmilian, wrote with fiery eloquence to Cyprian of Carthage, unleashing his fury against the bishop of Rome, Stephen; but he still mentioned the connection with the two apostles:

> Such a departure Stephen has now dared to make by breaking the peace against you which his predecessors had always kept with you in mutual love and honour. In this way he defames the blessed apostles Peter and Paul, declaring that they had handed down this custom, who in fact execrated heretics in their own letters and warned us to avoid them. From this it is apparent that this tradition (of Stephen) is human, for it supports the heretics and assumes that they have the baptism which belongs to the Church alone.[47]

More than a century after the death of Irenaeus, the council gathered at Arles by order of Constantine sent a letter to Bishop Sylvester of Rome who, having been prevented from coming, was represented by two priests and two deacons. His absence was regretted, but it was recognized that if he had not been able to come it was because he had found it impossible to leave the places 'where the apostles also have their seat from day to day and where their outpoured blood bears continual witness to the glory of God'.[48] The local church at Rome, 'founded' in the blood of the apostles Peter and Paul, remains still their seat. This is what makes it distinctive:

> The tradition found in St Irenaeus and developed between the fourth and fifth centuries [sees] the origin of the Roman church, and so of her episcopate and her *cathedra*, in the two apostles who were joined by a single, unbreakable link as if they had become one person only. It was a unification already achieved in the liturgy, which celebrated on the same day, June 29, the martyrdom of the two apostles. This was not so much because they were martyred on the same day, as it would be said later in an attempt to explain the anomaly of this unique double commemoration; but because the two apostles could not be separated, for they had become a single entity in the foundation of the church of Rome, as Irenaeus had realized.[49]

The joint commemoration of the apostles Peter and Paul at Rome is attested from the year 258.[50] An interesting point, explained by what we have seen, is that this is one of the rare commemorations which the West has given to the East. From the fifth century at Rome there were two separate synaxes celebrated, one at the Vatican and the other at St Paul-outside-the-Walls; but in them both, the two apostles were honoured together. The East does not separate them in its liturgy either[51] and 'it is very curious to notice that all the texts concerned consistently take care to say nothing good about one of them without a balancing word of praise for the other'.[52] For they consider both of them together as 'the foundation of the apostles', united by the Lord himself in their unique mission, that of becoming 'the dyad of the Trinity'.[53] It is therefore important that the *Missale Romanum* promulgated by Paul VI in 1970 has joined Peter and Paul in the Eucharist for the vigil and the feast, thereby renewing an ancient tradition buried in the Church's memory; the separate celebration of Paul on 30 June is replaced by that of the first Roman martyrs.

The truth sustained by the *lex orandi* is perpetuated in other expressions of church life also.[54] The inseparable union of the two apostles was used in some circles to play down Peter's importance, among the reactions to which was the Inquisition's decree in the days of Jansenism (*DS* 1999) later taken up by

Pius X in 1910 (*DS* 3555). But from the time of Nicholas I, (died 867), the pope of the struggle with Photius, the Roman see has never ceased to introduce its most solemn acts with the formula *Auctoritate Apostolorum Petri et Pauli*. Pius IX used the formula for the definition of the Immaculate Conception (*DS* 2803), Pius XII for that of the Assumption (*DS* 3903).

Paul VI often returned to the joint foundation of the local church at Rome by Peter and Paul. The apostolic exhortation *Petrum et Paulum* in which he introduced the Year of Faith sounded the note loud and clear: Peter and Paul are 'the chief columns not only in the particular Church of Rome but in the entire holy Church of God spread throughout the whole world'. He ended with these words:

> In the name and with the authority of blessed Peter and Paul, apostles and martyrs, upon whose tombs this Church of Rome is established and flourishes as inheritor, disciple and guardian of the unity and catholicity whose centre and source they themselves fixed here for ever . . . We greet you and We bless you with all Our heart.[55]

He reaffirmed the link between the city and the martyrdom of Peter and Paul in the Apostolic Constitution on the vicariate of Rome (1977): 'It is here that this Church was founded and constituted by the ministry of the apostles Peter and Paul'; the gospel was 'proclaimed here by the apostles Peter and Paul, made fruitful by their blood and that of the martyrs, witnessed to by the exemplary lives of innumerable holy men and women'.[56] From Irenaeus in the early morning of tradition to the Church of today, an unbroken thread binds the authority and the prestige of the see of Rome to the glorious apostles Peter and Paul, inseparably joined in the Church's memory. From this fact we may at once deduce that 'Paul contributes to the authority of the Roman Church and the Holy See something *which God has willed to be present in its historical reality*'.[57] A simple but highly significant indication occurred at the Council of Ephesus, when Pope Celestine was acclaimed as the 'new Paul' and as guardian of the faith after his letter had been recognized as conforming to the Church's faith.[58]

An authority, distinctive and beyond dispute, therefore,

belongs to the local church at Rome, when it comes to the rule of faith deriving from the apostolic witness, because it had been the place where Peter and Paul had taught and the theatre of their martyrdom. That Peter and Paul conferred such tremendous authority on this local church is due alike to their martyrdom in the city recognized as the hub of the empire and to their own great standing among the apostles; this is attested as early as the canonical Book of the Acts of the Apostles which divides into two parts, the first built around the ministry of Peter and the second around that of Paul. These two martyrs of the city are none other than Peter, by virtue of his place among the twelve representing the fulfilment of the old covenant – the twelve thrones for the twelve tribes[59] – and Paul, associated by his own mission with the great and absolutely new gospel event which opened the covenant and changed the Church of God from a Jewish sect to a new people.

Martyrdom itself is important because it represents the supreme test of Christian genuineness, the absolute seal on the witness to the gospel. By his death the witness to the faith enters into communion with the glory of Christ Jesus himself. He makes in some way the journey through the cross his own. We should remember Ignatius of Antioch's desire for martyrdom and the reason for it:[60] only thus is one truly (*alethos*) a disciple by the 'imitation' of the Passion, only thus is one in full communion with Jesus the Christ.[61] The martyr is thus placed 'above the prophets as prophets, and therefore above the apostles as apostles'.[62] Now the death of Peter and Paul – a witness given to Christ in that city which is the centre of the world itself – joins into one the glory of the martyr and the greatness of the apostolate.

And what apostles! The communion which their martyrdom will seal is the encounter at Rome itself of the two teaching authorities (*magisteria*) of the New Testament. That which is, for Irenaeus, glorified in the liturgy of outpoured blood (Phil. 2.27; 2 Tim. 4.6) is the witness of the Word proclaimed. Brothers in their death for the Lord's sake, Peter and Paul are also brothers in the proclamation of the Word, a proclamation of such a quality that it becomes a 'magisterium':

In 2 Peter the shepherdship of Peter is being applied in a different way from that encountered in 1 Peter; and the primary emphasis is now on Peter as the guardian of the orthodox faith – a possible facet of the presbyter-shepherd, as we saw in Acts 20.28–30. His apostolic authority enables him to judge interpretations of Scripture, even the writings of another apostle. We can now speak of a 'Petrine magisterium', perhaps related to an application of the binding–loosing power we saw in Matthew.

If we study the Pastoral Letters of Paul (perhaps post-Pauline, just as the Petrine Epistles may be post-Petrine), we find that we may speak of a 'Pauline magisterium' as well. In 2 Timothy 1.13 Paul tells Timothy: 'Follow the pattern of sound words which you have heard from me.' Thus, in the later parts of the New Testament we have the development of a view of apostolic authority, and not just of Peter's authority, especially as a protection against false teaching (2 Tim. 4.3–4). The names of several apostles may have been invoked, e.g. the magisterium of James by the Jewish Christians. But in the canonical New Testament Peter and Paul are the most important figures in the developing trajectory of apostolic authority. By the time 2 Peter was written and in the circles it represented, the Petrine trajectory was beginning to outstrip the Pauline one. The catalyst for this may have been the fact that the troublesome opponents, gnostics probably, were arguing on the basis of Paul. The author felt that recourse to the authority of Peter would be persuasive in correcting their appeal to Paul.[63]

The seal which martyrdom sets on the Word, the climax of witness by mouth in witness by blood outpoured: this is what 'founds and constitutes' the Church of Rome in her 'more powerful origin', her stronger apostolic authenticity, her *potentior principalitas*. When the Latin version of Irenaeus uses the verb *fundare* (*Adv. Haer.* 3.3.1–2) it probably translates the Greek *themelioo*, which Irenaeus uses immediately afterwards in a passage where we possess the original Greek. Now of the many senses which the word may carry[64] we should keep 'render immovable', 'set up for ever', 'strongly reinforce the foundations'.[65] Peter and Paul by their *witness* of a gospel proclamation sealed and glorified in the *martyrdom* of 'glorious' death have provided the church at Rome with unbreakable foundations of exceptional quality. Moreover, the presence of their 'trophies' - their bodies and their tombs - has the effect in the outlook of the first centuries of making permanent their presence with the Roman community. Their witness becomes the common possession of the Church which celebrates the Eucharist on their 'confession'. They are therefore the foundation of her *potentior principalitas*. It is built on them. We know what Eusebius of Caesarea reported of Nero:

> . . . in his day Paul was beheaded at Rome itself, and that Peter likewise was crucified, and this story is accredited by the attachment, which prevails to this day, of the names of Peter and Paul to the cemeteries there; and in no less a degree also by a churchman, named Gaius, who lived in the time of Zephyrinus, bishop of the Romans. Gaius, in fact, when discoursing in writing with Proclus, a champion of the heresy of the Phrygians, speaks thus of the places where the sacred tabernacles of the said apostles have been laid:
>
> 'But I myself can point out the trophies of the apostles. For if it is thy will to proceed to the Vatican, or to the Ostian Way, thou wilt find the trophies of those who founded this church.'
>
> And that they were martyred both on the same occasion, Dionysius, bishop of the Corinthians, in a written communication to the Romans, proves in the following manner:
>
> 'In these ways you also, by such an admonition, have united the planting that came from Peter and Paul, of both the Romans and the Corinthians. For indeed both planted also in our Corinth, and likewise taught us; and likewise they taught together also in Italy, and were martyred on the same occasion.'[66]

Rome, then, was the seat of Peter and Paul, for they 'founded' the church there. But were they the first to evangelize there? That Paul was not with the Roman community at its inception is obvious from his letter to the Romans and from the Acts of the Apostles (Rom. 1.7; 15.28; Acts 28.14-15). The tradition that Peter came to Rome is too strong to be doubted, but it is most unlikely that he was present at the very start of the church there.[67] Moreover, we have no serious proof that there was a single bishop at Rome rather than a college of presbyters or bishops, before the middle of the second century. It is even difficult to show convincingly that any of the twelve became the head of any local church. Only much later did the twelve come to be seen as the bishops of the first Christian centres.[68] In any case Irenaeus knows nothing of Peter's episcopate at Rome. He makes it clear that Linus was the first bishop *after* the founders, Peter and Paul.

This is of primary importance. To think of Peter as the first link in a chain of bishops, in a purely juridical conception of the transmission of powers, is to devalue his proper function. That is unique, *ephapax*, once and for all. Peter 'founds' the Roman church because with Paul, by his teaching and his martyrdom, he makes it what it is: the church that is witness to the faith of the gospel. By the same law which willed that a people, Israel, should be and remain (Romans 11) the chosen people, a local church, that of Rome, thus became the guardian of the supreme apostolic witness. Faithful to the pattern of fulfilment in God's designs from the time of Abraham, an almost fleshly link joins the new people of God to the church of that city where Peter and Paul had their seat.

This, then, explains the weight of authority enjoyed by the local church at Rome within the communion of the churches: a weight of faith more than of powers, of example in witness more than of jurisdiction. She will therefore be called to exert an influence in a world where the means of communication will long remain precarious. As the Christian community at the heart of the new Babylon, she will become the 'memory' of the presence of salvation in the full tide of the world's sin, marked as she is by the outstanding authenticity of witness which it is her mission to guard.

A reading of the complex story of relationships between the churches over the first centuries, before traditions became fixed, shows that the principal axis around which the influence of the Roman church extended was the function of touchstone in contentious matters,[69] or that of providing a point of reference. A touchstone enables one to recognize and assess the value of something, in this case of teaching; the point of reference enables one to continue walking consistently in spite of difficulties, in this case to be guided by the model which the apostles provided. We are moving in the realm of signs and remembrances. The church of Rome is the one which calls to mind the great and glorious confession of the apostolic faith of which she had been the place and remains the guardian. She is also the guarantee of authentically belonging to Christ: to be in communion with her means to be linked with the glorious confession of the two apostles of the faith, and through them with the Lord.

Later, it is true, at the time when particular points will have hardened and will confront each other as matters of dogma, the communion of churches will feel itself committed in a way which will push the Roman church into the role of arbiter and judge, so that she claims for herself a large measure of judicial power. Ever more insistent on her place in the hierarchy of churches, she will place the weight of her authority behind the preservation of a unity where she wishes to be not just the touchstone, but the central piece. She will strive to become a mistress of truth to whom even the Eastern churches, not at all on the same wavelength as her, will be required to 'submit themselves'.[70] The pontificate of Leo the Great stands at the point of change. The paradox is that the church of Rome's emphasis on her vocation to maintain and protect unity should lead instead to division:

Great chunks of Christendom seceded. But in many others a feeling of frustration remained, a tenacious resentment. The drift which separated the West, in this case unanimously behind Rome, from the East, which was itself divided despite the efforts of the imperial power, this drift, already under way, began to get up speed. The role of Rome, vigorously promoted by Leo, was not indeed denied, though perhaps the East remained closer to the old conception ('touchstone' of the faith) while the pope imposed the new conception (arbiter and judge of orthodoxy), and thanks to the weight of political power the change of direction was decisive. There is no doubt that the danger which the Roman decision had warded off, the old temptation to blur in the glory of the risen Lord that humble sharing in the human condition through which Jesus carried out his work of salvation - this danger was enormous. That must be stressed, for Leo saved a basic and essential element in the gospel. But the circumstances mentioned earlier, above all the cultural estrangement that had come between East and West may have made a more flexible approach impossible. Would such an approach have allowed justice to be done to differences of awareness of the various aspects of the mystery which, as things were, clashed with each other to the point of incomprehension? A true agreement might then have been possible.[71]

By staking everything on the juridical, would not the Church of Rome to some extent have veiled or distorted the heart of her mission?

Be that as it may, we may say dogmatically that the axle of Rome's *principalitas*, around which other elements have grown without changing or disfiguring it, is the function of *memorial* of the great and glorious confession of Peter and Paul which make her the touchstone and the point of reference for the apostolic faith. There above all is her primacy to be seen.[72]

From the 'potentior principalitas' of the church at Rome to the primacy of the bishop of Rome

The particular quality of the church at Rome, once her foundation was completed by the martyrdom of Peter and Paul, rubbed off on to the bishop who occupied the see of that city and presided over its *cathedra*.[73] The successors of Linus (if he really was the first bishop) will have had a place within the communion of bishops commensurate with the place of Rome within the communion of churches. As bishop, they will have had the responsibility of exercising *episkope* in this church of Rome, which includes both 'watching over' the church's fidelity to the faith of the apostles, and 'representing' it.[74] Because he was bishop of the church which had the *potentior principalitas* among the churches, the bishop of Rome would have been the first among the bishops. Because he presides over the life of the church 'which presides in love',[75] he would have a privileged place among those who have received from the Spirit the duty of presiding in the life of the churches. His primacy came to him from his church, which in turn owed it to what the glorious witness of Peter and Paul had brought about in her. He has no personal authority apart from the prerogatives (*presbeia*) of his local church.

Approaching along this line, we can see clearly that, while the person of Peter, together with Paul, played a decisive part, Peter's confession and the words which Jesus spoke to him are not directly decisive as a basis for the primacy of the bishops of Rome. They are so in an indirect sense only, 'in that they make Peter what he was, and thus Peter, with Paul, gives to the church which he has founded and where they died her primary place in the order of churches and so gives her bishop that unique authority in the college' of bishops.[76] The primacy of the bishop of Rome is contained within that of his local church. In short:

> The oldest witnesses called in Catholic apologetic in support of the primacy of Rome and her pontiff indicate a direct regulative role to the Church of Rome alone, and an indirect one only to the Roman pontiff (except during the difference of opinion between Irenaeus and Victor). No one before Callistus thought of deducing the pre-eminence of Rome from Matthew 18; and Callistus only seems to have used it because of the question of full and unlimited power to absolve. Victor of Rome, who did indeed claim to excommunicate a whole series of distant churches, did not support his position by the fact that he was St Peter's successor. Irenaeus and the bishops who thought as he did raised with him the question of whether it was opportune, not that of juridical competence. (See Eusebius, *H.E.* 5.24.9ff.) This implies that they recognized that the power which Victor claimed to exercise (inopportunely though not un-canonically) had its place within the structure of Christ's Church on earth. From all this we conclude that the awareness of the Roman church's competence, and that of its bishops, within the universal Church is older than the awareness that this position corresponds with the position of St Peter among the apostles.[77]

It has been noticed how closely this priority of the local church of Rome over her bishop corresponds to contemporary custom. Greek patriotism emphasized the city rather than the magistrates, honoured as these were. In the same way the church - the parish, *paroikia* - was from the start understood to arise from the brotherly communion which made it 'one in

Christ', not from the man who presided in that communion.[78] This is why important decisions even at Rome were taken in councils during the first centuries.[79]

Even today the same vision controls the manner of electing 'the supreme pastor of the Church'; the Church of Rome elects *her* bishop. Paul VI's Apostolic Constitution *Romano Pontifici eligendo* of 1 October 1975 is quite clear on the point.[80] There is no intention of breaking with the very ancient tradition according to which the pope becomes supreme pastor of the universal church because he has been elected bishop of Rome by members of the church of Rome. That church chooses him through qualified members of the Roman clergy, the cardinals, *cardines* (hinges) of the church of Rome. For invariably

> the election of the bishop of the Church of Rome has been the exclusive right of the Church of Rome. This is true historically, for during the long period which ended with the definite schism of 1054 none of the other patriarchs ever claimed to have a hand in this election. Because the electoral college of the Roman pontiff is going to elect the bishop of Rome, it must be composed of members who are linked in some substantial way with the Church of Rome. But at the same time it must be composed of churchmen who are in a position to choose the person whom 'in the Lord' they consider best suited to be bishop of Rome and supreme pastor of the universal Church.

This prevents the opinion developing that

> the Pope, rather than being bishop of Rome and by right of that fact the supreme pastor of the universal Church and head of the college of bishops, is a sort of delegate of the universal Church, or at least elected as universal bishop and not as bishop of a particular Church, that of Rome, of which he who lawfully bears the title, by divine will succeeds Peter also in his power as supreme pastor of the universal Church,[81]

an opinion which would contradict centuries of Tradition. Paul VI here went beyond Vatican II. Vatican II on the whole 'seems to mark a regrettable step backwards by comparison with Vatican I, for the see of Rome as the specific foundation of papal primacy is not taken into account except in that part of the Decree on Ecumenism concerned with relations with the Orthodox Churches' (3.14ff.).[82]

Set as it is within the *principalitas* of the Church of Rome, the primacy of the bishop of that see can be seen to be a genuinely episcopal office accompanied by the episcopal powers needed to carry it out. It is equally clear that the office can only be understood as functioning within the communion of churches and the college of their bishops. Just as the prerogatives (*presbeia*) of the Roman Church do not place her outside the shared ecclesiality of the churches, so the primacy of her bishop does not put him outside the shared episcopate. The primacy can only be exercised as an episcopal function conferred by the general sacrament of episcopacy. Pope Paul VI's Apostolic Constitution *Romano Pontifici eligendo* is rightly careful to give a ruling to this effect:

After acceptance, the one elected is, if he has already received episcopal ordination, immediately bishop of the church of Rome and at the same time true pope and head of the episcopal college: he acquires in actuality and is able to exercise full and absolute power over the universal Church. If the one elected does not possess episcopal character, he must immediately be ordained bishop.

Then, after the customary formalities prescribed by the *Ordo sacrorum rituum Conclavis* have been accomplished, the cardinal electors come forward according to the rules for doing homage to the elected sovereign pontiff and to make their act of obedience. Thanksgiving is then made to God; after which the senior cardinal deacon announces to the people waiting the name of the new pontiff who, immediately afterwards, gives the apostolic blessing *urbi et orbi*.

If the one elected does not possess episcopal character, homage is paid to him and the announcement made only after he has been ordained bishop.

If the one elected is outside the Conclave, rules laid down in the *Ordo sacrorum rituum Conclavis* must be followed.

The episcopal ordination of the sovereign pontiff who is not yet a bishop, as discussed in numbers 88 and 89, will be conducted *de more Ecclesiae* by the dean of the Sacred College of cardinals or, in his absence, by the vice-dean or, if he too is prevented, by the senior cardinal bishop.

We lay it down that the Conclave shall end, in respect of its canonical effects mentioned in number 56, immediately after the new pontiff has been elected and has given his consent to the election and, if he does not possess episcopal character, after he has been ordained bishop.[83]

The office (*munus*) of the bishop of Rome will evidently show some of the characteristics of the *principalitas* of the seat of the apostles, for it is derived from the mission of his local church within the communion of churches and is a service to that mission. Its most basic function will be to work out the calling of touchstone, point of reference and memorial of the apostolic faith, the proper calling of the Roman church. This will not in the first instance mean concentrating on enforcing authoritarian decisions; it is for every church and every bishop to discover, usually by means of a synod,[84] the action they should take to keep in line with the apostolic tradition which Rome has 're-called'. But the responsibility of the bishop who sits on the *cathedra* founded in the blood of Peter and Paul will make him a watchman for his brother bishops, a sentinel trusted because he will know when to sound the alarm.[85] It is above all a prophetic (Ezek. 3.17) sense of care to be found at the heart of the *episkope* of every bishop but which in this case extends to the communion of the churches considered in its quality of communion. A sentinel or watchman is not the commander who gives orders and decides on the attitude to take. But he has a responsibility at once fundamental and precise towards the commander and those under him. Defeat from a surprise attack or the waste of resources from a false alarm may depend on his alertness and judgement – Thomas Aquinas would call it 'prudence'. The well-being of the group depends on confidence in his warning: too many false alarms and they will stop taking him seriously.

'Watchman' and 'sentinel' come from the word which the clergy of the Roman church used about the year 250. The see was vacant, but they felt the need to intervene in the church at

Carthage, then in the grip of a crisis, as an expression of their own church's concern:

> The brothers in irons greet you, as do the priests and the whole church which herself watches (*excubat*) with the greatest care (*summa sollicitudine*) over all those who call on the name of the Lord (*pro omnes qui invocant nomen Domini*). For our part, we ask that you in your turn would remember us also.

Leo the Great used the same figure to describe his office:

> If we do not intervene with the vigilance (*vigilantia*) which is incumbent upon us, we could not excuse ourselves to him who wished that we should be the sentinel (*qui nos speculatores esse voluit*).[86]

The bishop who exercises this function of 'watch' over all the churches is in a position of genuine leadership. If the essential expression of this quality is not the power to impose decisions by virtue of the jurisdiction which goes with it, it still may not be reduced to a primacy of honour, an empty symbol deprived of real power. On the contrary, there are times when this bishop must intervene authoritatively, in cases of serious need imposing himself with vigour. We saw Leo the Great driven to do so at the time of Chalcedon, where the safety of the faith was at stake. Primatial action of this sort always remains episcopal in type, however wide the issue – the sort of action which every bishop takes in his own church. But in the early centuries a bishop never acted in isolation, always in fellowship with his *presbyterium*, even in matters involving complex issues of jurisdiction:

> As such, the bishop is *par excellence* the doctrinal authority of the Church, voicing her tradition, interpreting the Scriptures, revealing by the voice of the Spirit the authentic 'saving' teaching. He is, further, *ex officio* a healer and (the highest form of healing) a supremely potent exorcist. But in all this he is simply the special organ of the Spirit who indwells the Church. He is the Church's minister, not its ruler.[87]

This must by analogy apply to the relation between the bishop of Rome and the other bishops. He will not act in isolation, stating a doctrine, expressing a tradition, or giving an interpretation of what is revealed, which are not those of the Church. Vatican I went so far as to declare that the infallibility which under certain circumstances he may count on is not his own but that with which the Lord wished to endow his Church (*DS* 3074). He is a minister, the *servus servorum Dei*.[88]

Correspondingly we may say that, in its own sphere, the authority of the watchman does not rest formally on the *right* to impose obedience - except in particularly serious cases - but on the *duty* to question the churches in what concerns the demands of truth and of fidelity to the apostles' teaching, entrusted to them by the Spirit. This spiritual requirement means that they in their turn must 'receive' the warnings, the advice, the reprimands, even the directives of him whom the Spirit has made bishop of the Church 'which presides in love'.

Presiding in love therefore means above all having a concern which bears on the witness to the faith. It expresses itself essentially in the fact of telling out the faith, of guiding the understanding and practice of it, of expressing the spirit of the communion of the churches when faced with some interpretation that would distort it, of speaking in the name of the other bishops not to tell them something that they would not know but to proclaim their common understanding of the gospel of God. Matters of organization, of administration centred on a *curia*, do not belong to the inwardness of this primatial function. Beneath all the accretions which have overlaid it - and which, given the historical circumstances and the good of the Church, were often necessary - the bishop of Rome's mission remained that of a watchman or sentinel in the service of the apostolic witness which Peter and Paul gave to make the foundation of their local church, which has now become touchstone, point of reference and memorial of the faith.

'Vicar of Peter'
in the see of the Church of Peter and Paul

When presiding in his *cathedra*, the bishop of Rome acts as the man whom the Spirit of God has appointed to occupy the see of the church of the apostles Peter and Paul. His ministry and office (*munus*) are entirely dependent on the glorious witness of the two Coryphaei. And the papal seal bears the heads of Peter and Paul.[89] It does not, however, follow that the bishop of Rome's relationship to Peter is of exactly the same sort as his relationship to Paul. Moreover the link which binds each of the two apostles to the church of Rome is not necessarily identical, even though both of them founded her and both of them 'lived and presided in her'.[90]

The bishops of Rome have sometimes called themselves 'successors of Peter and Paul', and that into the present century.[91] But the formula should not be used without the most careful qualification. The case of relationship with Paul is clearer. It is difficult to 'succeed' him, in the strict sense, in any see. His own mission, we know from Scripture, expressed itself charismatically rather than in creating structures. For this reason it was entirely personal, for there can hardly be a 'succession', strictly speaking, to a vocation of this type. Paul seems indeed to have been raised up by the Spirit of the risen Lord to bear witness above all to the primacy of an inward communion of faith and love, the perpetually new work of the Spirit. His coming to Rome which sealed his martyrdom imprinted on the very foundation of the church of that city the mysterious economy of God, whose will it was that the salvation of which Israel was the instrument should reach out among the nations to the heart of the heathen world so that the barriers should be broken down. Paul had been 'the apostle to the Gentiles'. Because his church is founded on the witness of Paul, the bishop of this city receives a quality which should mark his ministry: permanent openness to the Spirit, the care of non-believers, the priority of the Spirit over the letter, the total transcendence of the Word over all structures. He is made by Paul more than he succeeds to him.

Very soon, however, while the unshakeable certainty that the Roman church was founded on the two apostles still persisted and while Eusebius continued to count the episcopal successions 'after the martyrdom of Peter and Paul',[92] Peter's name alone was to be found at the head of the line of the bishops of Rome wherever the succession to the see was being considered. For Hippolytus, for example, Victor occupied the thirteenth place 'starting from Peter'.[93] Augustine expressed himself in the same terms: 'Linus succeeded Peter.'[94] The description of the bishop of Rome as 'successor of Peter' continued across the centuries, and the Dogmatic Constitution *Lumen Gentium* of Vatican II bracketed the title with that of Roman pontiff in its most important paragraphs.[95] The bishop of that church of which Peter and Paul are equal founders – 'their vocation brought them together, their work made them similar and their death made them equal,' said Leo the Great[96] – succeeds to Peter but should make sure that his ministry keeps in harmony with what he receives through his church from Paul. That is the difference. It has left its mark in the liturgy itself, even in the East.[97]

We may speak, then, of a succession *to* Peter. The phrase is too well attested to be rejected now, but it must be interpreted. Used without care for the finer distinctions it may distort the truth.

An unconsidered assertion that the bishop of Rome is he who succeeds to Peter could in the first place prove too restrictive.[98] Several ecclesiastical traditions have followed Cyprian in maintaining that Rome is not the only see that can claim Peter. Other churches, Antioch in particular, have a privileged link with his ministry, which opens out to them a universal dimension. The Acts of the Apostles gives some evidence. Besides, every bishop when in his own see is in some sense Peter's successor. The idea is often found in Cyprian, who enlarges upon it in a well-known passage of *De Catholicae Ecclesiae Unitate*.[99] There are, of course, two versions of this work and it is hard to know which is the original or if both versions come from Cyprian's hand.[100] However it may be, we must take up Cyprian's insistence that Jesus instituted the episcopate as a whole in the words which follow Peter's confession (Matt. 16). The words spoken to Peter reach out to include all the apostles, whose spokesman he is, entrusting to all of them the *cathedra*, by which we should understand the episcopal function. For 'he assigned the like power to all the apostles', 'the other apostles also were what Peter was; they benefited from an equal share in honour and power, but the beginning takes its departure from unity'.[101] Whether or not Cyprian implied a thread of Roman supremacy running through the episcopate which, as he showed, belonged to all the apostles, the texts are concerned above all to reassert the need for brotherly union in this troubled period. One thing is clear: the Scripture which he cites will not allow Peter to be isolated. If Peter is the rock, the Epistle to the Ephesians makes all the apostles and prophets the foundations of the Church (Eph. 2.20), and the Apocalypse sees in the 'Twelve Apostles of the Lamb' the twelve thrones of the New Jerusalem (Rev. 21.14). If there is Peter in every apostle, then in every bishop there is a successor to Peter.

The matter must be pursued further. The notion of 'succession' itself raises problems. One complete area of Peter's function cannot by its nature be passed on; and it is a wide area. In the first place it is impossible to pass on his martyrdom with all that it, together with that of Paul, means for the local church at Rome. It could not be repeated, for no one else is the same person as Peter with those qualities which gave his witness its unique importance compared with that of other martyrs of the faith. The most that could be done is to imitate him. We have already noted the very particular part which this martyrdom and that of Paul, as actual events, played in the *potentior principalitas* of the Roman church and so in the primacy of her bishop.

Moreover, even in his personal primacy within the apostolic group, Peter remains one of the apostles: more precisely, one of the twelve, with all the wealth of meaning which the New Testament gives the twelve as the twelve.[102] Simon became Peter only as a member of the apostolic group and his particular place never puts him above or outside this group. Nor is that place ever seen except as a function of the group. His outstanding part remains within the apostolic function. And the apostles could never have a successor in that function of witness which lay at the heart of their calling (Acts 2.32; 3.15; 4.20-33; 8.25; 10.39-42; 13.31). They are those who bear witness to the fact that the risen Lord is the Jesus in whose company they had lived (Acts 1.21-2). That is why to have been with Jesus during his life and after his death remained a qualification essential in anyone who was to be included in the group of the apostles and to take part in the first mission, that of bearing witness (Acts 1.1-3; 10.41). He who had not been a witness could not be an apostle. The witness of the apostles was unique because its roots lay in the unique events concerning Jesus Christ. This is why the twelve are for ever, once-for-all (*ephapax*) the Church's foundation. No one could follow them in this function of witness. The most they could be 'succeeded' in was in the function of shepherding and teaching in order to guard the churches founded on the power of their witness.[103]

There are other reaches of the apostolic function besides that of witness which equally cannot be passed on. The twelve are the bearers at once of a mission and of an eschatological privilege.[104] As a college, they surround the Christ at the time of the judgement which opens for mankind a way into the Kingdom announced and prepared by the gospel of God of which they had been witnesses (Matt. 19.28; Luke 22.30). This function, symbolically pictured by twelve thrones grouped around a central throne, 'together with it forming a single tribunal', cannot in any way be passed on. 'Death itself will not remove from the twelve their privilege as assessors with the sovereign Judge.'[105]

What goes for the apostles and the twelve will obviously go also for Peter whose mission was contained within the communion of the apostolic group. It is thus impossible to speak of a 'Petrine succession', to use a very clumsy phrase, without qualification. Indeed one can only use the expression after a whole gamut of distinctions. We certainly know that Jesus himself involved the twelve in his mission of evangelizing, so that the once-for-all (*ephapax*) efficacy of his work could bear fruit to the ends of the earth. Death did not allow them to complete this earthly mission. So they had 'continuators, inheritors of their responsibility to evangelize the world'. However, 'because these continuators were not replacements, the thought developed that the apostles were still operating through them; death had not prevented them from presiding still over the destinies of the Church',[106] especially in cases where the trophies of their martyrdom remained in the church as a *sacramentum* of their presence. We have reached the heart of the problem. Peter has vicars in the see of Rome rather than successors. The once-for-all nature of his office remains present through the vicars who successively occupy his seat.[107]

The continuity of Peter's presence in the see which, with Paul, he had founded in his martyrdom, without any succession strictly speaking, is one of the most influential factors in the Roman primacy. Peter's once-for-all authority attached to the Church and see of Rome is what becomes effective through all those who succeed each other in this see but who never really succeed him. Peter remains the foundation of the Roman church (with Paul). And since Linus it is his authority – his own, not theirs added to his – which remains, always the same but always operating through new situations and needs. They are his vicars in the strict sense. We are here dealing with a view of history which belongs properly to 'salvation history' and which proves true at all essential levels. In the memorial of the liturgy, for example, the event on which it is founded, buried in the once-for-all of passing history, comes forth through the power of the Spirit every time the liturgy is celebrated and, under the signs which recall it, meets the present generation. It is not repeated but perpetuated. This is quite different from saying that the sacrament succeeds the event. The rites performed constitute the symbol, thanks to which the saving value of the event remains offered and active, still present within human history. In the same way the apostolic word, always the same, continues to uphold the life of the Church though nothing essential can be added to it. But the Spirit does not cease recalling it to the memory of the Christian communities, through the ministry of ministers who make it clear, translate it and apply it in words which belong to each age and culture. In this way Peter's witness, thanks to his vicars, lives on.

The bishops of Rome were from the start remarkably aware of this quality in their relationship to Peter. Unmistakable traces of it may be seen in Damasus (died 384), Siricius (died 399),[108] Zosimus,[109] and Celestine at the time of the Council of Ephesus in 431.[110] Peter Chrysologus, archbishop of Ravenna, expresses it fully in his letter to Eutyches in the time of Leo the Great: 'We exhort you, honourable brother, that you listen obediently to what has been written by the blessed pope of the city of Rome, since blessed Peter who lives and presides over his

own see offers the truth of faith to those who seek it.'[111] Leo
himself endorses this teaching: for him, 'the most blessed
apostle Peter does not cease to preside over his own seat'.[112]
Elsewhere he makes his views more explicit:

> The soundness of that faith for which Christ praised the first of the
> apostles is constant. And just as what Peter believed in the Christ
> remains for always, so does that which Christ instituted in the
> person of Peter . . . Saint Peter, keeping always the soundness of
> the stone which was given him, has not let go of the helm which
> was given him in the Church . . . That is why, if we manage to act
> well, to decide soundly, by our daily prayers to sway the divine
> mercy, it comes from the works and from the merits of him whose
> power is still living in his own see and whose authority continues to
> be the first (*cuius in sede sua vivit potestas et excellit auctoritas*)
> . . . It is in the whole Church that each day Peter says: 'You are the
> Christ, the Son of the living God.' Every tongue which thus con-
> fesses the Lord is animated by the teaching authority of this
> word.[113]

The correspondence of Gregory the Great can be shown to be
shot through with this way of seeing it.[114] The word 'successor'
is used of the popes in their own sequence, not as following
Peter.[115] In the seventh century the expression 'successor of
Peter' appears once in Leo II (in 683) and then in a few scattered
places.[116] It has not yet invaded the pontifical documents.
Where it is found, it is used in the sense of *vice Petri, vice
apostolicae sedis*, and so of 'vicar'.[117] Peter continues to preside
through the diaconate of bishops who follow each other in the
Roman see. Domitian of Prusias, an Eastern bishop, explained
it at the Second Council of Constantinople in these remarkable
words: Pope Agatho's letter to the Council (681) was 'as if
dictated by the Holy Spirit through the mouth of the holy and
blessed prince of the Apostles, Peter, and written by the hand of
the thrice-blessed Agatho'.[118] And in the troubled days of the
Second Council of Nicaea (787), Pope Hadrian, in a strongly
authoritarian pronouncement, still based his power on the
vicarial relationship to Peter, '*cuius . . . vices gerimus*'.[119]

When Gregory VII, author of the *Dictatus Papae*, deposed
and excommunicated the Emperor Henry in 1076, he did so

still in the name of Peter's authority and in terms which show that the ancient tradition remains in the foreground:

> Blessed Peter, prince of the Apostles, bend towards me, I beseech you, a favourable ear; listen to your servant whom you have nourished from infancy, whom you have plucked until this day from the hands of those who have hated him and hate him still for his faithfulness towards you. You are my witness, together with my sovereign lady the Mother of God, as well as blessed Paul, your brother among the saints, that your holy Roman church has constrained me despite myself to govern her, and that I rose to your seat by honourable means. I should certainly have preferred to end my life in a monastic habit rather than occupy your place, with the worry of earthly glory and the spirit of this age. I believe also that it is by your grace and not through my own merits that the Christian people, who have been in a special way entrusted to me, obey me, for the power of binding and loosing in heaven and on earth has been given me by God on your request, that I exercise it in your place. Firmly confident in you, for the honour and defence of the Church, on behalf of the omnipotent God, Father, Son and Holy Spirit, I forbid King Henry, son of the Emperor Henry, who through an insane pride has risen against your Church, to govern the kingdom of Germany and Italy. I release all Christians from their oath to him and I forbid all and everyone to recognize him as king. It is fitting that he who wishes to diminish the honour of your Church should lose the honour which he seems to possess. Since also, as a Christian, he has refused to obey, in that he has not returned to the Lord whom he deserted by his connections with excommunicated persons, in heaping up iniquities, in ignoring the warnings which, as you will witness, I have given him for his salvation, in separating himself from your church and in attempting to divide it – in your stead I bind him with the bond of anathema, that all the peoples of the earth may know that on this rock the Son of the living God has built his Church and that the gates of hell shall not prevail against it.[120]

Other words of Gregory echo these sentiments, right up to his final letter where he reminds Christians that Peter is still 'the first pastor after Christ himself'.[121]

The ancient tradition thus persisted, the same as that which had impelled the Fathers at Chalcedon to shout 'Peter has spoken through Leo' and to write to the latter (on the thorny question of canon 28) that he is 'the interpreter of the voice of Peter' and that he 'makes all to share in the blessedness of Peter's faith'.[122] The Fathers of the Third Council of Constantinople said as much to Agatho.[123] The East here saw beyond the person of the bishop of Rome, directly to Peter, but to Peter in that which gave him his authority, the witness to his faith. This is not exactly what Gregory VII said, for to him Peter's authority carried an almost absolute juridical power, owning sway even over princes. The two traditions are, however, one in this: they both understand that the bishop of Rome derives his true meaning from the continued presence of Peter as he had been in his own day: an *ephapax* which persists not simply as the starting point of the pontifical ministry, but as a standing reality which must always be made present, in vicarious fashion, when words and deeds that are truly Peter's continue to be spoken and performed.

Soon, however, a vastly more linear view of succession will prevail, to the point indeed when the term 'vicar of Peter' will be suspect. Preferred ways of referring to the bishop of Rome will be 'vicar of Christ' and 'successor of Peter'. Innocent III's position is well known: 'We, although successors of the prince of the Apostles, are not, however, his vicars nor the vicars of any other apostle or other man, but of Jesus Christ himself.' 'The supreme pontiff is not called vicar of a mere man but is truly vicar of the true God.'[124] After the Council of Trent Robert Bellarmine set a seal on this far from happy development, especially in his *Controversia*. The bishop of Rome becomes the vicar of Christ, not of Peter: 'The sovereign pontiff is the vicar of Christ, and he represents Christ to us as he was when he dwelt among men.'[125] Hence also Bellarmine's definition of the Church: 'An assembly of men . . . under the authority of lawful pastors and above all (*praecipue*) of the only vicar of Christ on earth, the Roman pontiff.'[126] The road to juridicism was wide open. But the expression 'vicar of Peter' was never quite eliminated. It kept its place in the liturgy, for instance in the old Roman Pontifical for the ordination of a bishop: 'Will you show submission and obedience towards the blessed Apostle

Peter, to whom through God has been given the power to bind and loose, and to his vicar our Lord Pope X and his successors?'[127] The new missal introduces it in the prayer for a departed pope. John XXIII and Paul VI both used it.[128] A discreet but significant presence, like that of a vestigial organ in the body.

Great caution, then, is needed in speaking of a successor *to* Peter. All things considered, it would be better to revert to the expression 'vicar of Peter' in describing the bishop of Rome's relationship, not to the first bishop of Rome but, an entirely different matter, to the founder (together with Paul) of the Roman church. The bishops of Rome succeed each other in order to preserve the work of Peter and Paul, and to make present until the end of time the leadership which Peter especially was called to exercise in the once-for-all apostolic event, for this *ephapax* is the place of the Church. If we are to speak of 'succession', it can only be in this broad and derived sense:

> The institutional apostolate, according to which he who is mandated has the importance which he who mandated him would have if he were present, must be transmitted should the one mandated die before he had accomplished his mission – the three Petrine functions cannot end with the death of Peter, since after his death a Church still remains to be protected, colleagues in the ministry require to be strengthened, and the flock must be fed. Peter continues to live in the church as the place accorded him in the Gospels and the Acts, written after his death, shows – the context in which Jesus entrusted Peter with his mission was marked by what is definitive in the church and must therefore remain until the end: the certainty of the resurrection of Jesus and the meal which bears his name.[129]

From the place of the Church of Rome among the churches to the role of Peter in the apostolic group

In a homily for the Feast of Peter and Paul, Augustine insisted that 'these two were made one only; although they suffered on different days, they were made one only. Peter went first, Paul followed.' Before saying that, he had explained:

As you know, the Lord Jesus, before his Passion, chose his disciples and named them apostles. Among them it was Peter who on almost every count deserved to personify the whole Church in himself. It was because he thus personified the whole Church in himself that he had the happiness of hearing it said of him, 'I will give you the keys of the kingdom of heaven.' In fact it was not one man in himself exclusively, but the whole Church in its unity, which received these keys. This throws into relief the pre-eminence (*excellentia*) of Peter, for he represented the universality and the unity of the Church when he was told 'I give to you' meaning, 'to the whole Church'. If you want to be sure that it is the Church which has received the keys of the kingdom of heaven, hear what the Lord said to all his apostles in another place: 'Receive the Holy Spirit.' And immediately after it, 'Everyone to whom you remit his sins, they are remitted; everyone to whom you retain his sins, they are retained . . .'

It was still with good reason that after his resurrection the Lord entrusted to Peter personally the responsibility of feeding his sheep. He was indeed not the only one among the disciples who was worthy to feed the Lord's sheep. But if the Lord speaks to one only, it is to emphasize the value of unity. And if he speaks to Peter in the first instance, it is because Peter is first among the apostles.[130]

We have to ask why Peter held this pre-eminence (*excellentia*) within this unity of the apostles which embraced Peter and Paul as well as Peter and the eleven. It was essentially a matter of leadership. We have seen how Peter's martyrdom conferred on the Roman church a pre-eminence (*excellentia, potentior principalitas*) in the way of leadership, while Paul's martyrdom stamped it with a more charismatic pre-eminence, especially on the 'prophetic' level of the Word and in serving the universal scope of salvation.

This distinction arose no doubt from the New Testament accounts of the two apostles. The pre-eminence of the local church at Rome among the other churches, and, by rebound, of its bishop among the college of bishops, was seen to be inseparable from the position of Paul, who was 'added' to the original group with a view to the salvation of pagans. This explains why Peter and Paul are mentioned together when the

Roman church as such is being considered; but when the leadership of that church is the subject, Peter alone is named. 'Leadership', an untranslatable word which has been naturalized into French, is to be understood as the authority which guides the group and carries it along.

Tradition became increasingly, if gradually, aware of the link between Peter's place among the apostles and that of the pastor of the church of Rome, centre of the communion of churches, within the college of bishops. Tertullian early in the third century seems to have been the first to quote the confession at Caesarea Philippi (Matt. 16.16-19) as evidence for the Roman primacy, the *tu es Petrus*. The Fathers who followed were for a long time more reserved.[131] This sudden attention to the Petrine texts and the previous silence need to be seen in context. The canon of Scripture was not in practice settled until about AD 180. Only after that, and after having discovered beyond doubt the link between bishops and apostles, was anyone in a position to establish a parallel with that of the hierarchy of apostles shown in the New Testament.[132]

We have thus to wait for the work of Tertullian and his contemporary Clement of Alexandria (died around AD 215) for the first more or less consistent interpretations of those sections of the Gospels which describe Peter's leadership.[133] It is interesting to read them together, for they already set the tone:

> Was anything hidden from Peter who was called the rock on which the Church would be built, who received the keys of the kingdom of heaven, and the power of loosing and binding in heaven and on earth? Was anything hidden from John . . . ? (Tertullian, *De Praescriptione* 22, about AD 200, *PL* 2.39-40).
>
> . . . For though you think that heaven is still shut up, remember that the Lord left the keys of it to Peter here, and through him to the Church, which keys everyone will carry with him, if he has been questioned and made confession (of the faith) (Tertullian, *Scorpiace* 10, about AD 208, *PL* 2.165).
>
> Now with reference to your decision, I ask: how do you come to usurp the prerogatives of the Church? If it is because the Lord said to Peter, 'Upon this rock I will build my Church, to thee I have given the keys of the heavenly kingdom'; or 'Whatsoever thou

shalt bind or loose on earth, shall be bound or loosed in heaven'; do you for that reason presume to have diverted the power of binding and loosing to yourself, that is, to every sister church of Petrine origin? Who are you to subvert the plain intention of the Lord, who conferred this on Peter personally? He says, 'on *thee* will I build my Church', and 'I will give the keys to *thee*', not to the Church, and 'whatsoever *thou* shalt bind or loose . . .' (Tertullian, *De Pudicitia*, about AD 220, Montanist period, *PL* 2.1078-9).

. . . And when he heard these things, blessed Peter, the elect, the one picked out, the first of the disciples, for whom only and for himself the Saviour pays the tribute, quickly learnt and understood the saying (Clement of Alexandria, *Quis Dives Salvetur?* 21, AD 203, *PG* 9.625).

Tertullian leans especially on chapter 16 of Matthew. But as Clement of Alexandria's very careful comment shows, the tradition attached as much importance to other passages,[134] notably the words which Luke places in the middle of his account of the Last Supper, and in the chapter added as an appendix to the Johannine gospel (Luke 22.31-2; John 21.15-19):

The Lord said: 'Simon, Simon, behold, Satan demanded to have you, that he might sift you like wheat, but I have prayed for you that your faith may not fail; and when you have turned again, strengthen your brethren' (Luke 22.31-5).

When they had finished breakfast, Jesus said to Simon Peter, 'Simon, son of John, do you love me more than these?' He said to him, 'Yes, Lord; you know that I love you.' He said to him, 'Feed my lambs.' A second time he said to him, 'Simon, son of John, do you love me?' He said to him, 'Yes, Lord; you know that I love you.' He said to him, 'Tend my sheep.' He said to him the third time, 'Simon, son of John, do you love me?' Peter was grieved because he said to him the third time, 'Do you love me?' And he said to him, 'Lord, you know everthing; you know that I love you.' Jesus said to him, 'Feed my sheep. Truly, truly, I say to you, when you were young, you girded yourself and walked where you would; but when you are old, you will stretch out your hands, and another will gird you and carry you where you do not wish to go.' (This he said to show by what death he was to glorify God.) And after this he said to him, 'Follow me' (John 21.15-19).

We cannot undertake a full study of these passages, but will trust the conclusions of the specialists, even though these, unfortunately, often disagree. We shall read them with particular concern for what the Spirit wished to accomplish in the period between the ministry of Jesus and the time when the Christian communities found their own true shape, rather than to distinguish between 'what comes from Jesus himself and what the Church has provided'. We must declare at the outset that, for us, whatever the Church *of apostolic times*, led by the Spirit of Pentecost, understood of its own nature and in consequence allowed to be produced in its life, belongs to the gospel events. To accept nothing as authentic and therefore worth considering unless it 'comes explicitly from Jesus' is to be imprisoned in a closed circle. The writings of the New Testament themselves are the fruit and the written product of a tradition which was there before them and which accounts for their particular form. What scholar is capable of discerning with certainty those parts which 'come explicitly from Jesus'? Our faith is apostolic precisely because it arises from what the apostles perceived and passed on.

Although it is true that 'the prominence which Peter later gained may have been retrojected into'[135] the earlier period, anyone quietly reading through the New Testament as a whole will be struck by one point. It is impossible to recall the accounts of the ministry of Jesus without meeting Peter at the moments of particular importance, even if it is his faults or his cowardice that is stressed. It is impossible to tell 'the story of the ministry of Jesus . . . without mention of Simon'.[136] However carefully we guard against exaggeration and keep to the best attested episodes, we cannot avoid the evidence: the earliest community saw him as the *first* of the twelve. He is shown as the first to be called, the first to be named in the lists of the apostles (indeed, Matt. 10.2 calls him *protos*), the first to confess that Jesus is the Messiah, the first of the apostles to see the risen Lord (1 Cor. 15.5), the first to proclaim the *kerygma* of good news (Acts 2.14). The written records give the impression that his companions recognized a certain authority in him even during the life of Jesus: he stands first in a number of incidents that involved the whole group of disciples (thus Mark 1.36; Matt.

14.28-9; 15.15; 16.16; 17.24; 18.21; 19.27; Mark 16.7; John 6.68). After the resurrection he became, for the Acts of the Apostles, the most important personality in the first days of the apostolic Church. It seems clear, moreover, that there was at least some continuity between the situation then and what had happened during the ministry of Jesus. Was he virtually an official spokesman? It may be too much to claim for the period before the Passion,[137] but it was true after Pentecost. Too many speeches and incidents in the first part of the Acts of the Apostles display a genuine leadership for them not to reflect a conviction engraved in the memory of the first Christian generation.

Furthermore, Peter stands out from the apostolic group in several ways, but without cutting himself off from them. Phrases like 'Simon and his companions' (Mark 1.36), 'Peter and the eleven' (Acts 2.14), 'Peter and the other apostles' (Acts 2.37) show Peter as an apostle with the others and the others with him, to the point where it would seem possible to describe the apostolic group as 'Peter and the rest'. Besides, the varied pericopes which show that Jesus had special intentions for Peter show also that those intentions were made known to him in the presence of the other apostles. It is less a matter of 'words spoken to Peter *and* to the others, but of words spoken to Peter *rather than* to the others'.[138] So it was in the case of 'You are Peter, and on this rock', 'Simon, I have prayed for you that your faith may not fail', and 'Feed my sheep'. There is no way of identifying with any certainty what is the product of a theological reading of events in the light of post-Easter experience projected back on to events in the ministry of Jesus. Undoubtedly, however, the Christian community a few decades after those events was convinced that Peter's part after Pentecost derived neither from chance nor from election by the other apostles, but from an intention of Jesus who had lived alongside Peter in Galilee and whose resurrection the apostles now proclaimed.[139] Was this true of the Christian community everywhere, and were the same inferences universally made? Certainly not.[140]

For several centuries now Peter's 'confession' in Matthew 16.13-23 has, in the Western tradition, been the passage most often cited to account for the earliest Christian community's belief in Peter's primacy. It is certainly the most detailed of the passages. But we should remember from the start that only Matthew's version includes the verses which show the Church to be founded on Peter and his possession of the keys of heaven (16.17-19); and this version is without doubt the least ancient.[141] We must read the texts of Mark, Luke and Matthew side by side:

Mark 8.29-30	Luke 9.20-21	Matt. 16.16-20
Peter answered him, 'You are the Christ.'	And Peter answered, 'The Christ of God.'	Simon Peter replied, 'You are the Christ, the Son of the living God.'
		And Jesus answered him, 'Blessed are you, Simon Bar-Jona! For flesh and blood has not revealed this to you, but my Father who is in heaven. And I tell you, you are Peter, and on this rock I will build my church, and the powers of death shall not prevail against it. I will give you the keys of the kingdom of heaven, and whatever you bind on earth shall be bound in heaven, and whatever you loose on earth shall be loosed in heaven.'
And he charged them to tell no one about him.	But he charged and commanded them to tell this to no one.	Then he strictly charged the disciples to tell no one that he was the Christ.

It leaps to the eye that Matthew's account is distinguished by additional material inserted into a very low-key confession of faith. Matthew did not invent this material. The rebuke which, like Mark (8.32-3), he puts into the mouth of Jesus a few verses later (Matt. 16.23) shows that at this stage of his developing vocation as a disciple, Peter's idea of the mystery of Jesus still

lacks adequate depth.[142] ('Get behind me, Satan! You are a
hindrance to me; for you are not on the side of God, but of
men.') Everything points to the conclusion that the account of
this confession, supported in a very different form by the
Johannine tradition (John 6.68-9), reflects a precise recollection
guarded in the corporate memory of the apostles of an event in
the actual life of Jesus. But Matthew, it seems, has connected
this confession with another one, made after the resurrection,
which expresses the faith of the Church as such. The Easter
faith has therefore coloured Matthew's version,[143] and this
explains the enthusiastic approval of Jesus, which accords ill
with the vigorous denunciation that follows. It may thus be
possible to detect the mark or at least the influence of Peter's
part after the resurrection on the words which the evangelist
has put into the mouth of Jesus.

A statement which Jesus made about Peter in this passage
corresponds to Peter's confession concerning Jesus. Peter is
declared 'happy,' 'blessed' (*makarios*) by virtue of the faith
which he has proclaimed. This gives him a place apart within
the group of the disciples: he is the only one among them who,
in the gospel accounts, is declared by the Lord to be blessed, and
his confession of Jesus as Messiah is confirmed because it
issues from a revelation which the Father had granted.[144] He
also receives a name which reveals his role in the future, a name
enshrining a vocation, such as occurs several times in the Bible:
he will be the rock. He also receives the keys of the Kingdom.

The tradition of the Church has not spoken with one voice in
its interpretation of the word 'rock', especially of the connection between the proper name *Petros* and the common noun
petra, *Pierre et la pierre*, Peter and the rock. Modern exegesis
varies also.[145]

For some of the Fathers - Origen in the East, for instance,
and Augustine in the West, the rock on which the Church is
built is Christ as he is confessed. Matthew is to be read in the
light of 1 Corinthians 10.4. So in his *Retractationes*, verse 427,
Augustine writes:

> I mentioned somewhere with reference to the apostle Peter that the
> 'Church is founded upon him as upon a rock'. This meaning is also

sung by many lips in the lines of the blessed Ambrose, where, speaking of the domestic cock, he says: 'When it crows, he, the rock of the Church, absolves from sin.' But I realize that I have since frequently explained the words of our Lord: 'Thou art Peter and upon this rock I will build my Church', to the effect that they should be understood as referring to him whom Peter confessed when he said: 'Thou art the Christ, the Son of the living God', and as meaning that Peter, having been named after this rock, figured the person of the Church, which is built upon this rock and has received the keys of the kingdom of heaven. For what was said to him was not 'Thou art the rock', but 'Thou art Peter'. But the rock was Christ, having confessed whom (even as the whole Church confesses) Simon was named Peter. Which of these two interpretations is the more likely to be correct, let the reader choose.[146]

Augustine himself chose the second.[147] Peter is the type of the Church, built upon the Christ whom his faith confesses. A phrase in the *Tractatus* on St John's Gospel puts it excellently: 'On this rock, therefore, he said, which thou hast confessed, I will build my Church. For the Rock (*petra*) was Christ; and on this foundation Peter himself was built. For other foundation can no man lay than that is laid, which is Christ Jesus. The Church, therefore, which is founded in Christ, received from him the keys of the Kingdom in the person of Peter . . . In this representation Christ is to be considered as the Rock, Peter as the Church.'[148]

Others, especially in the West, took the rock (*petra*) to be the person of Peter. There is a long list of those who held this position. Ambrose is often cited, but his opinions seem to us to be more qualified. We may mention Hilary of Poitiers, for whom 'Peter is he upon whom the Lord has built the Church as on a living foundation (*tamquam vivo fundamento*)' and who sees him supporting the whole building of the Church (*aedificationi Ecclesiae subjacens*);[149] Jerome;[150] and Leo the Great, who puts this commentary into the mouth of Jesus: 'Although I am the indestructible stone (*petra*), the corner-stone . . . the foundation such that man can lay no another, nevertheless you also are stone (*petra*) because by my strength you will be strengthened so that those things which are proper to me by power shall be common to us both by participation.'[151]

A third group holds that the rock (*petra*) is the faith confessed by Peter. This position is often called 'Antiochene exegesis' because it was favoured in the East. Thus St John Chrysostom: 'On this stone (*petra*) I will build my Church, meaning, on the faith of your confession (*te pistei tes homologias*)'; 'He who has just provided the confession of the same apostle as a foundation for the Church . . . how shall he have need to pray?'[152] Theodoret follows the same line of thought,[153] John of Damascus crystallized it.[154] But it was for Theodore of Mopsuestia to express it with greatest subtlety:

> It is the gathering of the faithful and the 'godfearers' whom our Lord also called 'Church', when he said, 'You are Peter and on this rock.' It is on this faith and confession that he promises to gather together all those who 'fear God', so that it is their assembly which shall never be broken up or conquered by the attack of enemies.[155]

This line is to be found in the West also; though here there is always a strong link between the confession of faith and the person of Peter. The rock (*petra*) is neither Peter alone nor his confession of faith alone. It is Peter in so far as he confesses the apostolic faith and the apostolic faith in so far as it is expressed by Peter. We could indeed find a like refusal to separate Peter and his confession among the Eastern Fathers, notably in Basil.[156] But the Greeks are less explicit than the Latins, among whom we may take Ambrose for a representative witness. In a splendid page of his commentary on Luke he writes:

> Great is the generosity of God, for he has given nearly all his names to his disciples. 'I am the light of the world,' he says (John 8.12); and he grants this name in which he glories to his disciples, saying, 'You are the light of the world' (Matt. 5.15). 'I am the living bread,' he said (John 6.51), and 'we are all one bread' (1 Cor. 10.7). 'I am the true vine' (John 15), and yet he says to you, 'I planted you as a fruitful vine of the choicest seed' (Jer. 2.21). Christ is the rock: 'They drank of the spiritual rock which followed them, and the rock was Christ' (1 Cor. 10.14). Neither has he refused the grace of this name to his disciple, so long as he is Peter also, because he will have the constant solidity of stone, so firm will he be in his faith.

Work hard then in your turn to be stone; henceforward look for the stone not outside but within you. Your stone is your activity; your stone is your spirit. Your house will be built on this stone so that no gusting of evil spirits can blow it down. Your stone is the faith and the faith is the foundation of the Church. If you are stone, you will be in the Church, because the Church rests on the stone.[157]

Hilary also insists that it means the person of Peter, but without cutting out the sense of confession: 'One is this blessed stone of the faith (*petra fidei*) confessed by the mouth of Peter'; 'the Church is built up on this stone of confession (*confessionis petra*)'.[158]

Taking everything into account, especially that the faith involved is that of the time after the resurrection,[159] we prefer the last position, on which we take our stand firmly but not rigidly. It does justice to the details of the passage in question, and, beyond that, to the attitude which underlines all the New Testament evidence. Most importantly, it enables us to tie together what we know of Peter during the ministry of Jesus with what the Acts of the Apostles tells us of his function as spokesman for the twelve after the resurrection, and as missionary preacher. In the words of a group of specialists, Catholic and Protestant, who together examined the evidence closely:

> Eventually all of this combined, and Peter is portrayed even during Jesus' ministry as the one who gave voice to a solemn revelation granted to him by God about who Jesus was: the Messiah and the Son of the living God (Matt. 16.16f). In the light of the post-Easter events it becomes clear to the Christian community that with this faith Peter is the rock on whom Jesus has founded his church against which the gates of Hades shall not prevail.
>
> Not only is Peter presented as a confessor of the Christian faith; eventually he can be seen as a guardian of the faith against false teaching. Some hints of this aspect may be implied in the power of binding and loosing.[160]

Peter's pre-eminence, which explains his primacy among the twelve, comes from his confession of the apostolic faith. And it is in his act of confession that he becomes the first among those upon whom the Lord founds his Church.

In this way of looking at it particularly, it is enlightening to stress what the exegetes often forget, the close connection between on the one hand the confession of faith and the martyrdom foreshadowed immediately after the words to Peter by the prediction of suffering and the cross, and on the other hand the rebuke to Peter labelled as Satan and *skandalon*. These verses, Matthew 16.21-3, are important for grasping the profound meaning which Matthew gives to the whole section. Perhaps we should extend the section to include the rest of the chapter, filling out its meaning with 'If any man would come after me, let him deny himself and take up his cross and follow me. For whoever would save his life will lose it, and whoever loses his life for my sake will find it' (16.24-5). Without being too simplistic, we might establish a parallel with another pericope central to the gospel material about Peter, the last chapter of St John. It includes Peter's confession of love for Jesus, which implies a confession of faith; the announcement of a privileged pastoral task ('feed my lambs', 'feed my sheep', 'tend my sheep'), the warning of martyrdom ('you will stretch out your hands, and another will gird you and carry you where you do not wish to go.' (This Jesus said to show by what death he was to glorify God.) And after this he said to him, 'Follow me'). Is not this a veiled hint of Peter's glorious witness in sealing his confession of faith? As for the words which Luke writes into the Last Supper (22.31f), they awake similar echoes, though in a different key. Peter will be involved in the ordeal of Jesus, but when he is recovered from it he must 'strengthen his brethren'. His faith was to play a decisive part in the formation of the primitive community.[161] Peter's 'primacy' is woven into his confession of faith and his continuing responsibility for it.

This is what confirms his connection with the event at the heart of that faith, the resurrection.[162] The New Testament insists on the fact that Peter was the first among the apostles to see the risen one (1 Cor. 15.5; Luke 24. 34). The Fourth Gospel's account of that other disciple arriving first at the tomb but standing aside while Peter went in makes the same point. Peter's priority in meeting the risen Christ stitches together, as it were, his place in the apostolic group during the years of the ministry of Jesus and his rank in the Easter community. It is not being over-simple to see a family likeness between Mark's prediction of the Passion and resurrection, which follows immediately Peter's confession and provokes him to refuse it, and John's remark at the end of his account of the empty tomb: 'For as yet they did not know the scripture, that he must rise from the dead' (Matt. 16.21-3; Mark 8.31-3; John 20.9).

The 'priority' of Peter's encounter with the risen Christ stands between the confession at Caesarea, imperfect and hesitant according to Mark, and the proclamation of the *kerygma* on the day of Pentecost; and in both cases Peter, though standing in the foreground, spoke in the name of the group which followed Jesus. It is undoubtedly this priority which makes the connection between the two confessions of faith which Matthew has combined into one. The 'privilege' of the *first* appearance of the risen Lord to the apostles had the effect of ripening Peter's faith and so of transforming the place which he had held during the ministry of Jesus into an authentic primacy. He is the first to believe fully. His primacy is founded firmly on the faith which he confesses and will indeed be sealed in his blood. Luke's idea is included also (Luke 22.32). Founded on faith in the resurrection, the primacy will become a means of serving that faith. Peter will be he who, in the name of the other apostles, proclaims 'This Jesus God raised up, and of that we are all witnesses' (Acts 2.32).[163]

The power of the keys, too, is rooted in the confession of faith which Peter made after the Resurrection in the name of his brothers.[164] For Judaism, indeed, the image of the keys of the Kingdom speaks of authority founded on an objective reality. To give the keys means to confer a power on, to authorize, someone who is worthy. He who has the keys has the authority. The scribes, those of them at least whom Matthew had in mind (Matt. 23.13), claimed a similar power which allowed them to control entrance into the Kingdom of heaven, founding that claim on the excellence of their interpretation of the Word:

> They exercised this power by declaring God's will revealed in the Scriptures through their preaching, their teaching and the judgements they gave. By thus opening the way into the Kingdom, they

became the spiritual heads of the community. Jesus accused them of not fulfilling their task properly and so of locking the Kingdom of God instead of opening it. As Lord of the messianic community he then handed over to Peter the keys of God's kingly rule, the full authority of proclamation.[165]

Judaism, moreover, took the power of binding and loosing to be that of excluding from the community or restoring people to it. Seen in this light it is clear that Peter will exercise the keys through his missionary preaching, nourished as it was by his faith as 'first witness'. The apostolic faith which he, in the name of his brothers, had been the first to confess throws open to mankind the entrance into the Kingdom of heaven. Sins are forgiven in baptism, which sets a seal on the welcome given to the gospel *kerygma*, the proclamation of the faith confessed by Peter. There is a 'binding and loosing', to use the rabbinic language, because it gives freedom from the situation which obtained beforehand. Baptism marked also the entry into the community of the Church, the foretaste of the eschatological Kingdom.[166] The verbs 'bind' and 'loose' refer in the first instance to forbidding and permitting, to the imposition of obligations and the lifting of them; they may perhaps also imply the power of declaring what must be believed and done to enter the Church of God and to remain there; their scope is wider than a bare declaration of the Good News. Jesus in St Matthew invests Peter, the supreme confessor of the faith, with a teaching authority befitting the excellence of that confession. But because this authority has to do with the word of salvation, its consequences are of the greatest significance, extending even to entry into the Kingdom of heaven.

If we now read again the Matthaean passage thus carefully studied within the total New Testament evidence about Peter, we may conclude:

> The New Testament attributes a threefold function to the primacy of Peter: he is first in the sense that Christ has entrusted him with the keys of the Kingdom, which means that he is the chief witness to what a Christian must believe and do; then he is first in the sense that Christ has charged him to strengthen his brethren in the apostolate; and finally he is first in the sense that the risen Lord

made him pastor of the Church, to guard her unity, defend her, and nourish her.[167]

First (*protos*), but not unique! The other apostles are similar to him in everything except in holding the first place. If he is the rock, they too are the foundation (Eph. 2.20); if he binds and looses, they remit and retain (John 20.23, Matt. 18.18);[168] if he declares the kerygma, they too must preach the gospel which makes disciples (Matt. 28.18-20); if he heals, they work signs and wonders too (Acts 2.43); if he seals his witness in martyrdom, so do they (Acts 12.2). And the faith which he confesses is not different from that of his brother apostles. His primacy is that of a true *primus inter pares, a primus* who is genuinely, and not merely in point of honour, first, while the *pares* are genuinely equal and do not derive their power or their mission from him. Only the Spirit of God can give these. The first (*protos*) does not absorb the others.

The case of Paul will show what this means. Paul called himself the least of the apostles, having been made one by the Lord's direct intervention (1 Cor. 15.8; Gal. 1.1). He is well aware that he is a genuine apostle without qualification, on the basis of his meeting with the risen Lord. He knows that his own preaching of the gospel is every bit as important as that of Peter himself; he is Peter's equal when it comes to the mission of preaching the Word and bringing about the birth of God's Church among the Gentiles. He is ready, moreover, to oppose Peter's views quite uninhibitedly when the situation requires it: 'I opposed him to his face, because he stood condemned.' He was 'not straightforward about the truth of the gospel' (Gal. 2.11, 14). He even suspected him of trying to dodge the scandal of the cross (Gal. 5.11) again by condoning the views of the Judaeo-Christians who wanted to lock the Church into the closed circle of Israel instead of releasing it into liberty. Had he not forgotten his own words at the home of Cornelius in Caesarea (Acts 10.28-9)? Moreover, Paul made sure that the 'pillars' of the church of Jerusalem recognized that God had entrusted him with the mission to the Gentiles just as much as he had given

Peter that to the Jews (Gal. 2.6-9). He wanted his vocation to be in some way 'received' by the mother church.[169]

This insistence upon equality did not, however, prevent Paul from respecting a certain quality of 'first' in Peter. His explanations 'start from an accepted presupposition that Peter is the first of those who were apostles before him, the principal figure among the notabilities in Jerusalem'.[170] He really sees him as head of the apostolic mission to the Jews, not without connection with the Lord's own wish:

> It is certainly not fortuitous that Paul speaks more often and in greater detail about Cephas-Peter than about any other person on the apostolic scene. To the apostle to the Gentiles, Peter represented the authority of the original church, the first witness to that basic kerygma which unites all the apostolic preachers (1 Cor. 15.5). Paul visited Peter on his first stay in Jerusalem (Gal. 1.18), he gives as a standard for assessing his own apostolate to the heathen world that of Peter to the Jews (Gal. 2.7-8); he gives as a precedent for not earning his own living the same apostolic reason which Peter gives (1 Cor. 9.5).
>
> Paul can, however, claim against Peter 'the truth of the gospel' (Gal. 2.14) and he will allow no appeal to Peter from himself in the matter of divisions within the community (1 Cor. 1.12; 3.22). If 1 Corinthians 3.10-17 reflects a dispute with a 'Peter party' at Corinth, he does not allow Peter to be considered the foundation of God's building, 'for no other foundation can anyone lay other than that which is laid, which is Jesus Christ (1 Cor. 3.11)'.[171]

We may say, then, that Paul was chosen by God as Peter was chosen, that he had the same claim to be called an apostle. Yet while fully aware of his own standing, Paul seems to have accepted the place which Peter held among the earliest converts as a given right, though he did not hesitate to judge his actions and decisions in the light of the gospel (Gal. 2.11, 14). However great his own acknowledged authority, Peter stood under the judgement of the only absolute authority, that of the Lord Jesus, of which 'the truth of the gospel' constitutes the norm.

There we have what we might call 'the primacy of Paul'. We said earlier that it was charismatic rather than institutional.

116

Paul was the one who bore witness to the absolute, radical authority of the Word over everything and everyone, even over him to whom the Lord had committed leadership, because of the quality of his confession of faith, within the apostolic group. The fact of Paul's unique calling shows how God's grace transcends every institution. The Holy Spirit restored the gap in the twelve by the election of Matthias, thereby stressing not only the continuity between the post-resurrection Church and the ministry of Jesus but also that between the twelve tribes of the old covenant and the new people of God; and then proceeded to raise up Paul as an apostle in his own right. It was as if Paul functioned alongside the 'traditional' structure, yet did so according to the will of God and of the Lord Jesus Christ. If, as was often the case, his ministry did not cross that of the other apostles (as it did at Antioch) one might think in terms of two parallel paths and, so far as Peter is concerned, two primacies which seldom overlapped.

The two primacies did, however, meet at Rome, intermingling in the blood of martyrdom. There, the 'glorious witnesses' welded into one communion the leadership of the *protos* and the authority of the prophet. The Christian community at Rome, the church of their witness, had indeed existed before the Spirit impelled them there. It now became the place of total, perfect confession of the apostolic faith, with no split in its faithfulness both to its roots in the historical group which Jesus had gathered during his earthly ministry and to the new experience of the Spirit of the resurrection. Hence the privilege of this local church, and so of her see and *cathedra*. Hence also her special calling: the *communion* of the witness of Peter and that of Paul which had been entrusted to her – engraved in her, so that she became the 'living memory' among all the churches. Her bishop would have the responsibility of becoming guardian of and spokesman for all that is implied by such a privilege and calling.

When it comes to institutional leadership, as we have seen, one thinks especially of Peter. Little by little we shall become aware in the authority of the bishop of Rome as head of the 'church which presides in love', of the echo and even the presence in the

117

circumstances of the time of Peter's authority, that of the 'first' (*protos*) in the group of the apostles.

A major turning-point in this development arrived with Leo the Great. He did not entirely abandon the existing view which, as we have seen, understood the bishop of Rome as the 'vicar' of Peter through whom shone the apostle's once-for-all witness and leadership; but he often gave the impression of seeing himself as one to whom Peter gives something of his own personal authority. It is an exaggeration to say that he saw himself as *Petrus redivivus*.[172] There was, however, a great temptation to call himself Peter's heir, interpreting this inheritance according to the principle of Roman law under which the heir replaces the deceased, takes on his rights in their entirety and becomes judicially identical with him. When Leo uses the term 'Peter's heir' or asserts that Peter speaks through his voice, we should not indeed believe that he considered himself to have inherited 'the objective legal status of Peter', much less that he called himself 'indistinguishable from Saint Peter himself', being 'in some sense a reincarnation of Saint Peter', so that his *principatus* was 'identical with Peter's'.[173] Nevertheless, in Leo's eyes the bishop of Rome can make judicial claims on the other bishops and because he is Peter's 'successor' has an authority *analogous* to that of Peter among the apostles. The authority which he possesses, founded on Peter's and derived from it, comes in his eyes to seem inseparable from it. Not only, indeed, does he serve this authority, but it establishes his power. He does not possess the whole of Peter's authority, for that would deny the intransmissible part of the foundation laid in history, but he receives that part of the power *of* Peter which is necessary for his *principatus sacerdotii*. All the same, Leo is no Innocent III, let alone a Boniface VIII.

The pope, then, is the bishop of Rome. One point stands out from this huge fresco which we have too rapidly sketched. We believe it to be essential. The primacy of the bishop of Rome is in no sense equivalent to that of a bishop set over the heads of other bishops. It derives from the privileged position of one local church, that of Rome. And before it is a matter of exercising judicial power over the other churches, this privilege is a matter of duty: witnessing to the faith which Peter and Paul confessed. It is a privilege of serving, in the sense of those words which Luke includes in his account of the Last Supper of Jesus with his own: 'Let the leader (among you) be as one who serves . . . I have prayed for you that your faith may not fail; and when you have turned again, strengthen your brethren' (Luke 22.26, 32). Ambrose put it admirably: *Primatum confessionis non honoris; primatum fidei, non ordinis.*[174]

But is not this what the other churches expect from the bishop of Rome: and do they not need to be assured that it is forthcoming, before *communion* with the see of Rome is restored?

3
The Servant of Communion

The Servant of Communion

What is a pope? At the end of the last chapter we answered that question in the language of the Great Tradition: the pope is the bishop of Rome. We purposely ended with the example of Leo the Great. It was under him that the see of Rome began to assert its prerogatives vigorously and often touchily, quoting on occasions the authority of Peter himself. Yet it was thanks to him that the purpose of the Roman primacy became clear; it was for the service of communion between the churches.

For Leo, the heart of this *fidelium universitas* (whole body of the faithful) is none other than the profession of the true faith, the *unitas fidei catholicae*.[1] The occasions when he felt it necessary to intervene outside the churches of his Western patriarchate[2] were connected either with defending the faith or - too often forgotten - with safeguarding the privileges (*presbeia*) of certain churches.[3] He meant to ensure that the decisions of the Fathers at the holy Council of Nicaea were observed.[4] The function to which, as bishop of Rome, he felt called within the *koinonia* of the churches may be described as serving their communion by supporting the churches in their confession of the true apostolic faith, and ensuring respect for the privileges proper to each of the churches. At this turning-point in history, when the Roman see set itself to follow an increasingly authoritarian path, Leo's vision of the authority which he claimed and exercised was still dominated by serving the faith, despite a concern for juridical sanctions which was to grow heavier:

> We have received from Peter, the Prince of the Apostles, the certainty of possessing the right to defend the truth which brings our peace. No one must be allowed to weaken it since this truth has so solid a foundation.[5]

123

And at Chalcedon at least, the East seemed more ready than before to recognize that claim.[6]

This understanding accords with the true nature of the primacy of the Roman church and her bishop. If any new thinking on Roman authority is to ring true, it must be along these lines. In any case it is the master element which has remained in the Roman primacy under all the frequently disfiguring additions made across the centuries. The accretions have been built around it. There is still time to scrape them away.

It seems essential to an ecumenical approach like that of the present book to read again the dogmatic pronouncements of the two Vatican Councils in the light of that vision of the primacy still current in Leo's time. Not, indeed, by simplistic comparison of words; but we aim to highlight the point where Rome may listen to the other Churches, especially those of very ancient tradition, and ask herself whether they are not questioning her about what she herself considers the innermost element of her primacy.

A visible foundation for the unity of faith and communion

If Leo the Great saw his ministry as the responsibility for keeping within the communion of faith all the churches born from their reception of the apostolic preaching, he must have seen himself as one who could only carry out his office in communion with those whom he called 'brothers and fellow-bishops.'[7] He behaved accordingly:

> Leo did not proceed arbitrarily in the exercise of his authority in doctrine, but by agreement with his brothers in the episcopate and with the whole Church. He did not wish to teach anything beyond what the Church believed, what all Catholics believed.[8]

And while he insisted firmly on the need for communion with the Roman see,[9] he not only respected but protected and defended the rights of his brother bishops, encouraging them to use every initiative which was theirs by right and which no one, not even the bishop of Rome, could threaten:

When he intervened in the affairs of another church, it was either because the matter in question lay outside the competence of the local authority, or because the local authority could not or would not take the action needed. Whether answering an appeal or taking his own initiative, Leo intervened always as a last resort.

. . . Leo left to the metropolitan bishops everything which came within their competence, intervening only when a matter lay outside it. He made others respect their privileges and he respected them himself. As for bishops in general, Leo recognized that each shepherd governed his own flock with a special care and had to give account of the sheep entrusted to him. The pope also recognized that all the bishops shared the same dignity, regardless of the importance of their see. Moreover, his insistence on the preparation needed before a man was raised to the episcopate and his frequent appeals to the canons forbidding interference in the territory of another bishop showed that, for Leo, the bishops enjoyed complete authority in their own churches.[10]

He held, too, that questions should be settled on the spot.[11] He never wanted to restrict the local episcopate, let alone to downgrade its value.

It is instructive to compare this conception of the primacy with what the Acts of the Apostles says of Peter's attitude in what is generally called the Council of Jerusalem. Peter intervenes, his voice is heard, his advice carries weight (Acts 15.7, 12, 14). He tries to bring about unanimity (*homothymadon*, 15.25). But he does not impose his will and he does not take the decision alone; James, 'the apostles, the elders and the brethren' (15.23) each had their part to play.[12] James had a particularly large part. Peter does not have to create unity – that comes from the Spirit of the Lord – but to keep the community in *koinonia*. Nor is the ministry of the bishop of Rome to be at the origin of church unity, for this, the gift of the Spirit, is on offer at every Eucharist. His role is to guard, defend and promote the visible communion of believers. Just as Peter was not the one 'starting from whom' the Church of God was built, but the one who allows the apostolic group to become, by its *koinonia* in the confession of faith, her true foundation (Eph. 2.20), so the bishop of Rome is not the one 'starting from whom' the Church of God is built but the one who allows the ministry of his 'brothers and fellow-bishops' to open out into the communion of their churches. The mission of the bishop of the apostolic see[13] does not stand above the mission of bishops generally, but exists within it with the purpose of serving it.

Vatican I's Constitution *Pastor Aeternus* and its 're-reading' in Vatican II's *Lumen Gentium* are careful to give this service of unity as the essential mission of the local church at Rome and her bishop. The charge (*munus*) of the 'Roman primacy' is situated at the intersection of two of the data conveyed in the Scriptures: the *ut unum sint* of the Fourth Gospel with all its resonances in New Testament tradition; and the emergence of an *episkope* charged by the Spirit to guard and guide the new people in faithfulness to the gospel.

Pastor Aeternus takes up the matter several times:

> The eternal shepherd and *episcopus* of our souls (1 Peter 2.25), in order to continue permanently the saving work of redemption, wished to build up the holy Church in which, as in the house of the living God, all the faithful could be bound together in a single faith and a single love. That is why before he was glorified he prayed to his Father not only for the apostles but also for those who through their word should believe in him, that they should all be one as the Father and the Son are one (John 17.20f). As he sent into the world the apostles whom he had chosen, as indeed he had himself been sent by the Father (John 20.21), so he wished that there should be pastors and teachers in his Church to the end of time (Matt. 28.20). And in order that in very truth (*ut vero*) the episcopate itself should be one and undivided and that, thanks to the close mutual unity of the priests, the whole multitude of believers should be kept in the unity of faith and communion, in placing blessed Peter at the head of the other apostles, he thus established his person as a lasting principle and visible foundation of this double unity (*DS* 3050-1).

> Thus in keeping the unity both of communion and of a single profession of faith with the Roman Pontiff (*cum Romano Pontifice tam communionis quam eiusdem fidei professionis unitate*), the Church of Christ would be a single flock under a single shepherd (*DS* 3060).

It is a pity that subsequent theology explained and commented so little upon these two important paragraphs of *Pastor Aeternus*, one of which opens the constitution, giving it its name, the other closing the central section; but it was too closely tied to the ultramontane issue and concerned above all to emphasize the 'pontifical powers'. It would otherwise have been clear even in 1870 that the question of primacy did not involve shortsighted assertions of the bishop of Rome's power over each community and each Christian in communion with him. The primacy would instead have been connected with a deeper reality: the service of the Church's unity through fidelity to the apostolic faith over which it was the vocation of the Church of Rome (*Ecclesia Romana*, *DS* 3057, 3060) to watch. The Fathers of the Council set as its boundaries the universal dimension of *koinonia*, the catholicity of the *ut unum sint*, in view of the very many embodiments and translations of the apostolic faith which had become necessary. Quite explicitly they had no intention of departing from the traditional faith which was rooted in the use of the churches and transmitted by the great councils 'where the East met the West in the unity of faith and love' (*DS* 3052, 3059, 3065).

Vatican II was to say nothing different:

... Jesus Christ, the eternal pastor, set up the holy Church by entrusting the apostles with their mission as he himself had been sent by the Father (John 20.21). He willed that their successors, the bishops namely, should be the shepherds in his Church until the end of the world ... In order that the episcopate itself, however, might be one and undivided he put Peter at the head of the other disciples, and in him he set up a lasting and visible source and foundation of the unity both of faith and of communion (*LG* 18, Flannery p. 370).

Collegiate unity is also apparent in the mutual relations of each bishop to individual dioceses and with the universal Church. The Roman Pontiff, as the successor of Peter, is the perpetual and visible source and foundation of the unity both of the bishops and of the whole company of the faithful. The individual bishops are the visible source and foundation of unity in their own particular churches, which are constituted after the model of the universal

Church; it is in these and formed out of these that the one and unique Catholic Church exists. And for that reason precisely each bishop represents his own Church, whereas all, together with the pope, represent the whole Church in a bond of peace, love and unity (*LG* 23, Flannery p. 376).

A straightforward reading of paragraph 23 shows that the constitution *Lumen Gentium*, building on the fact that the universal Church arises from the communion of local churches, says of each individual bishop taken separately (*singuli episcopi*) that he is for his particular church what the bishop of Rome is for his church: the visible source and foundation of unity. Elsewhere, the constitution declares that the bishops have over 'their' church a power (*potestas*) which is proper, ordinary and immediate (*LG* 27), adjectives which Vatican I used to describe the power (*potestas*) of the bishop of Rome over all the Christian communities and the faithful (*DS* 3060, 3064). This finds an echo in the Vatican II decree *Christus Dominus* on the pastoral office of bishops:

> In this Church of Christ the Roman Pontiff, as the successor of Peter, to whom Christ entrusted the care of his sheep and lambs, has been granted by God supreme, full and immediate power in the care of souls. As pastor of all the faithful his mission is to promote the common good of the universal Church and the particular good of all the churches. He is therefore endowed with the primacy of ordinary power over all the churches (*CD* 2.1, Flannery p. 564).

Two concurrent powers?

At this point we reach immediately and abruptly the heart of the problem, the area where our non-(Roman) Catholic brothers ask us to help them see clearly. But, as we said in the first chapter, the same area hides causes of constant disquiet and unease for the Catholic community too. How may we reconcile these two powers, at first sight equal, both making for unity, both operating on the same churches and the same faithful people? Does not one of them have to be subordinate if there is to be any stable unity? Things being what they are, it seems likely that Rome will carry the day:[14] so much so, that the assurance, introduced into *Pastor Aeternus* at the request of Mgr Spalding, archbishop of Baltimore, to allay fears, reads like a mere dream.

> This power of the sovereign pontiff in no way obstructs the ordinary and immediate power of episcopal jurisdiction, by which the bishops, established by the Holy Spirit (Acts 20.28) as successors to the Apostles, feed and govern as true pastors the flock committed to each one. On the contrary, this power is asserted, strengthened and vindicated by the supreme and universal pastor, as Gregory the Great says: 'My honour is the honour of the universal church. My honour is the solid strength of my brothers (in the episcopal dignity). Then am I truly honoured, when honour is not denied to each one to whom it is due' (*DS* 3061).

In the humorous words of a British theologian, each diocese is submitted to twin episcopal powers with identical jurisdiction, each episcopal twin being doubled by the papal twin. Since the papacy can manage perfectly well on its own, there is no practical reason why the episcopal twin should not be deemed superfluous and treated accordingly.[15] Which of the two pastors of Vatican I is 'he who *truly* counts'? Which of the two 'vicars and legates of Christ' of Vatican II (*LG* 27, Flannery p. 382) is the one with whom we must remain in communion if we are to live within the *catholica Ecclesia*?

To the question put in this way there is only one answer from Vatican I and Vatican II. You share in ecclesial communion in so far as you are in communion with the bishop of your local church, who is himself in communion with all his brother bishops because he and they are in communion with the bishop of Rome. All the words in this answer count. It is not possible to qualify them. To speak only of communion with the bishop of Rome while considering communion with the local bishop as 'incidental and secondary'[16] is, to use an expression from the debates during Vatican I, to go *ad destructionem Ecclesiae*.

In fact the minority at Vatican I had already badgered the Fathers of the Deputation of the Faith, who were responsible for the final version of the text, on this question. They sounded a warning: if it was not clearly shown how the two episcopal powers, both of them ordinary and immediate, bore upon the same section of the flock, there must remain a risk of upsetting the balance so that the local bishop appeared to be no more than a shadow of the bishop of Rome.

Interventions in this interest were frequent at all stages in the drawing up of the document. We may cite that of the bishop of Hippo, Mgr Felix de las Cases, on 30 May 1870, after the revision of the text:

> The schema seems to aim at nothing else than that the pope is in practice to be the only bishop of the whole Church, the others being indeed bishops in name but in reality nothing but vicars . . . The assertion of episcopal jurisdiction, ordinary and immediate, over the whole Church, sounds very like that other thing: . . . the pope is the *immediate*, ordinary bishop of every diocese, as much that of Gubbio as that of Rome.[17]

On 14 June, shortly before the closure of debates in the *aula*, Mgr Bravard, bishop of Coutances, made a speech to the same effect, stressing that an extra paragraph recognizing the power of the bishops would not resolve the problem. The danger was that

> the bishops would appear only . . . as vicars of the Roman pontiff, removable at his will, whereas Christ chose twelve whom he called his apostles, and that all of us who are assigned to a see, once we have received the fullness of the priesthood, had believed that we were truly and irrevocably espoused to that see before God and that we were bound to it as to a spouse.[18]

A close reading of these interventions undoubtedly suggests that in the eyes of the minority the issue at stake was not a demand by bishops afraid that their basic rights were being eroded. It was rather that traditional understanding held by the undivided Church to which Leo the Great remains the faithful witness, central to which is the recognized position of the episcopate.[19] Those who spoke out to this effect represent the voice of the Great Tradition, interrogating the Council in the name of loyalty to that which from the beginning the Spirit himself had brought into being.

The aim is the link with the Church of the Fathers. It would have been better to have started with a schema on the Church,

Mgr Ketteler bishop of Mainz declared wisely and with this concern.[20] When the Melchite patriarch of Antioch, Mgr Grégoire Youssef,[21] Mgr Papp Szilagyi bishop of Grand-Varadin,[22] Mgr Vancsa bishop of Fogaras in Transylvania,[23] Mgr Bravard of Coutances,[24] Mgr Bonnaz of Csanad in Hungary,[25] and, in his earlier observations of March 1870, Mgr Förster bishop of Breslau[26] or Mgr Smiciklas bishop of Kreutz,[27] raise the ecumenical aspects of the problem, they underscore the issue really at stake. For if the power of the bishop of Rome appears as a force (or jurisdiction) 'concurrent' with that of bishops in their own diocese,[28] he is made to be the only bishop in the full sense; for he is the primate and this primacy is said to be exercised on 'the pastors and the faithful of whatever rank or rite, whether individually or together" (*DS* 3060), on 'all and each of the churches as on all and each of the faithful' (*DS* 3064). This is to destroy the *ordo Ecclesiae*.

So we must be careful to keep hold of the clarifications and modifications brought out by this appeal to the Great Tradition. They are precious. And on this matter they all agree in insisting that the 'primacy' of the bishop of Rome is not such as to conflict with what the Tradition holds to be of *divine right* for the episcopate. It is not enough, they say, to declare that this last is of *divine right*. The episcopate must – and this is vital – be allowed to be and to act as a body existing *by divine right*. This point emerges from the debates.[29]

Gregory II Youssef, the courageous Melchite patriarch of Antioch, was one of the great figures among the Minority. He went to the heart of the problem with his warning that it was impossible to look on the Church as an 'absolute monarchy' with the pontiff as the monarch, a view which he believed lay behind the current plans; and he proposed an amendment to this effect. For everything that distorts the episcopal function affects the nature of the Church itself. Not surprisingly his amendment was rejected: he wanted matters to be made clear while many in the Majority preferred them left vague. Too much precision, they felt, would tend to qualify the Roman power 'dangerously'. He did, however, provoke a most valuable response from Mgr Zinelli in his final report: 'No one in his right mind could suppose that pope or council could destroy (*destruere*) the episcopate or other rights divinely established in the Church.'[30] But it would destroy the true nature of the pastoral function if another 'personage' were allowed to carry out the tasks which embodied it! Besides, it was futile to claim 'to assert, strengthen and defend' (*DS* 3061) the episcopal power while at the same time overshadowing it in practice.[31] The primacy of the bishop of Rome must therefore allow for norms and limits. It is to be measured by that in the Church which comes from God's will.

We mentioned earlier that Vatican II rejected a suggestion of Paul VI. He would have liked to make use of an old phrase which deemed the bishop of Rome *uni Domino devi(n)ctus* and so accountable to no one but God in the exercise of his primacy. The Theological Commission's answer in defence of its refusal provides an explanation a century later of Mgr Zinelli's point – though he himself would have inclined towards Paul VI's view and have greeted the phrase with joy:

> because it is an over-simplified formula (*nimis simplificata*). For the Roman pontiff is bound to keep within the Revelation itself, the basic structure of the Church, the sacraments, the definitions of the first councils, etc. We cannot list them all. Great care is needed with phrases like 'uniquely' and 'alone'. They could give rise to very many difficulties. Such a phrase would in any case need to be qualified by long and complicated explanation. The Commission deems it therefore better to avoid the phrase. There is also a psychological reason: we must avoid pacifying some people in such a way as to arouse new anxieties, especially over our relations with the East.[32]

The mention of the Eastern churches shows the importance attached to that ancient tradition, of which in other circumstances Gregory II Youssef had himself been the spokesman.

Great efforts were made at the moment of the decisive vote in 1870 to explain to the worried Fathers how the ordinary power of the bishop in his diocese tied in with the ordinary power of the bishop of Rome in the same diocese. But those taking part in the discussions were unfortunately only too pleased to go round and round in a treadmill of vocabulary which encouraged ambiguous statements. Nevertheless the point was made firmly that 'ordinary' meant something different in the two cases. Applied to the pope's power it meant *adnexum officio*, imparted with the office itself *and not delegated*. Applied to the local bishop it means 'not only in extraordinary cases', a power 'to be exercised from day to day over those needs and cases which arise ordinarily in a diocese'.[33] The bishop of Saint-Brieuc, Mgr David, a member of the Minority who was not present at the solemn declaration on 18 July, said in full council:

> The sovereign pontiff's power over the universal Church is ordinary in the sense that it is by divine right tied to the primacy itself and, as and when properly exercised, has no need of any delegation (*nulla omnino delegatione indigere concipitur*) ... But is the power of the sovereign pontiff ordinary in the sense that the pope could habitually (*ordinarie*) without necessity or evident usefulness to the Church and simply at his own pleasure perform in every diocese, by himself or his collaborators, the episcopal functions in the way that the Ordinary of the diocese performs them (*absque necessitate aut evidenti ecclesiae utilitate juxta merum beneplacitum et in qualibet diocesi, prout Ordinarius ipse, per se aut per suos munia episcopalia obire possit summus pontifex*)? Who is there that could not see the awkwardness and friction which would arise from such confusion?[34]

Cardinal Rauscher, archbishop of Vienna, also made an important contribution showing that it was impossible to conceive of two powers which would be *ordinary* in the same sense and be exercised in the same diocese.[35]

On 5 July 1870 Mgr Zinelli, replying to Mgr Dupanloup, gave the official meaning of 'ordinary' as it was used in the final text to characterize the bishop of Rome's power over all local churches. It shows that he had taken account of the criticisms, though he declined to change the terminology:

> All (jurists and doctors in canon law) describe as ordinary that power which comes to someone by virtue of his office, and as delegated that which comes to him not from his own office but which he exercises in the name of another to whom it is ordinary.

The Deputation of the Faith believes that with this explanation the difference is narrow. For does not the sovereign pontiff possess by virtue of his office that power which is attributed to him? If it is by virtue of his office, it is an ordinary power.[36]

An enlightening comment on a document which had elsewhere been kept deliberately obscure. Vatican I refused to change the episcopate into a company of bureaucrats or delegates of the pope, an army of shadows doubling functions more appropriately performed by the supreme head himself. The Council refused to look upon the primacy as an overall power absorbing every episcopal activity within the people of God. The power (or jurisdiction) of the bishop of Rome was not to be an obstacle to that of the other bishops. Unanimously

> the Fathers (of the Council) rejected the idea that the Roman pontiff should intervene in their dioceses *ordinarie*, in the same way which belonged to them, for the day-to-day, customary and ordinary government throughout each diocese. Considered according to this code of practice, the jurisdiction over one particular church belongs to them solely and in some sense exclusively, though always under the supreme authority of the Roman pontiff.[37]

Zinelli explained the term further by adding that, if the sovereign pontiff acted without regard to this fact, he would be using his power *non ad aedificationem sed in destructionem*. He would change it into a power of destruction.[38] He would also go against the reason for the existence of his own office. The objections raised, which seemed sometimes to be treated lightly,[39] in fact led the way to a more carefully differentiated vision. Their greatest value lay in showing the true nature of the problem: to discover the specific responsibility of the papal office.

Much the same may be said of discussions surrounding another adjective used to describe the bishop of Rome's power. This power is said to be *immediate* over all the churches, pastors and faithful (*DS* 3064). The adjective was to worry Vatican II as much as *ordinary*. The constitution *Lumen Gentium* used both to qualify the power of bishops in their dioceses (*LG* 27), but not that of the pope. It is, however, true that the decree *Christus Dominus* on the function of bishops did not share this scruple and took up the formula from *Pastor Aeternus* (*CD* 2.1). But the constitution on the Church vindicates the disquiet felt by the minority at Vatican I.[40]

In his contribution already mentioned, Cardinal Rauscher of Vienna set out the problem well, though he was not totally against keeping the term:

> To attribute to the (Roman) pontiff a jurisdiction to be exercised immediately in each of the churches is to affirm unambiguously that he possesses the power to carry out in every diocese that which belongs to the bishop's duty, on every occasion that the Church's health requires it.[41]

Leaving the matter vague thus ran the risk of subordinating the role of the local bishop, which meant a head-on collision with the ancient tradition of the Eastern churches. They, even those among them that were in communion with Rome, would be 'horrified' by the transformation of bishops into 'vicars apostolic'.[42] There were those who set out a vision of primacy similar to that of Leo the Great:

> If the purpose of the primacy requires it, the power of primacy extends to everything that a bishop does. For it is to preserve unity, to ensure spiritual agreement, to make up deficiencies, to root out abuses, counteract or avoid disasters – in a word to see that everything works healthily and wisely towards the sublime aims of the Church,

explained the Hungarian Mgr Haynald.[43] Without this qualification, the assertion of the bishop of Rome's *immediate* power in every diocese must establish a jurisdiction running fair and square alongside that of the bishop, which certainly works against the true status of a bishop and weakens his mission.[44]

Once again Mgr Zinelli took account of these difficulties in his final report, even if in somewhat cavalier fashion:

> How is an immediate power to be distinguished from a mediate one? That power is called immediate which may be exercised

without having to pass through an intermediary. But is not the pope able by himself to perform episcopal acts in every diocese, without passing through the mediation of the local bishop? Should he rather get the bishop's permission to confirm, for example, or to hear confessions? Each time a demand was heard for the pope to obtain such authorization, the Assembly burst into laughter.[45]

The immediacy in question is thus that of a chief who does not need to get permission. The example offered allows a short and rather petty explanation. But the disquiet expressed more serious concerns. There was a refusal to indicate clearly the precise factors which would safeguard and guarantee to each bishop the full exercise of his episcopal office. Does he not have full responsibility for his local church? Nevertheless, Zinelli is careful to conclude:

> There is no reason to fear that in the government of particular churches (*particularum ecclesiarum*) confusion will result from the fact that this ordinary, immediate power runs alongside the proper power of the bishop in this or that diocese. Confusion would arise if it was a matter of two equal (*pares*) concurrent jurisdictions, but not if one is subordinate to the other (*cum altera alteri sit subordinata*). It would certainly be the case that if the sovereign pontiff availed himself of his right to perform all episcopal acts in every diocese every day, and with no regard to the bishop (*nulla habita ratione episcopi*), riding roughshod over what ought to have been wisely decided, he would be using his power *non ad aedificationem sed in destructionem*, and confusion of spiritual leadership would certainly follow. But who could imagine such an absurd possibility? Let us all consider the matter calmly. Let us, with confidence in the moderation of the Holy See, be assured that this authority will work for the upholding of episcopal power, not for its weakening (*laesioni*).[46]

As we have said before, there is still need for a clear statement on the subordination of the two powers or jurisdictions at issue. Is the subordination one of the kind we now call 'subsidiarity'? The heart of the problem is there. Moreover, the assertion made at such a time and place, however weak its support, that the authority of the local bishop would not in practice be put at risk, constitutes an important item of evidence. For it was in that belief that the Fathers assented to the document.[47] The official interpretation of the word 'immediate' is not maximizing but vague. Based on the certainty that anything which goes against the divine will works *ad destructionem Ecclesiae*, it infers that the very nature of the Roman primacy and of the will of Christ for his Church themselves impose such limits as are essential.

Zinelli, in replying to those Fathers who had proposed amendments, affirmed in the plainest language that the plenary and supreme power of Peter and his successors could not be limited (*coarctari*) by any superior human power, but admitted that it was in effect limited by both natural and divine law. Because this was so, he said, the fears of those who imagined the pope destroying (*destruere*) the episcopate by his full and supreme (*perplena et suprema*) power were 'vain and futile . . . and hard to be taken seriously'; for is not the episcopate in the Church by divine right?[48] In the final discussions on 16 July he made the same point in reply to the *modus* put by Mgr Landriot, archbishop of Rheims:[49] bishops exist by divine right (*ex institutione divina*), within their diocese they possess an ordinary and immediate power and it is not within the power of the pope or an ecumenical council to destroy (*destruere*) the episcopate or anything else which is in the Church by divine institution.[50]

Vatican I thus stands in the following of Bellarmine in seeing the Church as starting with the bishop of Rome whose primatial power is supreme and universal but who has respect for the power of each bishop. More than that, it holds the primatial power to be at the service of the episcopate. The wording is as explicit as could be wished: 'The episcopal, ordinary and immediate jurisdiction of the bishops . . . is to be asserted, strengthened and defended by the supreme and universal pastor' (*DS* 3061). We are concerned with a divine right whose charge (*munus*) requires it to be at the service of the divine right of the other bishops. It is for this reason – a point too seldom grasped – that the crucial problem is how to display clearly the specific quality of service inherent in the primacy, rather than the exact nature of the power that goes with it. Are two ordinary and immediate powers to be deemed concurrent if they arise from two co-ordinated functions? In an immense literature on the subject, curiously few theologians have interpreted the third chapter of *Pastor Aeternus* by the prologue and the first chapter (*DS* 3050-5).

We may now draw the consequences. Because the Church is founded on the apostles with Peter among them and not outside them, the bishop of Rome can only exercise the primatial power which he is (in badly chosen words) recognized to hold by safeguarding the episcopate of those who have the charge of local churches, and by allowing it to be included in the building up of the universal Church, the *catholica*. He would be acting *in destructionem* if he regarded the universal Church as a vast diocese where the bishops were in fact his auxiliaries or 'vicars apostolic', 'bishops in name but in fact just vicars' as the bishop of Hippo, Mgr Felix de las Cases, put it.[51]

It is important to see that the bishop of Rome's power does not operate in the same way at Rome itself and 'in the diocese of Gubbio'.[52] His function within the *urbs*, the city of Rome – his own diocese without which he would not be a bishop, the local church endowed with the *potentior principalitas* – must be clearly distinguished from his true function in the *orbis*, the universal Church arising from the communion of all the local churches. In the first case he has to exercise that *potestas ordinaria et immediata* which belongs to every bishop in his constant and customary dealings with the problems and needs of his local church. In the other case, the Spirit of the Lord requires him to be the sentinel, the 'watchman', the memory of the apostolic faith among his brother bishops especially, to keep them in faithfulness to their mission and above all to keep them unceasingly open to the universal aspects of salvation and of the Church of God.

This reading of Vatican I is supported by Pius IX himself, and quite unequivocally. Five years after Vatican I he was called upon to endorse warmly the declaration by which the German episcopate reacted to a telegram from Bismarck dated 14 May 1872.[53] The bishops explained:

This telegram claims that the decisions of the Vatican Council have the following consequences:

1 The pope may assume episcopal rights in every diocese and substitute his own episcopal power.

2 Episcopal jurisdiction is absorbed by papal jurisdiction.

3 The pope no longer exercises certain reserved, limited rights as in the past, but he is the repository of full and entire episcopal power.

4 The pope in general replaces each bishop individually.

5 The pope at his own discretion entirely may at any time take over the bishop's place in dealings with the government.

6 The bishops are no more than instruments of the pope, his agents with no responsibility of their own.

7 Bishops in relation to governments have become in fact the agents of a foreign sovereign, of a sovereign, indeed, who through his infallibility is more perfectly absolute than any absolute monarch in the world.

The German bishops took this as a challenge to give their own interpretation of *Pastor Aeternus*:

No doubt the decisions of the Council mean that the pope's power of ecclesiastical jurisdiction is *potestas suprema, ordinaria et immediata*, a supreme power of government given to the pope by Jesus Christ the Son of God, in the person of St Peter, a power which extends directly over the whole Church and so over each diocese and over all the faithful, in order to preserve unity of faith, discipline and government in the Church, and is in no way a mere attribution of certain reserved rights.

But this is not at all a new doctrine. It is a truth recognized in the Catholic faith and a principle known in canon law, a doctrine recently explained and confirmed by the Vatican Council, in agreement with the findings of earlier ecumenical councils, against the errors of Gallicans, Jansenists and Febronians. According to this teaching of the Catholic Church, the pope is bishop of Rome but not bishop of another diocese or another town; he is not bishop of Breslau nor bishop of Cologne, etc. But as bishop of Rome he is at the same time pope, that is, the pastor and supreme head of the universal Church, head of all the bishops and the faithful, and his papal power should be respected and listened to everywhere and always, not only in particular and exceptional cases. In this position the pope has to watch over each bishop in the fulfilment of the whole range of his episcopal charge. If a bishop is prevented, or if some need has made itself felt, the pope has the right and the duty, in his capacity as pope and not as bishop of the diocese, to order whatever is necessary for the administration of that diocese . . .

The decisions of the Vatican Council do not offer the shadow of a pretext to claim that the pope has by them become an absolute sovereign and, in virtue of his infallibility, a sovereign more perfectly absolute than any absolute monarch in the world . . .

In the exercise of papal power, therefore, absolutely nothing has changed. It follows that the opinion that the pope's position in relation to the episcopate has been changed by the Vatican Council is completely without foundation.

The interpretation is clear. Some of the phrases had been pronounced in open council in the name of the Minority. But Pius IX was unstinting in his praise:

Venerable Brothers, greetings and apostolic blessing.

The admirable firmness of soul which in the fight for the defence of truth, of justice and of the rights of the Church, fears neither the wrath of the powerful, nor their threats, nor the loss of goods, nor even exile, prison and death, and which has been the glory of Christ in centuries past, has ever since remained her special character and the evident proof that in this Church alone may be found that true and noble liberty whose name is heard everywhere today, but which in truth is to be met nowhere else.

You have again upheld the glory of the Church, venerable Brothers, when you undertook to expound the true meaning of the decrees of the Vatican Council so artificially distorted in a circular which has been made public, and thus prevented the faithful from developing wrong ideas and ensuring that an odious falsification should not provide an opportunity for preventing the free choice of a new pontiff.

Your corporate declaration is marked by clarity and exactness so that it leaves nothing to be desired, that it has been a great source of joy to us and that there is no need for us to add anything to it. But the lies asserted in some periodicals require of us a more solemn testimonial of our approval for, in order to maintain the assertions in the said circular which you have refuted, they have had the impudence to refuse to accept your explanations, on the pretext that your interpretation of the conciliar decrees is only a weakened interpretation in no way corresponding to the intentions of the apostolic See.

We condemn in the most formal manner this lying and slanderous supposition. Your declaration gives the pure Catholic doctrine, and therefore that of the Holy Council and the Holy See, perfectly grounded and clearly developed by evident and irrefutable arguments in such a way as to demonstrate to every man of good faith that, in the decrees under attack, there is absolutely nothing which is new or which changes anything in the relations which have existed until now, or which could provide a pretext for further oppression of the Church or for hindering the election of a new pontiff.

In a consistorial allocution delivered on 15 March 1875, Pius IX spoke of the distortion of the meaning of Vatican I by the German authorities and praised the declaration of the episcopate which had refuted false and trivial doctrines. The declaration would live in the memory of the universal Church to which it had brought such joy. He wanted to shower his praises (*amplissimas laudes*) on the German episcopate and each of its bishops in the presence of the cardinals and of the whole Catholic world (*catholico orbe*). He not only signalled his acceptance of their words but confirmed them with the fullness of his apostolic authority (*easque Apostolicae Auctoritatis plenitudine confirmamus*). Had the seriousness of the political situation made Pius IX less ultramontane in order to keep the support of the German episcopate? We think so. But the words are there, quite unequivocal and uttered on the solemn occasion of a consistory.

A question which will dog us throughout this chapter is this. The knife edge which we have discovered by attending closely to Vatican I corresponds, we know, to the desires of many non-Catholics eager to strengthen the ties of ecclesial communion; though, for reasons discussed in the first chapter, this knife edge is obscured by swollen administrative structures and popular religiosity. What is it that prevents the (Roman)

Catholic Church from opening itself to these desires? Certainly not *Pastor Aeternus* read intelligently.

The power of a bishop among the bishops

The bishop of Rome, then, is not a super-bishop. His function, which is the reason for his power, is enclosed within the mission entrusted to the company of bishops as such and is so ordered as to serve that mission. But what really is this function?

We must join Vatican I in making it clear that the function is truly episcopal even when it is exercised in connection with all the local churches and thus primatial in scope; a point where Vatican II hesitated. The more we study the question the more convinced we become that to call it episcopal, provided that word is interpreted by the discussions at Vatican I and the official explanation before the vote, is not the disaster it seemed at first sight. We are indeed aware of the sense which some of the consultants responsible for drawing up the preparatory document gave it. For them, the bishop of Rome 'may exercise his authority in all the dioceses of the Catholic world . . . each time he deems it appropriate (*quoties id expedire judicat*)'.[54] Here again, the Minority imposed a decisive modification.

The term caused debates even in 1870. The Deputation of the Faith refused obstinately to remove the qualifiers of the power (*potestas, jurisdictio*) of the bishop of Rome, once they had been added to the original text; that indeed did not include them. They first appeared in the schema passed round the Deputation of the Faith on 2 May 1870 and given to the Fathers soon after.[55] The Deputation had been hesitant about it, even divided, leaning rather towards omitting the term, but it still appeared in the text distributed to the Fathers on 9 May.[56] But the Majority fought stubbornly for keeping the adjective, fearing the Minority who preferred to speak of a primatial power[57] and scenting in some interventions a whiff of Febronius, Eybel or Tamburini, whose views had directly countered in the first schema.[58]

In his reply to Mgr Dupanloup during the famous debate of 5 July 1870, Mgr Zinelli repeated that the bishops held their power in a limited way, in the sense that they have charge of their own flock only[59] - a point which Vatican II's *Lumen Gentium* was to make more subtly (*LG* 27) - while the bishop of Rome has charge of the whole flock, and that they only exercise this power in dependence on Peter and his successor (*dependenter a Petro et Petri successore*). Nevertheless, Mgr Zinelli explained,

> It must be admitted that the power of the sovereign pontiff is in reality (*realiter*) of the same type as that of the bishops (*esse eandem speciem ac potestatem episcoporum*). Why then not use the same word to describe the quality of jurisdiction exercised by popes and by bishops, and why not say that the episcopal power resides in the bishops and the supreme episcopal power in the sovereign pontiff?[60]

It seems to us that, correctly interpreted, this *eandem speciem* and the *vere episcopalis* lend themselves to an interpretation which, far from exalting the bishop of Rome unduly, as the Minority feared, by placing his power above the general run of bishops or outside the normal episcopal condition, sets him fair and square in his proper place within the company of bishops. This is not perhaps what Zinelli wished to emphasize but it is certainly implied by his words. During the internal discussions of the Deputation of the Faith, indeed, Mgr Simor understood the addition to have this meaning, which made him oppose it.[61] The real point at issue here is not an extension of the power (*potestas*), but the nature of the responsibility (*munus, officium*). For it is on this that the former depends.

Zinelli's reasoning in his long contribution, moreover, starts from the function, the charge (*munus, officium*), not from the power. The bishop of Rome's function is not merely a genuinely episcopal *officium*, it is only an episcopal *officium*. It follows that the primacy which attaches to him must be understood as arising within the nature of the episcopal *officium* itself, identical in kind in him and in every other bishop. It will not include anything that takes it outside the range of the episcopal as Tradition understands it. Even those elements in this *officium* which are peculiar to it and distinguish it from the function of a

143

diocesan bishop are still episcopal. Because of this episcopal nature of his charge, the bishop of Rome has over the whole Church, and so over each diocese, a power which does not duplicate that of the college of bishops but which is inserted into it and remains genuinely episcopal. His own acts are encircled by the nature of the episcopate shared by the whole body of bishops. That is why there is only one plenary and supreme power in the Church:

> The bishops gathered together with their head in an ecumenical council - and in this case representing the whole Church - or dispersed yet in union with their head - in this case they are the Church itself - truly have the plenary power (*vere plenam potestatem habent*) . . . Confusion would arise if we admitted two plenary and supreme powers separate and distinct from each other . . . But we admit that the truly plenary and supreme power resides in the sovereign pontiff as the head (*veluti capite*) and that the truly plenary and supreme power resides also in the head united to the members, that is, the pontiff united with the bishops.[62]

The body does not exist without the head; nor does the head without the body, we might add. The whole matter of the bishop of Rome's power should be examined in the light of the relation that exists in the one and indivisible episcopate between the body and its head and the head and its body. Only in that way will we perceive the dialectical link between the quality of the power called out by the *officium* of the head and its measure (or 'limit') by that which the episcopal college needs by divine right (*a jure divino*) to be, in the terms of *Pastor Aeternus*, the body of those who are 'established by the Holy Spirit as successors to the Apostles for each of them to feed and govern as true pastors (*tamquam veri pastores*) the flock entrusted to him' (*DS* 3061).

The debates in the Council had brought out the fact, which we regard as fundamental, that the *officium* determines the *potestas jurisdictionis*, together with the other important fact that the *officium* had as its purpose the unity of the body of bishops and of the faithful. Against the trend among some of the Majority, the Minority group remembered that it was sound practice to start from the nature of this *officium* in order to qualify the power possessed (*potestas*) rather than to use the *potestas* in order to describe and qualify the function. If some bishops[63] in their remarks made the single point that, given this perspective, everything should be weighed in terms of need or usefulness to the local churches whether as a whole or even for one among them, others were more precise in their comments.

The bishop of Barcelona, for example, Mgr Monserrat y Navarro, reached the heart of the question when he asserted on 10 June 1870 that 'ordinary' and 'immediate', when applied to the bishop of Rome's power over the whole Church, should be defined by the aim of the primacy itself:

> We should call the Roman pontiff's jurisdiction 'ordinary', so far as it is an exercise of the God-given function of primate, when the pontiff in virtue of his primacy (*virtuti sui principatus*) provides whatever has to do with the preservation of unity (*providet erga ea, quae respiciunt ad conservationem unitatis*).

He showed how this criterion would cover not only definitions of faith and morals or about worship, but also the general code of discipline to consolidate, settle and dispense the *principia universalis oeconomiae Ecclesiae*.[64] He therefore proposed that the text of the Constitution should specifically state that

> the power attached to the primacy of the Holy See, which extends over the universal Church, is ordinary and immediate in that by its function (*ex officio*) this primacy is intended for the preservation of unity, intimately associated with the general good and harmony of the whole (*primatus destinatur ad conservationem unitatis intime conjunctae cum bono generali et concordia universali*), none of which prevents the Roman pontiff from exercising it in an extraordinary manner among the pastors and faithful of whatever rite or dignity, when the health of the Church demands it (*dum salus Ecclesiae id postulet*).[65]

The use of the term 'extraordinary' unfortunately resulted in the rejection of this important amendment.[66] Mgr Haynald, bishop of Kalocsa, also insisted that unity was the specific purpose of interventions from the bishop of Rome:

The episcopal power may do absolutely everything that the bishop does when the purpose of the primacy requires it, in order that unity may be maintained, harmony promoted, faults corrected, abuses removed, evils uprooted or avoided.[67]

One who belonged to the Majority was the bishop of Lerida, Mgr Caixal y Estrada. He held the same view, explaining how the primacy existed with a view to the unity of communion in the government of the universal Church (*ad unitatem communionis in regimine universalis Ecclesiae*), so that members of the Body of Christ should be sanctified in unity by the unity of Holy Communion and divine charity (*sacrae communionis et divinae caritatis unitate sanctificati in unum*).[68] He was praised by the Deputation of the Faith, who professed agreement with him, but he was not followed.[69] Another member of the Majority, Father P. Zelli, priest of St Paul-outside-the-Walls, based himself on the Fathers of the Church, especially Cyprian and Epiphanius, when expounding the 'traditional' view in a contribution of great depth.

Go back to what the holy doctor [St Cyprian] said: 'The episcopate is one, each one possesses a share without division of the whole': you will then understand that there is a single bishop in the Church of God as there is a single bishop in each church, but that nevertheless these bishops are included within the same communion of faith, the same concord, unity and conjunction, because they are set under one bishop in whom the episcopate is one. That is why he adds 'but the beginning has its point of departure in the unity and the primacy was given to Peter that it might be shown that the Church of Christ is one and that its teaching is one'.[70]

These quotations from people who belonged to the Majority show that it was not only the Minority with their worries who put forward the unity of the Body of Christ as the justification for the primacy. An ultramontane theologian as deeply anti-Gallican as M. D. Bouix, who died in 1870, upheld it also, even if he interpreted it in an ultramontane sense; so too did Passaglia.[71] The Irishman Mgr Leahy, speaking in the name of the Deputation of the Faith, intervened along these lines in an important statement on 13 June 1870. He was explaining the meaning of the term 'principle of unity':

Christ has built into the constitution of the Church herself what we call a principle of unity, which by itself (*de se*) is capable and effective in preserving the unity of faith and communion yesterday, today and for ever, which by itself (*de se*) is capable and effective in preserving the faithful from heresy and schism, which by itself (*de se*) is capable and effective in keeping all those who are dispersed throughout the world in the profession of the same faith and within the same communion, however different they are on all other points. Christ has built it into the very constitution of the Church; and to what has thus been built in belongs not only an invisible authority, not only the authority of Christ himself, but the visible, tangible authority which resides in the very person of Peter and Peter's successors.

As for the proof of this authority, it is to be seen

. . . *a priori* in the fact that all those who submit to it are necessarily joined together in the same faith and the same communion (*in eadem fide et in eadem communione necessario conjuguntur*). It is to be seen *a posteriori* since because of it people of all tribes and tongues are gathered into the one and only fold of Christ through having recognized the primacy of the sovereign pontiff, while on the contrary those who reject it . . . because they refuse the authority of the sovereign pontiff from the beginnings of the Church until now have been divided and continue to divide into many heresies and schisms. Truly, then, one may and must say that the Roman primacy is true and is to be called the principle of the unity of the faith and communion (*principium unitatis fidei et communionis*).[72]

Light begins to dawn. We may bring out that key insight which was present at Vatican I even if little developed. The power, *potestas*, exists in relation to the charge (*officium, munus*). It exists only in order to make it possible to carry out that responsibility. Because the power of the bishop of Rome is essentially fulfilled in the unity of the Church, it should obviously be articulated with the power of the other bishops who are also charged with building the Church. This articulation is accomplished at a formal level through that bias towards the unity of the whole body of the Church for which the body of bishops is responsible. In God's plan, therefore, the power of the primate is that which enables the *aedificatio Ecclesiae* entrusted to every bishop to open into the universal *koinonia* and to find its home there. Far from duplicating or stifling the responsibility of the local bishop, it secures the true extent of this responsibility by setting it within the *koinonia* of churches, where the building of the local church reaches completion. And since every element in church life at every level has its point of contact with the *koinonia*, the field of operation for the power or jurisdiction of the bishop of Rome is no less than 'all and each of the churches, as all and each of the pastors and faithful' (*DS* 3060, 3064), taken in the sense which we have defined.

Pastor Aeternus uses the word 'jurisdiction' to designate the power of the bishop of Rome. Hitherto we have avoided the word, but must now establish its meaning. If ever there was a complex notion, one whose meaning has varied from period to period, it is this one. Vatican II used the word sparingly and indeed seemed to avoid it deliberately: six occurrences 'and nearly always in situations of little doctrinal importance';[73] a marked contrast with the Council of 1870, where it was a favourite word. The *primatus jurisdictionis* of Peter and his successors was contrasted with a *primatus honoris* (*DS* 3043, 3054, 3055) and their *potestas jurisdictionis* was discussed (*DS* 3060, 3061, 3064). This jurisdiction, which calls for subordination within the hierarchy and obedience 'not only in that which concerns faith and morals but also in those areas involving the discipline and government of the Church throughout the world' (*DS* 3060), is explained as a power (*potestas*) to feed, rule and govern the universal Church (*DS* 3059).[74]

This pile-up of near synonyms shows very clearly that jurisdiction means not simply the power of 'saying what is right' or 'defining what must be done', but the power of government. The realm of the sacraments alone seems outside its competence (since the thirteenth century it was designated as coming under the power of order, *potestas ordinis*),[75] although in its disciplinary aspect it would be included. The 'supreme power of the magisterium' with its charism of infallibility is how jurisdiction works out at the level of teaching '*de fide vel moribus'* (DS 3065, 3074). Its subjects are 'the pastors and the faithful of every rite and every dignity, separately as well as together' (DS 3060).

There can be no possible doubt that Vatican I understood by 'jurisdiction' the right and the power to rule the Church in all that concerns her faith and discipline; which implies the right and the power to command obedience. To say of the bishop of Rome that he has full and supreme power and jurisdiction over the whole Church, not only in matters touching faith and morals, but also over what relates to the discipline and conduct 'of the Church spread throughout the world', as does canon 3 of *Pastor Aeternus* (DS 3064) amounts to an assertion of the right and power to rule over the whole Church.

Our reading of Vatican I allows us, we believe, to provide a context for this jurisdiction which at first sight seems so extravagant. It is a question of a 'supreme and plenary power', with no territorial limit, over all the local churches and all the faithful. But the purpose of this 'universality' is to build up the church *formally* under her aspect of universal communion. In other words it bears on that which ensures that the communion for which each bishop is responsible in his own church opens out into the *catholica* and so into a *koinonia* where one and the same faith may be found in each diocese and in each of the faithful. Seen from this point of view, it forms part of the *aedificatio Ecclesiae*. And since by definition the *koinonia* involves all the churches, their pastors and their faithful, the jurisdiction of the 'primate' cannot but extend to them all, unless it is an empty word or a merely honorific title. From this stems its universality. It covers the total life of all the local churches, most particularly in what concerns the smooth working and the development of the *koinonia*.

The adjectives 'ordinary' and 'immediate', used to explain how the 'plenary and supreme' jurisdiction applied to each local church, proved to be badly chosen for they gave rise to ambiguity and misunderstanding, hiding the basic meaning which we have just brought out. Understood in the light of Mgr Zinelli's clarifications, they signify 'the power given by reason of the office', 'power which may be exercised without having to pass through any intermediary', in such a manner that the responsibility of the local bishop is in no way compromised. Seen like this they do not contradict the Great Tradition. But it is still vague in a way that is dangerous because it opens the road to excesses. If the (Roman) Catholic Church were to accept the request of separated brethren and undertake to re-examine the validity of the use to which these terms are put, she would clarify her own understanding without betraying anything which she holds precious.[76]

The bishop of Rome and the communion of the local churches

A doctrine of the Church derived from Bellarmine prevented Vatican I from bringing out clearly the actual point where the power of the bishop of Rome fitted in with the power of the local bishop. A study of the discussions held in the *aula* shows that what at first sight looks like ill-will on the part of the Majority is often explained by their defective theology. The Minority appealed to a theological tradition which the Fathers of the Deputation of the Faith were unable to integrate with their own.

We showed in the first chapter how Vatican II 'received' the declarations of *Pastor Aeternus* by reading them again in a new theological light, that supplied by an ecclesiology of communion. In this teaching, the universal Church is to be found within each local church, the indivisible Church of God being truly present and active (*LG* 26; *CD* 11):

> The Christian assembly is not any old assembly. It is the *Ekklesia tou Theou*. That is its distinctive mark . . . From that we should understand that the theological concept *Church* is not to be understood as quantitative but as qualitative . . . What makes the Christian community 'Church' is not a number of people whether small or great, but the intervention of God who gathers together His own . . . The total community which constitutes the Church is not made by adding together the local communities, for each community, however small, represents the Church in her entirety.[77]

The local church as *koinonia* of faith, love and hope - the church where each bishop presides – is not simply a part of the Church of God. It is the Church of God in one of her manifestations in the here and now. The eucharistic synaxis brings about the emergence of the Church of God (*ekklesia tou Theou*) in this place and this historical situation. The eucharistic community is not a fragment of the mystery of the universal Church, but an appearance of this Church in communion with the Father and in the communion of brotherhood, through the Spirit of Christ the Lord. This is why each local community bonded into itself by the Eucharist finds that by that very fact it is 'in full unity' with the other local communities, wherever they may be in the world: not 'by virtue of a superimposed external structure, but by virtue of the whole Christ who is present in each one of them.'[78]

Now this real presence of the whole Church in each community implies that the Church of God 'which is at' one place (1 Cor. 1.2) *recognizes itself* as identical with the Church of God which is at another place. Instead of thinking of the organic unity and the catholicity of the Church as the sum total of the local communities, parts together forming a whole in which they complete each other, we should think in terms of identity and *recognition*. For the essence of this unity

> . . . is not that all churches together constitute one vast, unique organism, but that each church – in the identity of order, faith and the gifts of the Holy Spirit – is the *same* Church, the same Body of Christ, indivisibly present wherever is the 'ecclesia' . . .
>
> It is this ontology of the Church as a *theandric* unity, totally and indivisibly incarnated in each church, which establishes the connecting link between the churches . . . The fullness of each local church is the same that is given to every other church; it is a fullness possessed in common as the gift of God.[79]

The bishop's most fundamental task is to maintain his church in this identity so that every other true church may recognize *herself* as she meets her. At this level he is clearly the master craftsman of unity. His place *in aedificationem Ecclesiae*[80] is shown when he presides at the Eucharist.

It is quite obvious, of course, that this identity can often only be established after penetrating a great variety of outward trappings, for Christian communities are scattered around the world; and, since the faith is not abstract adhesion to Christ but receiving him into particular situations which will be very different, the translations of the gospel into actual life will be very varied. But once that profound identity of being which the Spirit of the Lord brings about has been recognized, it will lead on to a communion in which each community opens itself to the life and thought of the other Christian communities, breaking with everything that shuts it in on itself. Catholicity means nothing more than the presence of this identity in diversity. To recognize this identity in diversity 'sacramentalizes' it to the extent that it expresses communion by words and actions. Vatican II put it well: the 'multiplicity of local churches, unified in a common effort (*in unum conspirans*), shows all the more resplendently the catholicity of the undivided Church' (*LG* 23, Flannery p. 378). Catholicity and communion go together. But this catholicity must show itself, if only to obey the Lord's wish *ut unum sint* and to be conformed to the ideal developed in the Epistle to the Ephesians: 'For he has made us both one' (Eph. 2.4).

We now see why Tradition includes among the bishop's essential functions that of keeping his church open to catholicity. This is not something added to episcopacy but is grounded in the heart of it. Vatican II's Constitution *Lumen Gentium* as well as the Decree on Bishops in the Church emphasize splendidly that through the sacrament of ordination, every member of the episcopal college is bound to have care and 'solicitude for the whole Church' (*LG* 23; *CD* 6). This care, of which the sign is given and which is brought into force by the presence of several bishops at an episcopal ordination,[81] must pass into the new bishop's demeanour and pastoral practice.

In this light it becomes clear that a bishop's *episkope* exists at the intersection of two communions which together constitute the necessary guarantee of the community's identity as Church. The 'apostolic succession' secures the vertical communion, so guaranteeing that the church committed to the bishop shares the identity of the Church of the Apostles. It is the identity across time. It binds today with the day of the beginnings and allows the local church to recognize herself in the features of the apostolic Church. But there must also be a horizontal communion which will guarantee the identity of this local church with all the other local churches here and now dispersed throughout the world: the identity across space. It enables the local church, working out her faith and obedience to the gospel in her own situation, to recognize herself in the other local churches which are working out the same faith and the same obedience in their own particular situations. The horizontal communion is just as essential to the Church of God as the vertical communion.

In short, the bishop's function - it could even be said his primary function - is 'to allow the catholicity of the Church to reveal itself in a particular place'[82] and a particular culture, according to its two essential dimensions. On the one hand the bishop is he through whom 'the continuity of the Church as a whole living in history'[83] is authenticated and signified in and for the local church, considered on the vertical plane. Along the horizontal plane, on the other hand, the bishop is he through whom the communion of his local church with all the other churches living throughout the world of today is authenticated and signified: and most notably when he celebrates the eucharistic memorial. Just as the 'apostolic succession' allows him to carry out authentically his function (*munus*) in the first of these dimensions, so the communion with the *centrum unitatis*, the bishop of Rome within the college of bishops, allows him to carry out his function in the second dimension. In other words, communion with the *centrum unitatis*, the bishop of the see of Peter and Paul, is to the horizontal dimension of catholicity (inseparable as this is from the identity of the Church as such) what inclusion in the 'apostolic succession' is to the historical vertical dimension of catholicity. Both aspects reach back to the apostolic community but, in the second case, it is to the faith of that community as confessed in the martyrdom of Peter the coryphaeus and Paul the prophet, which founded the *potentior principalitas* of the local church at Rome and made her the touchstone of the faith.

That is the traditional way of seeing it. It will be noticed that insertion into the apostolic succession and communion with the *centrum unitatis*, seen along this perspective, both make for the full *episkope* of the bishop. Their purpose is to enable him to fulfil his task as *aedificator Ecclesiae* as well as pastor of the local church. The connection with the *centrum unitatis* and so with the bishop of Rome, does not reduce him to the rank of auxiliary, 'vicar' or delegate of the one who is in fact the only full 'bishop of the universal Church'. The Minority never ceased to alert the First Vatican Council on this point, but although several members preferred the phrase *centrum unitatis* to *principium unitatis*, their view never prevailed.[84] It is not the bishop of Rome who has received from the Spirit the charge to build the local church and keep it in faith and communion. It is the bishop of that church. But he accomplishes his mission fully to the extent that he is in communion with the *centrum unitatis* 'who presides in charity'. Further, the bishop of Rome is not strictly speaking he who creates unity. That responsibility falls to the local bishop as the instrument of the Spirit. The 'primate' has the task of 'watching' over the unity so that the faith on which it is built remains one with the apostolic faith.[85]

All the words with their finer shades of meaning in that sentence are important. For we here touch on the formal reason for the primacy of the see of Peter and Paul. It concerns that bishop's function as 'watchman', as memory. The *centrum unitatis* does not take over the whole work of building unity. As Vatican II showed in a passage already quoted, each bishop is a source and foundation of unity (*LG* 23). The existence of a centre requires elements to be unified around it. In this case the elements are the churches, in every one of which is to be found the Church of God.

We may find here the explanation of a difficult passage in the Preliminary Explanatory Note added to chapter 3 of *Lumen Gentium* as a guide to the reader.[86] How are we to understand this phrase from *Lumen Gentium*: 'One is constituted a member of the episcopal body in virtue of the sacramental consecration (*vi sacramentalis consecrationis*) and by the hierarchical communion with the head and members of the (episcopal) College (*heirarchica communione cum Collegii Capite atque membris*)' (*LG* 22)? It is an important matter: what must be done for the *catholica* to be fully present in the local church? How, thanks to the episcopal ministry, are the two poles of unity and plurality, the universal and the particular, to be kept simultaneous? We have seen that catholicity depends on them both.

The Explanatory Note describes the bishop of Rome's part in the entry of each bishop into the episcopal college by making a distinction which seems at first sight artificial, but turns out to be enlightening. It distinguishes between the *munera* implied in sacramental ordination (using *munera* in a sense different from that we have used, to include the responsibilities and the powers needed to fulfil them); and the *potestates* in practice, by which it means the discharge of the *munera*. The sacrament of ordination gives *all* the first group, duly pointed towards the action for which they exist and equipped with the necessary powers. This action, however, will only be in practice all that it should be - functions and powers of communion - thanks to the *canonica determinatio*. This canonical or juridical determination (Flannery p. 424) (by means of which the gifts of ordination are properly brought into action - E. tr.) may assume the many different forms mentioned in *Lumen Gentium* 24, some of which allow the churches a considerable area of autonomy, but always means a relationship with the bishop of Rome in his proper responsibility for unity within the *catholica*. It has the effect of inserting the bishop (as he already is) into the web of communion which binds together the members of the episcopal college. The bishop of Rome does not give the *munus*, in the sense understood by the Explanatory Note, for this comes from the Spirit of God and is conferred through the ministry of the bishops ordaining their new brother. What he does give to the new bishop is the place which will enable him to play his part within the communion of the churches.

It has perhaps not been sufficiently stressed that this hierarchical communion is one 'with the head and the members', not with the head only. This is no simple matter of assigning a bishop to a particular see. It is, rather, the question of a genuine entry into the unity of the episcopal college with all the responsibilities that go with it. By virtue of his own charge (his proper task), the bishop of Rome places the charge which the Spirit of the Lord has laid on the new bishop within the communion and directs it clearly so as to serve that communion. Its source is the sacrament. The primate's part may be seen more as a condition than a 'cause'.[87]

From then on the new bishop becomes not 'vicar of the

Roman pontiff' (*LG* 27) but 'vicar and legate of Christ', who exercises 'a proper, ordinary and immediate power in the name of Christ' (ibid., Flannery p. 383). It should be remembered that the Minority at Vatican I, sometimes leaning on Thomas Aquinas, had insisted that bishops were not 'vicars of the pope' but 'vicars of Christ' or 'vicars of God'.[88] By entering the episcopal college, the bishop together with all his brother bishops is welded into communion with the see of Peter and Paul, where, with and never apart from the supreme pontiff, 'they have supreme and full authority over the universal Church', as *Lumen Gentium* puts it (*LG* 22), adopting a phrase from Mgr Zinelli in 1870.[89] The *canonica determinatio* of the bishop of Rome opens the way to full episcopal power instead of restricting it. The fact that certain rights are 'reserved' - conceded when necessary - is a fault in the logic of this ecclesiology.

Moreover, when the bishop of Rome thus integrates a new bishop into the college, he does so by himself performing an episcopal act. We said that it was his supreme act of jurisdiction. The power which he then uses is nothing other than an instance - called for by his special responsibility (*munus*) - of the *potestas vere episcopabilis* (*DS* 3060) which is his as bishop of Rome, with a view to the full effectiveness of the *sollicitudo Ecclesiae universalis* borne by the College as a whole and by each bishop individually. It is not an act accomplished by virtue of the sacramental grace of the episcopate who, together, are charged with *episkope* over the Church; within this shared charge he has a particular and unique responsibility for his brother bishops and their churches. He has to 'watch' from within the communion of bishops to see that the churches remain in a state of faith and charity, thanks to the ministry of their bishop, so that they may recognize themselves in each other. He is thus the guardian and the guarantor of that 'care for all the churches' which no bishop, even on his own, may neglect; for it comes to him from his membership of the body of bishops to which the Spirit of God confides the *episkope* of the Church on earth. But in all this the bishop of Rome is still a brother bishop. We should remember *Lumen Gentium* 23:

The Roman pontiff, as the successor of Peter, is the perpetual and visible source and foundation of the unity both of the bishops and of the whole company of the faithful. The individual bishops are the visible source and foundation of unity in their own particular Churches, which are constituted after the model of the universal Church; it is in these and formed out of these that the one and unique Catholic Church exists. And for that reason precisely each bishop represents his own Church, whereas all, together with the pope, represent the whole Church in a bond of peace, love and unity (Flannery p. 376).

The bishop of Rome, then, enjoys the power (*potestas, jurisdictio, exousia*) without which he could not fulfil his function. But this power exists to ensure full catholicity in the making of every local church entrusted to a bishop, in which 'the Church of Christ, one, holy, catholic and apostolic is truly present and active' (*CD* 11, Flannery p. 569). It is not the power of a monarch on whom everything depends, but that of a *primus*, truly first, *inter pares*.

The bishop of Rome among the bishops: a case of 'corporate personality'?

We are considering a bishop who is only a bishop but who, on the basis of that sacrament which all bishops share, the episcopate, performs actions where the responsibility of the entire episcopate is, as it were, caught up and 'symbolized', in the strong sense which that word holds in much modern thought. This is a bishop among other bishops who is commissioned, on the basis of the shared grace of episcopacy, to gather his brother bishops into a college of which he is the *centrum unitatis*. He is a bishop within the college who must by the Lord's expressed will extend the *sollicitudo* of all the churches which is shared throughout the body of bishops to the point where it becomes a personal 'watch' over whatever in these churches affects the apostolic faith and the communion in the *catholica*. It is difficult to find a comparable relationship between a person and the group to which he belongs, which would help to describe it. Previous attempts had no success even where they did not lead theology along slippery paths or on to sinking sands. It will not do to follow some of the ultra-montanes who surrounded Pius IX, for example, and see a relationship between a monarch and his ministers. Even less, as our present studies suggest, should we think of a modern democracy where the pope, no longer called 'bishop of Rome', would be the 'representative of a vast assembly of bishops'. Such views are over-simplified, in which they are not un-like some of the 'models of the Church' traditionally offered.

We are again faced with a type of relationship that can only be expressed in biblical categories, as in the case of the bishop of Rome's relationship with the once-for-all nature of Peter's ministry. The category now is that of 'corporate personality'.[90] It is a notion to be used with care and caution, not as a blunt instrument.

'Corporate personality' expresses a phenomenon much studied in the French school of sociology, which concerns the common awareness shared within a social group. It occurs when the life of the group becomes concentrated on one of its members who is in every respect like the other members. The self-understanding of the group becomes embodied in this particular individual so that it *recognizes itself* in him:

> The group could be thought of as functioning through an indi-vidual member, who for the time being so completely represented it that he became identical with it. By the study of this concept Wheeler Robinson has thrown light on the use of the pronoun 'I' by the Psalmists, and on the Suffering Servant of Deutero-Isaiah. There was a fluidity of thought which seems strange to us, whereby the speaker could pass from the community to the individual who represented it, and from the individual back to the community, without any apparent consciousness of the transitions.[91]

This 'dialectical simultaneity of the one and the many' by which 'the individual tends to become the group and the group tends to identify itself with the representative individual' takes proper account of the mutual connections between causality and influence:

At a deep level the individual is not content simply to represent the group, let alone to influence it for good or evil. In the atmosphere of corporate personality it is objectively the case that he *is* the group or that the group *is* he.[92]

Biblical scholars see this notion behind the far-reaching fact that in biblical thought Adam is seen as the entire human race; the king as the whole people; the *Ebed Yahweh* as all Israel, God's Servant; the Son of Man as the entire 'people of the Saints of the Most High'.[93] The notion has thus become an important tool in biblical interpretation. New Testament specialists even think that, properly interpreted, it may account for the link between the personal act of Jesus and its effect on the vast numbers who are saved. Apart from this notion, they find it 'hard to grasp the deep and original sense', 'the basic theological meaning' of the titles given to Christ in Scripture - Second Adam, King, Suffering Servant, Son of Man, High Priest.[94]

Some who hold the doctrine of the Church as communion believe that the notion of corporate personality allows them to be faithful to the categories of the Bible while going to the heart of ecclesiological themes as central as that of *filii in Filio* (to explain the nature of grace); the Church as the Body of Christ inseparable from the individual Body of the Lord;[95] the apostolicity of the whole Church through intimate connection with 'the apostolic group'; the universal Church in face of the communion of local churches;[96] Peter's relation to the 'apostolic college'; and, we would add, the bishop of Rome's relation to the 'college of bishops'.

We are convinced of the value which this notion has for understanding the connection between 'primate' and college of bishops within the episcopal communion, provided it is used discerningly and with a sense of the finer shades, not rigidly or slavishly, and remembering the element of analogy. The basic identity between the representative individual and his group in an interplay of dynamic communion helps us to understand better how impossible it is to consider the primate (*protos*) except in connection with the college, for he would then be a monster, a head without a body. The primate is inseparably he who 'represents' the others, though in a sense quite different from that in the language of democracy: it is in him that they are able to recognize themselves. His contribution to the *koinonia* thus includes a responsibility which is not shared exactly by any of the others. When he speaks on his own, he is still the one through whom all the others express themselves, and his power (*potestas, jurisdictio*) is still that of the entire college. A passage from *Lumen Gentium*, which follows in the wake of Mgr Zinelli at Vatican I,[97] stands out clearly when seen in this light:

> The college or body of bishops has for all that no authority unless united with the Roman Pontiff, Peter's successor, at its head . . . For the Roman Pontiff, by reason of his office as Vicar of Christ . . . and as pastor of the entire Church, has full, supreme and universal power over the whole Church . . . The order of bishops . . . Together with their head, the Supreme Pontiff, and never apart from him, they have supreme and full authority over the universal Church. (*LG* 22, Flannery p. 375).

This biblical understanding, buried deep in the Church's memory, may well throw light on another thorny problem in Tradition: how does the authority of the bishop of Rome tie in with that of councils or synods? Because the risen Christ by the work of the Spirit became truly the communion of many in his one Body, so within the Church which is his Body the One must always coexist with the many, the universal with the local, the 'primate' and the college.

At the level of ministry, then, primacy and collegiality maintain within the whole Church that relationship of communion between the one and the many and their simultaneous presence. The primate does not replace the council nor the council the primate.[98] This relationship continues to be the normal one because without it the *koinonia* would be breached. The *episkope* of the Church is accomplished in the dialectical interplay of primate and college, the first expressing the second, the second only reaching its proper self through the first. Is not this the same tension as that to be found in 'the corporate personality'? It now finds historical expression in the symbiosis of council and bishop of Rome. The council gives true expression to the communion of bishops and the power which the Spirit has given it as the group of those who carry within themselves the multitude of the churches (the many). The bishop of Rome gives true expression to the unity towards which this communion and the power given by the Spirit to safeguard it is tending (the one). The many is not prior to the one nor the one to the many. Both respond to themselves in each other. Together they make up the *communion*, but it is that of the *catholica*.

The dialectical tension between the bishop of Rome and the other bishops, 'primate' and college, however, runs much further and much deeper than the immediate relation here and now between the primate and the bishops gathered in council or dispersed in their own sees. It encloses the whole story of Tradition. When the 'primate' speaks with authority, the body of bishops wishes and has a duty to recognize the voice of Tradition, which means at the same time the voice of the *sensus fidelium* and that of the bishops of time past. The 'primate's' responsibility is to voice the *tradition* of the apostles as it has been kept and passed on by the apostolic *succession* in the episcopal sees. He would not be able to create something new that sprang out of himself. His word is a 'creed' in the sense that it sets forth under appropriate guarantee the experience of faith of which the episcopate has been and remains the guardian. Though spoken by a person, it is none other than the word of the 'episcopal body' in all its fullness.

Evidence of this may be seen in the way the great ecumenical councils of the still undivided Church 'received' interventions from the bishop of Rome. The welcome which the Fathers at Chalcedon gave to the *Tome* which Leo the Great sent to Flavian is a good case in point. During the fourth session the assembled bishops swore by the gospel that Leo's letter was in complete agreement with the faith of Nicaea and Constantinople:[99]

> The confession of faith made at Nicaea was the basic standard used to compare and evaluate later statements. After reading this confession of faith the Fathers cried: 'It is the orthodox faith; thus do we all believe; thus have we all been baptized; thus do we baptize. This is what blessed Cyril taught. This is the true faith, the eternal

faith . . . It is thus that we all believe; it is thus that Pope Leo believes . . .' The *Tome* of Leo itself was only received by the council after a long and minute examination had established its agreement with the traditional faith, as the acclamations which followed its public reading showed: 'It is the faith of the Fathers! The faith of the apostles! we all believe in this way; the orthodox believe in this way! Let him be accursed who believes otherwise! Peter has spoken through Leo! It is the teaching of the apostles! . . . It is the teaching of Cyril! It is the true faith! It is the faith of the orthodox! It is the faith of the Fathers!'[100]

What are we to make of that acclamation, 'Peter has spoken through Leo'?[101] It seems impossible to read more into it than a recognition of 'the agreement of Leo's letter with the authentic doctrine of the apostles'.[102] The *Tome* conforms to Peter's confession of faith, which is echoed faithfully in the teaching of all the bishops, especially Cyril.[103] Particularly important is its perfect agreement with the faith of Nicaea, whose privileged witness to the Tradition gave it outstanding authority.[104] Determined as he was to impose the teaching of the *Tome* on Flavian, for he knew it to be true, Leo himself took as the standard of 'the true faith' conformity with the faith of the Fathers, especially the bishops and pastors. The undeniable welcome (*irretractabili firmavit assensu*) of his brother bishops at Chalcedon 'confirms' that his doctrine is that.[105] For him, the two supreme standards of orthodoxy are the baptismal creed[106] and doctrine 'confirmed by the Council of Nicaea'. He knew that the Holy Spirit had then been guiding the Fathers.[107] On the level of discipline, 'the decrees of the venerable Council of Nicaea' provide the unbreakable norms to which everyone from himself downwards must conform.[108] He does not speak except within the tradition of bishops of the past.

Pope Agatho's letter also was received by the Fathers, this time those who were assembled in the Third Council of Constantinople, 680-1: 'Peter has spoken through Agatho.'[109] But behind the acclamation lay the recognition that the letter 'agreed perfectly with the decisions of Chalcedon as well as with Leo's *Tome* and with the writings of Cyril of Alexandria'.[110]

Whether it is a council receiving teaching that comes from the bishop of Rome or whether it is the bishop of Rome receiving a conciliar decision, the tension between primate and episcopal college is always set in the context of listening to the Tradition of the Fathers, which means chiefly to the voice of bishops who have passed on the faith of their churches. When therefore the primate speaks here and now to his fellow-bishops with all the authority belonging to his office, he does so by 'receiving' what the bishops of the people of God have kept and taught *in aedificationem Ecclesiae* since apostolic times.

This is true also outside the setting of a council. Pope Leo III's behaviour at the heart of the *Filioque* crisis provides an example.[111] Trouble broke out at Jerusalem on Christmas Eve 808. The Latins appealed to Rome. Pope Leo III declared the doctrine of the *Filioque* to be convincing but gave judgement that he was unable to allow a change of any sort in the letter of what had issued from an ecumenical council. Let the Latins teach the *Filioque* for it belongs to their tradition. But let them not make it a part of the common faith by inserting it into the creed of the Fathers. He then had the Creed of the One Hundred and Fifty Fathers (the Niceno-Constantinopolitan Creed) engraved on silver plaques, without the *Filioque* clause, in Greek and Latin, one for the *Confessio* of St Peter, the other for the memorial of the apostles in St Paul-outside-the-Walls.

Leo acted in this way *pro amore et cautela orthodoxae fidei* (for love and the safeguarding of the true faith). The creed thus 'exposed' on the tombs of Peter and Paul, the two great witnesses to the faith which was sealed in their blood at Rome, were intended by the pope to return the two parts of the Church to unity. It was a symbolic gesture which gave wonderful expression to the bishop of Rome's true mission. His task was to keep unity in catholicity. His standard, however, is that of the councils. He is not in a position to allow anyone to add to, take away from, or in any way change (*quippiam addendi, minuendi seu mutandi*) the profession of faith which is common to the whole undivided Church. Nothing is to be modified in the creeds expressing the faith of the Fathers because it is on them that the communion of the Church depends. No pope, however powerful, has authority over the faith as approved by the councils and 'received' in ratification by his predecessors in the see of Peter and Paul. He is bound by the bishops of the past. His 'primatial' charge never puts him outside 'the other bishops', above all not in those most solemn functions as when he comes to proclaim a truth *ex cathedra* (*DS* 3074). He is a corporate personality.

Anyone even slightly acquainted with ecumenical discussions of recent years will see that we have attempted, while keeping faith scrupulously with the utterances of Vatican I and Vatican II (not ignoring the former) to set forth the hopes entertained by many separated fellow-Christians for the see of Peter and Paul. We now ask the question put after every stage in our argument: would the (Roman) Catholic Church be unfaithful to the deep insight which Vatican I translated into formularies marked by 'changing conceptions appropriate to a particular period'[112] (and which Vatican II re-read perhaps not boldly enough), if she allowed herself to be questioned on this point and to 'receive' the requests of 'the others'? Would she thereby lose her authenticity?

Functions in the service of the communion of faith and love

Every office in the people of God carries with it appropriate patterns of behaviour and commitments. Without them it would be an empty title. This is the case especially with offices that are conferred through a sacrament. Every sacrament has a duty corresponding to it: to adopt the attitude or perform the acts evoked by the grace that has been received. It is the duty of being faithful to what the Spirit himself has imprinted on the person.

The primacy of the bishops of the see of Rome – the church of the *potentior principalitas* – is therefore matched by a power (*potestas, jurisdictio*) which enables it to perform those particular functions in the course of which the major function of *centrum unitatis* is to some extent defined. Some of these functions take the form of signs, others of intervention.

The bishop of Rome, sign of unity

The ultramontane tradition, whose remoter origins we have recalled, was too closely tied to the matter of the jurisdictional powers attached to the primacy to give enough importance to the 'symbolic' role of the bishop of Rome. It neglected to show how the very act of presiding at the Eucharist, at the altar of the *Confessio*, is a reminder that churches dispersed throughout the world are one only in that faith to which Peter and Paul remain the supreme witnesses. But that is one of his essential functions.

We have already spoken of the church of Rome as the touchstone of the faith, its bishop's function being that of 'watchman' and 'memory'. Now in order to be that, it is not necessary to intervene, to declare, to define a point of doctrine, to impose, to call to order. It is enough to be the one who reminds. 'Strengthen your brethren in the faith' (cf. Luke 22.32) has often been interpreted along these lines. In the light of such texts as 1 Peter 5.3; 1 Cor. 11.1; Phil. 3.17, it has often been taken to mean 'become the model of the apostolic faith which constitutes the centre of communion'. The idea of corporate personality is clearly at work. The 'primate' is in fact seen in a way similar to that found in many hierarchical societies where the group recognizes itself, its own identity and image, in its 'first one', its 'head'. The individual manifests it by embodying the collective 'I'; the group is condensed into the individual. The irritating romantic aura, verging at times on an extremist cult, which for a century now has surrounded the person of the pope, grows out of this understanding. Nevertheless, the understanding itself is quite sound, especially since the bishop of Rome recalls the first see within the communion of churches.

In recoiling from the excesses, we should not reject too quickly the need to 'sacralize' the symbolic person, scenting too readily 'a stench of fetishism', 'clearly similar in kind to De Gaulle *divinized* at Colombey, Nasser almost *adored* at his funeral, James Dean turned into the *God* of rebellious youth, Elvis Presley *idolized* by tormented adolescence'. The tragedy here is not in the fact that one personality is collectively seized upon in such a way that a country, a generation, or a social class finds in him a symbol of their own identity. The harm comes from the sentimental tone of the 'veneration', or in some cases from confusion between the personal characteristics of the individual and the reality which he represents. But these are no necessary or inevitable results of the process, as the sober veneration accorded to King Albert or to Pope John XXIII shows.

The dark pages in the history of the papacy, the scandalous lives of certain pontiffs duly elected bishops of Rome, go to show that the people of God has not always been able to recognize a model of holiness in the papacy. If the Church of God is at once sinful and holy, it often happens that the papacy reflects only the image of her sin. Holiness, of course, does not simply mean moral perfection; that is holy which belongs to God and creatures who belong to him will still be marked by their fragility. To repeat that without shortsighted or base satisfaction is not to approve or even to excuse the escapades of several popes. Moreover Tradition, especially since Leo the Great, knows that the moral qualities of the minister are something quite different from the sacrament which he celebrates, a principle underlined by St Augustine which applies by analogy to the ministry of the bishop of Rome. The intelligent believer can distinguish between him who sits on the *cathedra* of Peter and Paul and what the Roman see signifies in the communion of churches: between the unworthy vicar of Peter and the glorious *cathedra Petri*.[113] Whatever his limitations or wretchedness, the bishop of Rome continues to direct the mind of the Church towards the once-for-all (*ephapax*) confession of Peter and Paul. It is that which matters above everything, for it is in this confession that the Church recognizes her own faith. An ecclesiology centred round the actual person of the 'primate' has seriously obscured the point by failing to set his ministry within the influence of the *potentior principalitas* of the local church of Rome. Much admired saint or scandalous sinner, the bishop of Rome is always absorbed in the witness of his see, caught up in that loyalty to the gospel whose witness his Roman church has held to since Peter and Paul, even when life has not always matched teaching. He is the witness of a *holy* see, the bishop of the Holy See.

It is unhappily true that since the Church has been torn apart, the person of the bishop of Rome has more often seemed the symbol of the breach - since, in Paul VI's brave words, 'the Pope . . . is undoubtedly the gravest obstacle in the path of ecumenism'[114] - than a sign of communion. The facts are there. Yet, without falling into facile apologetic, we should take seriously what several theologians of other traditions have said. Opposition to Rome in the Reformed reactions of the sixteenth century 'is only the dark, polemical side of an enterprise dedicated to putting right the Western Church'.[115] Certain Lutherans have wondered whether Luther's reaction was not more against the papacy as it was then embodied than against the papacy in itself.[116] There are Orthodox who assert that the problem is not the affirmation of a Roman primacy but the identification of it with supreme power.[117] Others appeal to the findings of history: 'What in fact happened to Western Christianity when papal primacy was denied or simply restricted in its range? Did not conciliarism lead on to the Reformation?'.[118] We must not build firm arguments on these questions nor indeed take them over. But we may admit that they encourage the view that it is difficult to think of 'the unity of the Church' without thinking also of 'the bishop of Rome'.

Intervention by a word which goes back to the apostolic witness

The tradition of the undivided Church at the moment when East and West met at the time of Chalcedon - a meeting fugitive indeed, but at a crucial moment for faith - expresses the bishop of Rome's responsibility through the image of the 'watcher', the sentinel. To those two images found in ancient writings, including those of Leo himself, we have added two expressions: 'point of awareness' and 'memory of the apostolic faith'. For the sentinel on watch needs in this case to keep one eye on the content of the apostolic faith and the other on the people of God as they grapple with all the problems of their mission in the heart of the world, in danger of getting bogged down there.

The constitution *Pastor Aeternus* liked to speak of a power of *magisterium* (*DS* 3065). *Lumen Gentium* followed it (*LG* 18, 25), applying the term also to the bishops (*LG* 22). We have thus moved from the dynamic image of a watchman who prevents you from sinking into mortal sleep to the more static one of a master who teaches. We may regret the change. But the underlying intention is the same. It is above all a matter of recalling to the memory of the churches those points about which there can be no fiddle if we are to remain in the unity of faith and communion. In difficult situations it might well be a question of declaring the conditions required for a unanimous confession of the apostolic faith to be recognized in all the varied ways of expressing it. For, in a fine phrase of Leo the Great, 'There is only one way of building up a single flock and a single shepherd and that is to proclaim the same thing',[119] however many theologies are involved. On occasions he may intervene to make a solemn declaration (*definitio*) on a point of faith. The first type of intervention is the most usual, the last the most exceptional. We can only deplore the fact that under pressure from latent juridicism the characteristics of the last type have been and are still allowed to colour the other two, so that every intervention from the bishop of Rome is accorded a juridical 'authority' which it may not necessarily possess.

The initiative of Leo III already described illustrates excellently the function of 'sentinel' of the apostolic faith, continually on the watch and continually referring to the Church's memory. Leo III respects the legitimate traditions of the Frankish churches. He recognizes also that he has a duty to intervene, and the power to do so, because the attitude of these churches has put at risk the unity of faith within the *koinonia* of the churches. He does so by judging severely the seriousness of the act ('the illicit custom of singing (*illicita consuetudo cantandi*) the *Filioque* in the Creed') and by giving an order which goes to the root of the matter: 'Let that be removed from the Creed' (*illud de symbolo tollatur*). Also, he takes steps to see that the faith of the Fathers – not the theology of the Franks – is known and defended. He sets out the true Creed, engraved on two silver plaques, near the 'confession' of Peter and the 'memorial' of Paul. But he explains that he is only exercising his power in this manner after reference to the faith of the councils, explained by the Fathers and received by his predecessors in the see of Rome. For his aim was only love and the defence of the true faith (*pro amore et cautela orthodoxae fidei*).[120] This had been the attitude also of his predecessor, the first Leo.[121] It proved lasting and the East at that time was not opposed to it.

> Love of the orthodox faith and its protection in theory and practice make up the responsibility and the ideal service which, in the eyes of all the churches in the world allow the truth of the gospel to shine through the proper function of the Roman pope. The best qualified and truest opinion in the East was until the early ninth century convinced that a ministry of this sort, carried out in accordance with the Spirit and also with the canons and customs of tradition, fell to the lot of the bishops of the Roman church, so strong was that church in the witness and the assistance of the Coryphaei of the Apostles.[122]

If the commanding officer, exhausted by the battle or overcome by drink, fails to rouse himself before an imminent danger, the sentinel will sound the alarm and rally all the men. Similarly, the bishop of Rome may *in some cases* be called to intervene for a local church. The immediacy attributed to his power allows him to do so especially if the local episcopate lacks clarity of mind or is unable to control a situation where some problem has put in peril the apostolic faith and the communion of the churches. Leo III's attitude may be applied to many different situations, which is why it has been taken as an example.

No one will quarrel with the fact that it sometimes falls on the 'primate' to speak to his brother bishops and their faithful in order to enlighten them on some basic aspect of the faith or the Christian life. The custom of sending out 'papal encyclicals' in itself presents no problems.[123] It extends over the universal Church the action which in patristic times the patriarchs took to ensure unity of doctrine and life. Since Benedict XIV (died 1758) and Gregory XVI (died 1846) the number of encyclicals has multiplied. Several of them have had great impact: Leo XIII's *Rerum Novarum*, Pius XI's *Quadragesimo anno*, John XXIII's *Mater et Magistra* and *Pacem in terris*, Paul VI's *Populorum progressio* have marked the stages of awareness in the

Church of the link between the gospel and the mission of the people of God in a world that perverts justice. They are very much a 'pastoral word' on some question affecting the people of God as a whole. They arose from the 'watch' of a sentinel quick to alert pastors and faithful. There are also other forms of the pope's 'universal word'.

But except in the case of the definitions guaranteed by infallibility which we will consider later, there is no question of according equal importance to these 'universal words' of the bishop of Rome, nor even to all the encyclicals. Nor should we award *a priori* to all such communications a higher standing than that enjoyed by pastoral letters from the local bishop or from the episcopal conference. The opinions developed in a public audience or for several years now at the Sunday Angelus do not necessarily carry more weight than the letter written *ex officio* by the bishop on the same subject. The case of encyclicals is still more complex:

> The universal pastorate includes many different tasks; hence the wide range of subjects covered by encyclicals. The most important arise from the function of the teaching office. When errors in or uncertainties over the faith or Christian morals have appeared, they warn of the danger and expound again the orthodox teaching. On other occasions it appears opportune to regulate the presentation of some aspect of the Christian mystery which has been highlighted by piety and theological reflection. Other encyclicals are aimed chiefly at the discipline or current arrangements in the life of the universal Church. Others inform the Catholic conscience about some event which concerns the unity of the faith and love in Christ. In every case, a determining factor is timeliness. In reading encyclicals, therefore, one should remember that they are written at some distinctive point in the history of the Church, when they express the living tradition and interpret it to the needs of their time. It is thus important to pay careful attention to their particular context.[124]

There is no guarantee that the charism of infallibility has been involved. To be effective in truly serving the communion of faith, the bishop of Rome's word undeniably needs an answering welcome, a 'reception', from the bishops and their churches.

The welcome will be loyal, straight, taking account of who it is that speaks, but still remaining sanely critical, watchful not to take everything as being on the same level. That is why it would be much wiser as well as consistent with episcopal responsibility for encyclicals to be addressed to bishops, whose duty it then becomes to pass on the message with suitable explanation.

This raises the thorny problem of the ordinary teaching office (*magisterium*) of the Roman 'primate'.[125] The term covers his day-to-day teaching, and we have said that very often many attributes of the infallible magisterium flow back on to it. Whereas in the first centuries the authority which led to a teaching being held to be binding came from the weight of truth of that teaching and so from its objective conformity to the confession of the apostolic faith, the emphasis came to be shifted. Authority now flowed from the office held by whoever taught or recalled such and such a point, being derived from his place in the hierarchy. To gauge the truth of a proposition, you looked first of all at who said it, not, as in the days of Leo the Great, at what it said. If the pope speaks, it was to be held, his word should be accepted *a priori* as more true than that of an episcopal conference or of a theologian competent in the matter, because the pope has the highest authority. It was therefore impossible, Pius XII deduced,[126] to continue discussion even among theologians of any controverted matter on which the pope had pronounced in an encyclical. But this is to forget that the acts of the ordinary magisterium are often theological texts bearing the marks of a particular school of thought. They should be assessed more for the quality of their content than from the standing of whoever signed them (and who in many cases had not himself written them). In this way one treats them with respect, by attempting to discover their true meaning.

It is the responsibility of the bishop of Rome, as the *centrum unitatis*, to receive and pass on to all the churches those major decisions, of interest to all though taken by some of their number. This function has been neglected; its recovery is urgent. If each bishop is concerned for the welfare of all the churches, and if the office of 'primate' exists specifically to weave the concerns of each one into a truly catholic pattern of care, it is incumbent upon the bishop of 'the church which presides in love' to exert himself[127] in putting the churches in touch with each other over their own particular decisions. Why should he pass on only what comes from him, as if he had absorbed into himself the entire 'concern for all the churches' (*sollicitudo omnium ecclesiarum*)? The Spirit speaks to the churches - to all the churches - by other channels than by the 'primate' only. and the responsibility of the 'primate' is to relay the Spirit's voice, not to absorb it into his own word.

If conflicts in matters of faith arise between the churches - and history shows that this is no abstract hypothesis - all the evidence indicates that the primate is entrusted with the mission of restoring unity: not by easy compromise but by recalling the demands of the truth transmitted in the apostolic Word. This task is more than that of 'sentinel'; he is 'the point of reference for self-awareness' and 'memory'.

We have been presenting a case which is true to the voice of Tradition and which raises no difficulties, so that many non-Catholics could easily follow; indeed, they might add that such a ministry 'of the universal word' is so good that they regret its absence from their own tradition. But it is a very different story when you tackle another matter on which the First Vatican Council insists: papal infallibility. It is, of course, unfortunately true that the setting of this 'privilege' in a bundle of 'powers' has led to an exaggerated estimate of its impact. S. Bulgakov was quite right in saying that in itself infallibility was 'almost inoffensive'; the problem arose with the three canons of *Pastor Aeternus* concerning jurisdiction.[128] For many people this remains the real stone of stumbling when they come to consider renewal of communion with Rome.

It is impossible to treat the subject in depth here. We must stick to essentials.[129] Infallible judgement represents the extreme limit of the 'point of reference for the faith' function, which is generally called upon to function in a simpler way. The Tradition of the undivided Church admitted that some declarations of the ecumenical councils spoke the truth about God, Jesus Christ and salvation with a certainty guaranteed by the Spirit of the Lord, in accordance with the promise in St

Matthew's Gospel (28.20). In times when loyalty to the apostolic faith is seriously threatened, the Spirit's help is routed through dogmatic declarations which are recognized as conforming to the witness of the apostles themselves. Those who have formulated them therefore speak the truth infallibly, which means that their judgement was not mistaken, thanks to the Spirit who was guiding them. 'It is the faith of the Apostles! . . . Peter has spoken through Leo! . . . It is the true faith!' said the Fathers of Chalcedon,[130] by these words recognizing that Leo's *Tome* to Flavian expressed the common faith without error.

But the (Roman) Catholic tradition has been preoccupied with localizing this power of pronouncing, as and when circumstances demand it, an infallible judgement within certain hierarchical authorities. So it is that the universal episcopate in communion with the bishop of Rome and the bishop of Rome in a communion of faith with the universal episcopate - hence with the universal faith of Christians - is held to be the ecclesiastical organ which the Spirit is able to use to give such a judgement. This judgement will always be marked by the conditions of its time and place and moulded by language which will always be limited. Its meaning, however, is guaranteed,[131] so that it declares what belongs to the apostolic faith and what does not.

The infallibility of the bishop of Rome thus means that he has the power, in certain circumstances, to guarantee without mistakes that a truth holds a genuine place in what has been revealed. Then, with the Spirit's help, he makes a judgement declaring what it is. For this to be so, he must have specifically claimed the authority and have conformed to the conditions laid down by Vatican I, stated before the Vote by Mgr Gasser speaking in the name of the Deputation of the Faith in these terms:

> The phrase 'the Roman pontiff is infallible' could not be considered false . . . But it is incomplete, since the pope is only infallible when, in solemn judgement, he defines for the universal Church a question of faith or morals.

The infallibility of the Roman pontiff is in practice limited as to

173

its subject, to occasions when the pope expresses himself as universal doctor and supreme judge in the chair of Peter, that is, at the centre; it is limited as to its object, to questions of faith and morals; and it is restricted as to the act itself, to occasions when he defines what is to be believed or rejected by all the faithful.[132]

Strictly speaking, therefore, it is the act of judgement which is infallible. The proposition is true but it is guaranteed by the judgement of him who pronounces it. He who speaks in this manner is a bishop of the Church, enabled from his 'presidency' of the see of Peter and Paul to count on exceptional circumstances of the Spirit's help: not inspiration nor revelation but assistance. This prevents him from falling into error when for the benefit of all the churches and the faithful, he makes a solemn judgement on the truth of the gospel as it bears on faith and morals. The Holy Spirit then guarantees that such truth genuinely lies within revelation and belongs to the faith of Peter and Paul.

The (Roman) Catholic position would be much less upsetting to other Christians if it were a question of this assertion only, surrounded by a clear list of conditions and backed especially by the certainty that before pronouncing an infallible judgement, the bishop of Rome would have listened carefully to all his brother bishops. It is not enough to say that when pronouncing his solemn judgement the 'primate' enjoys the prerogative of speaking in the name of his brethren, rather like Peter in the New Testament.[133] There is a need for assurance that he is genuinely expressing the mind of his brothers in such a judgement and is thus genuinely speaking in their name.

One particular phrase in *Pastor Aeternus* has greatly complicated the matter: 'The definitions of the Roman pontiff (speaking *ex cathedra*) are irreformable of themselves and not by virtue of the Church's consent (*ex sese non autem ex consensu Ecclesiae irreformabiles*)' (*DS* 3074). This tiny formula has given rise to rivers of ink.[134] The history of debates during Vatican I shows that its purpose was to counter a Gallican error in the declaration of the Assembly of Clergy of 1682.[135] Mgr Gasser himself explained, with his authority as a representative of the Deputation of the Faith, that it was meant to reject 'the

strict and absolute necessity (*stricta et absoluta*) of the advice
and help of the bishops in any infallible dogmatic judgement of
the Roman pontiff'.[136] At Vatican II, the constitution *Lumen
Gentium* took up the matter in terms which would have gained
from being clearer but which nevertheless dispersed some of
the uncertainty by establishing the link between the infallibility
of the bishop of Rome and that of the college of bishops:

Although the bishops, taken individually, do not enjoy the privilege
of infallibility, they do, however, proclaim infallibly the doctrine of
Christ on the following conditions: namely, when, even though
dispersed throughout the world but preserving for all that amongst
themselves and with Peter's successor the bond of communion, in
their authoritative teaching concerning faith and morals, they are
in agreement that a particular teaching is to be held definitively and
absolutely. This is still more clearly the case when, assembled in an
ecumenical council, they are, for the universal Church, teachers of
and judges in matters of faith and morals, whose decisions must be
adhered to with the loyal and obedient assent of faith.

This infallibility, however, with which the divine Redeemer
wished to endow his Church in defining doctrine pertaining to
faith or morals, is coextensive with the deposit of revelation, which
must be religiously guarded and loyally and courageously ex-
pounded. The Roman pontiff, head of the college of bishops, enjoys
this infallibility in virtue of his office, when, as supreme pastor and
teacher of all the faithful – who confirms his brethren in the faith
(cf. Luke 22.32) – he proclaims in an absolute decision a doctrine
pertaining to faith or morals. For that reason his definitions are
rightly said to be irreformable by their very nature and not by
reason of the assent of the Church, inasmuch as they were made
with the assistance of the Holy Spirit promised to him in the
person of blessed Peter himself; and as a consequence they are in
no way in need of the approval of others, and do not admit of
appeal to any other tribunal. For in such a case the Roman pontiff
does not utter a pronouncement as a private person, but rather
does he expound and defend the teaching of the Catholic faith as
the supreme teacher of the universal Church, in whom the
Church's charism of infallibility is present in a singular way. The
infallibility promised to the Church is also present in the body of

bishops when, together with Peter's successor, they exercise the supreme teaching office. Now, the assent of the Church can never be lacking to such definitions on account of the same Holy Spirit's influence, through which Christ's whole flock is maintained in the unity of the faith and makes progress in it (*LG* 25, Flannery pp. 379-80).

The clause *ex sese non ex consensu Ecclesiae* is thus not intended to mean that, when 'defining' *ex cathedra*, the Roman 'primate' has no need to be sure that his thought agrees with that of his brother bishops. Mgr Gasser acknowledged that to ask explicitly for their help and to turn to them for advice was appropriate and even relatively necessary.[137] Now, in the light of *Lumen Gentium*, the clause may be said to mean: definitions *ex cathedra* do not derive their validity from subsequent juridical verification of their correctness by a higher church authority distinct from the bishop of Rome.

Moreover, Pius IX and Pius XII explicitly stated before the two Marian definitions that it was their intention to give solemn expression to the beliefs of their brother bishops.[138] For any definition of faith, especially when 'solemnly' pronounced from the seat of Peter and Paul (*ex cathedra*), is nothing else than a way of allowing the given faith to emerge with a guarantee of particular authority; and over that faith the episcopal college as such, bishops with their 'first' and the 'first' with his brother bishops, keeps watch, *episkope*. The definition conveys 'the awareness of the Church which has found its means of expression'.[139] The guarantee of the Spirit is obviously no stronger here than in the solemn declarations of the great ecumenical councils. It comes now in confirmation of a conviction at least morally unanimous which the words of the 'primate' have brought into the foreground.[140] The judgement of the 'first' again consists of a word spoken within the body (*collegium*) of those who have the *episkope* of the Church of God. In him, the other bishops recognize the stamp of an infallibility which they all possess in so far as they are jointly responsible for the Church's fidelity to the apostolic faith of Peter and Paul, founders of the church with the *potentior principalitas*.

Vatican I goes even further. It asserts that in his 'solemn' judgement the bishop of Rome does no more than bear the infallibility of the whole Church (*DS* 3074). He is the mouth through which the whole body of the Church – not simply the body of bishops – tells the truth to itself. The way in which the two Marian dogmas were presented, moreover, shows that the infallibility of the Church comes in the *conspiratio* of pastors and faithful, the same people to whom the bishop of Rome addresses his 'definition'.[141] The *sensus fidelium*, that intuition of the gospel which the Spirit gives the faithful in baptism, plays an important part.[142] When the bishops tell the faith, it is not their own that they tell, but the faith of the Church, of the see which enrolled them into the apostolic succession of faith and communion, and which they have to guard. It is interesting that the propositions which the bishops addressed to the pope at the synod of October 1980 should have begun with a long reminder of the *sensus fidei* of lay people.[143] The infallible judgement of the bishop of Rome itself articulates and brings to full expression the 'instinctively right' (through the *instinctus fidei*) judgements of the people of God. Once again, the phenomenon of corporate personality is seen at work.

All this explains why 'reception' of the councils and the solemn declarations of the bishop of Rome belong to the actual logic of infallibility. Chalcedon 'received' the *Tome* of Pope Leo. By 'receiving' is to be understood the fact that the people of God 'recognized' the apostolic faith in the hierarchical decision, being aware of the profound harmony between what is declared and what is known instinctively through the *sensus fidei*.[144] This 'reception' does not create truth. It does not legitimate the declaration of the definition. Its true function is to show that, as the Chalcedonian Fathers put it, 'It is the faith of the Fathers! . . . It is the faith of the Apostles! . . . It is the true faith!" Moreover, 'reception' sets in motion a process of clarification by critical reflection which furthers the knowledge of the faith, as the often cited *Mysterium Ecclesiae* so rightly says. The infallible judgement has given to the Church a sense of the truth, has declared the content of the truth in the way the circumstances required. It has silenced neither the desire nor frequently the need to deepen the grasp of that truth and to unpack its meaning. Nicaea and Ephesus called for Chalcedon, Vatican I called for Vatican II.

Let us again ask our question, stubbornly and perhaps naively. Since the *ex sese non ex consensu* only asserts the refusal to submit the 'definitions' of the Roman 'primate' to the bar of a higher tribunal, would the (Roman) Catholic Church be running against her own convictions if she 'welcomed' the disquiet felt by many other Christians and in consequence 're-read' the last paragraph of *Pastor Aeternus* chapter 3 (*DS* 3074) and *Lumen Gentium* 25, which is still too weak? The spectre of Gallicanism has been exorcized. A burning desire for unity has sprung up in many ecclesial communities and churches 'separated' from Rome. Would it be a serious matter in particular to affirm that the 'primate' should make sure that his definition was timely and that his own opinions were in full agreement with those of his brother bishops by using as a matter of necessity and conscience all available means of consultation, of inquiry into the *sensus fidei* and the state of theological discussion? Would it be serious to recognize also that infallibility guarantees the judgement brought to bear on the doctrine, but not the timeliness of defining it? And finally, would it be a serious matter to lay down clearly that such definitions *ex cathedra* should not be made except when the apostolic faith and the communion of the churches are truly *in periculo*? And it would be for the whole body of bishops to say when the moment of danger had come.

Intervention by a decision which safeguards the communion of the churches

The prophetic function embodied in the intervention of the bishop of Rome's word represents beyond doubt the most characteristic part of his charge (*munus*), as 'primate' of the universal Church. It is this which links him to the primary function of his local church, the Church of Rome which the glorious martyrdom of Peter and Paul made into the touchstone of the apostolic faith. We have noted how the Roman see gradually realized that it was being led to play the part of arbiter in the gravest matters. This developed in part from a growing sense of its own responsibility, slowly distorted by an obvious lust for power; but also from the actual needs of the *koinonia* of the churches as they struggled with the rise of regionalism, together with intensifying cultural differences and the clash of politics.

Having earlier concentrated on the Tradition of the undivided Church at the moment when, in the backwash of the Council of Chalcedon, East and West, pope and emperor met in 'fugitive and moving agreement', [145] we now return to Leo the Great and his attitude. Aware as he was of being the guardian of laws which should safeguard communion by regulating the relationships between the churches, Leo did not hesitate to intervene. He did so, for instance, when the hierarchy of the great episcopal sees and patriarchates was being violated. His attitude to the jurisdiction claimed by the see of Jerusalem was typical:

> The essential point of our decision is as follows. Even if a more considerable number of bishops, manipulated by some, were to understand on a matter in a sense contrary to what the three hundred and eighteen bishops [of Nicaea] had laid down, their decision is quashed by the law. It is only possible to keep the tranquillity of peace between everyone by keeping inviolate the respect owned to the canons. [146]

He intervened also when he learned that in defiance of the canons the bishop of Constantinople had ordained a bishop for the church of Antioch. [147] His letter was severe: 'Let the church at Antioch where the blessed Peter preached . . . hold to the rank decided by the Fathers: since she was called to the third place, let her never accept being placed lower.' [148] His concern is clear: that everywhere loyalty to the rule of faith should be maintained and the rights of the churches never undermined. [149]

When Leo explains that his solicitude, 'which is not in furtherance of his own interests but those of Christ', does not deprive those churches and their bishops of any of the dignity which they were divinely accorded, [150] he shows that what might look like a desire for power (and which was little by little to be invaded by that desire) first arose from a sense of duty. Leo the

Great, like his successor Leo III in the affair of the *Filioque* and the Franks, acted out of duty. Everything therefore depends on the content of that duty. It is indeed complex! The bishop of Rome is *servus servorum Dei*[151] and he has the duty (the charge, the commission, the *munus*) to carry out faithfully whatever is needed to keep the churches in *koinonia*. If he does not do so, whether from negligence or from lack of knowledge, it will be *ad destructionem Ecclesiae*. But it is equally 'for the destruction and not the building up of the Church' if in his concern he oversteps the limits of his own primatial power and encroaches on the power of the bishops of other local churches (*DS* 3061). There, we have suggested, lies the whole problem.

Circumstances might indeed arise where it was necessary for the bishop of Rome, in some situation, faced with some crisis, to take on a particular responsibility in harmony with his function (and, said Vatican I, with the immediacy of his jurisdiction), but which lay outside the specific purpose of his primacy. It would be the temporary replacement of the local bishop brought about by special circumstances, a condition not meant to last. England, for example, could not be left in the situation as it was immediately after Augustine's mission; black Africa could not keep the sort of relationship with Rome established in the first period of evangelization. It is thus important to see whether, once things have returned to normal, other people could not better take on that responsibility. Any temporary ways of proceeding must be watched in case they should become permanent, thereby depriving other authorities of their proper rights.

Now it happens that several of the powers today retained by the bishop of Rome (and the Roman curia) are 'pontifical' without arising from the specific purpose of the primacy.[152] Instead of being justified by the formal reason of the unity of faith and communion, the retention of these powers is often explained by the desire for juridical uniformity and for centralization, according to which whatever makes for cohesion and communion in the Church of God depends on the bishop of Rome. A poor ecclesiology has here almost identified unity with centralization, failing to grasp that unity calls for communion and that this is something altogether different from complete seizure by the *centrum unitatis*. But the more authority of this kind is imposed, the less the communion is that of the gospel, for it has been confused with absorption or else has been put under a tutelage which contradicts its own nature. Communion recognizes diversity and sees in it some of its own richness; how else could it be catholic? It is not wallowing in pessimism to admit how too much Roman centralization, hard to shake off because bad habits have been formed, has made a situation which is ecclesiologically abnormal. It has piled up a difficult and useless obstacle blocking the way to the unity of all Christians. It might have been hoped that Vatican II, which recognized the authority belonging to episcopal conferences, should have decongested the *centrum unitatis* and led it back to its specific function.[153] But progress is slow and we have sometimes simply raised up a parallel bureaucracy. We cannot yet speak of genuine reform.

The (Roman) Catholic tradition has in this area succumbed to one of its habitual faults. It slides too easily from allowing that some attitude is 'possible' to asserting that the same attitude is 'necessary', from *potest* to *debet*.[153] Because it is liturgically 'possible' to recite aloud the offertory prayers, even though the rubric says that they are normally said *secreto*,[154] everyone believes himself bound to say them aloud and a bishop ticks off a priest who sticks to the rubric, demanding of him 'obedience'. Or because the principal celebrant in a concelebration 'may' hand over the intercession in the canon to one of the concelebrants (*uni e concelebrantibus committi potest*),[155] it becomes an obligation to do so, to the point where a priest may feel frustrated if the president prefers to say it himself, according to the normal pattern. It is much the same in the field of ecclesial duties,[156] where 'legitimate' changes slowly into 'necessary', 'possible' into 'required', 'concession' into 'proper responsibility'. The process may be studied most notably in the matter of the Roman see's power of intervention. The bishop of Rome *may* reserve certain rights, such as that of granting dispensations and ecclesiastical benefices, of giving judgement in major cases. Therefore he reserves them all, even though it means later 'conceding' some of those rights to people who would, had things been normal, have possessed them *de jure*.

The nomination of bishops – not to be confused with the canonical determination required by the *communio hierarchica*[157] – provides a typical illustration of this process.[158] The first ten centuries knew nothing of any formal intervention of the bishop of Rome in the nomination of a bishop. Everything happened at the local level: co-option, ordination implying the community's assent and above all the prayer of epiclesis calling on the Spirit, along the lines described in the *Apostolic Tradition* of Hippolytus (chap. 2). Yet the communion with the see of Peter and Paul existed. The bishop of that see 'received' the man of the region's choice. If Leo the Great intervened, for instance, it was after some serious irregularity had been reported to him.[159] It was for each local church, in immediate communion with the other churches of the region or patriarchate, to choose in the Holy Spirit the man who was suitable, whose faith and uprightness of character were known.[160]

Soon the princes got mixed up in the matter, which gave rise in the West to the Investiture Controversy. In 1122 the Concordat of Worms re-established the rights of local bishops and chapters, but without calling for any control by the Roman see. The bishops of Rome did not even demand that their right to confirm elections as metropolitan should be admitted, until the end of the fourteenth century. After that the situation gradually developed to the point of Rome making the nominations. When a famous canonist, consulted as an authority right up to Vatican II (though he died in 1914), slid from *potest* to *debet* in offering an explanation which contradicted history while vindicating current practice, he was no more than a witness to the catholic temptation of changing the occasional into a right, especially where Rome is involved:

> The right to institute bishops belongs properly and by nature (*proprio et nativo jure*) to the Roman pontiff. If bishops of the ecclesiastical Province, or chapters, or even civil authorities, laymen and clergy have come to have some say in the nomination of bishops, it is because of a concession, tacit or explicit, of the Roman pontiff.[161]

Other people's rights have apparently become a concession from the bishop of Rome!

We return to the question. If the (Roman) Catholic Church, aware of the disquiet which her excessive centralization induces in other Christians, were to agree no longer to 'concede' but genuinely to restore to local churches (or episcopal conferences) a large number of those possible points of intervention which she has changed into obligatory ones, would she go against the heart of her ecclesiological convictions? She would be taking up again with her own traditions of before Gregory VII and the *Dictatus Papae*. She would also clear away one of the enormous boulders blocking the road to unity, especially with the sister churches of the East.

It would clearly mean returning to that traditional practice whose spirit is carried forward in the modern notion of subsidiarity. Subsidiarity would maintain the power and responsibility of the 'primate' in the opposite sense to that of centralization, for it refuses everything outside the strict function of 'primacy'. It would thus be the means of avoiding all the confusions which we have pointed out: that of the universal Church viewed as 'the pope's diocese' (*sic*) so that the pope exercises in all 'parts of the Church' the power which belongs to him in the local church where he is bishop; that of 'telescoping' his function as patriarch of the West with his office as 'primate of the universal Church'. The problem is to be found even in the heart of the Western Church itself, for it is growing increasingly difficult to characterize it as 'the Latin Church'. African and Asian churches are asserting their proper identity along with the rest of their own culture. Is not this breaking open the frontiers of the Western churches? Are we not in fact seeing other groups of churches coming to birth slowly, in full communion with the see of Rome yet asserting their own characteristics over against the churches of Latin tradition?

The principle of subsidiarity requires that the 'higher' authority, faced with a smaller group really under its care yet entrusted with some authority of its own, should seek as far as possible to reduce its interventions.[162] It allows the group to be given in practice the means of embodying the faith in its own situation and of regulating with those immediately responsible the questions arising out of its identity and its life. The higher authority will intervene only when it must; that is, after the group has unsuccessfully exhausted its resources in the face of some internal crisis and is drifting away, or shows itself incapable of grasping some essential requirement of the Christian life and cannot produce pastors competent to guide it. In other words, the bishop of Rome has, by virtue of the 'primacy' which we have described, the duty (*debet*) of acting for the good of the whole Church (which is at stake in each local church, for that is where it is realized), when he sees that one of these churches has run so short of resources that it is deteriorating in a way that threatens its identity and so that of the universal *koinonia*; or when it fails to take the necessary decisions in some important matter.

This is a very long way from a universal presence which stifles and alienates. An intervention of this kind clearly does not subordinate the authority of the local bishop but strengthens and defends it (*DS* 3061), alerts him to his proper responsibilities and brings him the supplies he needs. Still less is it a case of the Roman spirit seizing the fabric of essential values embodied there, having confused those elements without which the *koinonia* would be so compromised that the Christian identity of that church would be lost, with a bundle of rites, customs, traditions and legislation which is perhaps strange to the Roman outlook but none the less compatible with faith and love.

The bishop of Rome, then, acts according to the true form of his function of 'primate'. As such, he is not situated at the apex of a pyramid from which everything descends and to which everything returns. He is, rather, to be seen as the centre in whom each bishop is able to recognize himself, to read off the responsibilities of his own *episkope*, and from whom brotherly help may be asked. He holds this centrality from his church at Rome and from the two princes of the apostles, Peter and Paul.

Leo the Great was aware of his 'primacy' and was eager to exercise it straightforwardly, so that we have often called him as a witness to the traditional vision – and we now do so again. His authority seemed indeed more like a power of resort, attentively answering appeals, than a force imposing everywhere his views and the customs of his local church. His attitude to the Palestinian monks who had revolted against the decisions of Chalcedon and were hounding bishop Juvenal from his see was typical. In the end it mattered little to him that the excited monks rejected his personal teaching, which perhaps they had misunderstood. What counted above all was their loyalty to the faith of their Fathers, with which Leo knew that he was in full agreement.[163] It was for local councils to settle their regional problems.[164] In any case the true Roman spirit would say, Let local custom be respected.[165] Besides, even in his own local church at Rome, Leo allowed a great variety of local rites to coexist, local privileges and traditions brought in by Oriental immigrants.[166] The rite of the *fermentum*, a morsel of bread consecrated by the bishop at his own Eucharist which every presbyter celebrating for the community threw into the chalice, signified that communion was made by the power of the Body of Christ, not by uniformity of custom and rite. Powerful as it was, Leo's primacy operating over the other churches aimed at a communion in the faith of the Roman church, not in her customs.

Tradition itself saw the matter in less juridical terms than the principle of subsidiarity, making use of one image in particular. Several centuries after Leo, the Church was organized as a pentarchy, but still depended for faith and discipline on the decisions of the councils. If within the Church of five centres the East continued to recognize the special place of the Roman see, that place was within 'the crown of the five thrones of the five bishops of the five great churches.'[167] The ecumenical council was always considered the highest expression of consensus among the churches,[168] to the point indeed where Germanus, patriarch of Constantinople (715-30), could declare: 'Outside a council it is impossible for me to change anything to do with the faith.'[169] But it is no genuine ecumenical council unless 'the five patriarchs proclaim a single faith and a single interpretation; and if only one of them is absent or does not accept the council, it will be no council but a futile and deceiving confabulation'.[170] Patriarch Nicephorus of Constantinople (806-15) explained that 'the ambiguities and uncertainties which arise in the Church of God are resolved in ecumenical councils and are defined with the agreement and judgement of those of the archbishops who by the apostolic seats on which they preside are greater than the others'.[171] The apostolic thrones dominate the history of the Church in this manner because the apostles continue to preside there. Pope Pelagius I (556-61) did not think differently.[172]

In this crown of the *Apostolikoi Thronoi* which arose from the communion of the churches and their bishops as expressed in the ecumenical council, the see (*cathedra, thronos*) of the church of Peter and Paul holds a special place. The Roman church was never cut off from her links with the other apostolic sees and with them it remained within the communion of all the episcopal sees, but its position was nevertheless emphasized. Among the acts of the Seventh Ecumenical Council (Nicaea II, 787), for instance, is found the speech of John the Deacon which lists the conditions indispensably needed for a council to be deemed ecumenical. It is there asserted that a council is only ecumenical if the pope of the church of Rome then in office 'communicates' with it in some way. The Greek verb used is *synergeo*, which suggests a communion of 'energies', of powers: not a simple addition of them, nor one among them being heavily imposed:[173]

Among the different notes required for a council to be considered ecumenical, was the demand that the Church of Rome and, through her, her lawful pastor in union with his own synod, should 'collaborate' with the Council either by being present himself or by a circular letter sent round to the other churches . . . Agreement on the part of the other four major sees was needed before the proceedings could be given universal authority . . . To the pope was reserved the more individual role of 'synergy' (*adjutorium, co-operatio*) with the council, compared with the 'choral symphony' expected from the other patriarchs, and indispensable for verifying the universally binding status of the deliberations to which all the Christian churches gave at least moral assent.[174]

Earlier and later documents alike support this interpretation of 'synergy', which accounts both for the authority of all the sees in the 'apostolic crown' and for the special weight of the see of Rome. A passage from the Life of St Stephen, martyred on 28 November 764, puts these words into the saint's mouth:

How is it possible to call a council ecumenical which the bishop of Rome has not even approved, when a rule exists under which it is not lawful to give canonical judgements on ecclesiastical questions independently of the pope of Rome?[175]

And in his famous *Great Apology*, Patriarch Nicephorus of Constantinople said this when speaking of Nicaea II:

> If ever there was a council assembled rightly and with guarantees of legality, it is this one [Nicaea II]. For the church which has the greatest weight of importance in the Western part, that of ancient Rome, has indeed played her part in directing and presiding, in accordance with the divine norms formulated from the beginning. Without them [the Romans], a dogma held in the Church, based from the beginning on canonical norms and sacred customs, could still not be approved and commended for circulation. They, the Romans, have been endowed in order to fulfil the function of guide in the priesthood and we have given them the credit due to those who among the Apostles are the Coryphaei.[176]

The recognition was no doubt fragile and its implications, such as the existence of a 'first see' in the crown of the apostolic thrones, little developed. The course of history made this very clear. The assertion of the joint power of the five great sees is hardly integrated with the recognition of the 'primacy' of the see of Peter and Paul. The letters of the patriarch Tarasius and of the Second Council of Nicaea to the emperors and to the clergy of Constantinople, as well as the course of events during the Council, witness to this lack of clarity. Recognition was refused to the iconoclastic pseudo-council of Hieria on the Bosphorus

> because it has not been recognized by the heads of the other churches, namely the patriarchs; indeed, they have declared it anathema. It included neither the pope of Rome nor the priests in communion with him. No representative of the pope was there, no letter from him was read, as the rule for councils requires. The patriarchs of Alexandria, Antioch and Jerusalem were not in agreement with them either. Finally, the decisions of Hieria were contrary to those of the six previous councils.

The position held by the pope certainly appears from these letters to be very important; but it was not of itself decisive. The pope's representatives themselves do not appeal exclusively to Hadrian's letter, but also to his agreement with Tarasius and the other Eastern patriarchs. After the synodical letter of the patriarch of Jerusalem had been read, the pope's legate spoke, declaring that they held to the faith expressed in that letter because the patriarch of Jerusalem had confessed the same faith as that which Tarasius, the most holy patriarch of Constantinople, revered, as do the pope Hadrian and his synod [Tarasius is mentioned first here, no doubt as a courtesy]. The legates praised God that the Eastern patriarchs were of one mind with the pope of Rome and the patriarch of the new Rome on the matter of the veneration of images. He who does not confess the faith of all these, let him be anathema![177]

The imprecision and lack of clarity shown here are certainly not to be deplored without qualification. If the position of the see of Rome is effectively recognized in what makes it distinctive – its place in the preservation of the unity of faith and communion between the churches[178] – this distinctiveness must be very deeply imprinted on two fundamental solidarities or areas of interdependence. It should be inseparable from the solidarity of the bishop of Rome with other apostolic sees and his solidarity with the authority of the great ecumenical councils. This is a matter of genuine 'synergy'. That term has on the whole richer overtones than subsidiarity, being less juridical and more theological. On the one hand, 'reception' by the see of Rome gives validity to conciliar decisions, in whose making the Church of Rome has worked side by side with the other churches and to which she will be bound as firmly as the other churches,[179] without ever allowing herself to trifle with them. On the other hand, the judgement on which the 'first see' bases its reception is itself essentially conditioned by past councils. In declaring some teaching to be 'new', the bishop of Rome judges by the yardstick of faithfulness to what the Fathers of Nicaea, Constantinople, Ephesus or Chalcedon have decreed: a remarkable *synergy*. The original authority of the church of Peter and Paul (the Coryphaei) is included without being swamped in the authority of the communion of churches existing here and now and, together with them, in the authority of the churches of the past when they clarified the apostolic faith. Ecclesial communion is not welded together without the Roman see, but that see only welds together what it 'receives' from the churches. The true function of the Roman see is to be found precisely *in* this reception. It is worth remembering that the church of Rome was never omnipresent or super-active at the great councils, not even at Chalcedon. Even Ambrose suffered from the fact that this see was sometimes pushed around.

The vision of *synergy* seems especially to correspond with what *Lumen Gentium* has allowed us to understand about the nature of primatial power. We spoke of extending the *potestas vere episcopalis* of one of the bishops - he who occupies the see of the apostles Peter and Paul - in terms of his brother bishops expressing the full reality of their common concern for the building up of the Church in universal communion. The 'primacy' is to be found within the communion of faith and love. It is not at the summit, like the point of a pyramid in the imagination of a Manning. This is why it is not enough to be in communion subjectively with the bishop of Rome, recognizing him as 'head and supreme pastor', to be within the *koinonia*. It is necessary also, and before everything, not to err over the fundamental points of the faith. The Church is made by Eucharist and baptism, not by the papacy. The purpose of the papacy is to give the Eucharist its full dimensions.

Let us ask our question again. If the (Roman) Catholic Church were to define her mission in terms of *synergy* and at a juridical level to develop *subsidiarity* in her relations with other sees, would this obscure her deep conviction about the function of the Roman 'primate'? If one admits, as every (Roman) Catholic loyal to his Church does, that God himself has willed the office of the bishop of Rome, how can we think God wants it to be what it has gradually turned into? How, in his wisdom and intelligence, could he have wished to load on to the shoulders of the 'primate' a task so heavy and complex that no normally healthy man could carry it without ruining his health and power to work, or surrounding himself by a bureaucracy so heavy that it acts as a brake on his wishes and his insights as the one responsible for sustaining the *koinonia?* In a very intelligent contribution to the discussions of Vatican I, Mgr Ketteler, bishop of Mainz, a member of the Minority, said that to confer on the pope an ordinary and immediate jurisdiction over all the churches and all the faithful was to give him a task that it was impossible in practice to carry out.[180] This is even more true in our century, which has seen the flourishing of missionary movements which have meant the introduction into catholicity of new cultures and new human situations.

Is it right that the burden on the bishop of Rome should be so heavy? If the projects of ecumenical reconciliation succeed – and let us dare to hope that at least some of them will! – the burden can only grow heavier. If Rome agreed to free the 'primacy' from useless weight, 'consenting' to a *synergy* of the different responsibilities in *episkope*, would she be acting against Providence? Let us be honest: he who presides at the universal *koinonia* has received from the Spirit an arduous function (*munus*), but one for which he has the guarantee of the help of that Spirit. But does he who presides in a centralized and thus over-bureaucratized Church have the guarantee at every level of his activity? As for the 'honour of the universal Church', is that not better served by *synergy* than by a single individual? Gregory the Great saw correctly when he answered the patriarch Eulogius of Alexandria in these lines, some of which have entered into *Pastor Aeternus*:

Your Beatitude . . . speaks to me saying 'as you have commanded'. I must ask you not to use such words in speaking of me, for I know what I am and what you are. In rank you are my brothers, in manner of life my fathers. I have therefore not given orders but have simply done my best to indicate what I think useful. But I have the impression that your Beatitude has not taken care to remember what I had hoped to establish in your memory. For I said that you ought not to address me in that fashion, nor ought you so to address anyone else. And here at the head of your letter I find the proud title of universal pope, which I have refused. I pray your most beloved Holiness not to do it again, because what is exaggeratedly attributed to another is taken away from you. It is not in words that I would find my greatness, but in manner of life. And I do not consider that to be an honour which, as I know, undermines the honour of my brothers. My honour is the honour of the universal Church. My honour is the solid strength of my brothers. Then am I truly honoured, when honour is not denied to each one to whom it is due. If your Holiness calls me universal pope, you deny to yourself that which you attribute in a universal sense to me. Let that not be so. Away with those words which inflate vanity and wound charity.[181]

Rome may allow herself to strip away her plaster, the false gilding added century by century to obscure the structural lines of her primacy as the Church founded on the martyrdom of Peter and Paul. She can only stand to gain. It would be like those old Roman church buildings weighed down by later additions out of keeping with their true style but suddenly restored to their true beauty. But above all she would then give the whole Church of God, broken and disfigured by divisions in which she is not innocent, the 'service' which the Spirit of Pentecost expects of her. What would prevent her from reaching that poverty of spirit which would set her back in the straight line of her calling?

By way of conclusion

We set ourselves to read again in the light of the Great Tradition what the two Vatican Councils had said about the function of the bishop of Rome. In the course of long research we have become convinced that this function, if understood in its own precise terms, could answer at many levels the wishes of Christians now separated from Rome but longing to enter again into communion with her.

At a time like the present, when serious ecumenical dialogues are reaching their conclusion, we must ask not only if Rome will accept them, but how she may allow herself to be questioned by the matters that have been raised. We have brought out the precise points where this questioning meets a current in the Church's intention which is seething within the Catholic community itself. Has the bishop of Rome not become 'more than a pope'? The two Vatican Councils did not demand that!

At the close of this work we therefore express our conviction without prevarication. The Roman 'primacy' belongs to the mystery of the Church in her pilgrimage on earth; it could not be dispensed with without doing violence to God's plan. We must, however, ask whether, in spite of generous and sincere statements, this 'primacy' is not still being fulfilled at the cost of another wound, inflicted this time on the episcopate. The bishop of Rome is the sentinel who 'watches' over the people of God, which is his true function; but he often prefers to act as if he were the only one in charge, instead of alerting the bishops as authentic pastors in the Church of God. Vatican II reaffirmed the irreplaceable role of the bishops. The juridical institutions since set up have not enabled the intentions of the Council to pass into fact. The bishop of Rome still acts in a certain 'solitude' like that which was supported by the *Dictatus Papae* of Gregory VII.

But the Spirit is at work. He inspired Paul VI, to whose memory we dedicate this book, to take some irreversible steps. He will know when the time has come to hasten the harvest:

Do you not say, 'There are yet four months, then comes the harvest'? I tell you, lift up your eyes, and see how the fields are already white for harvest (John 4.35).

Notes

Notes marked with an asterisk (*) contain further information in the 'Notes - Addenda' section on p. 233.

Part 1   The Pope - more than a Pope?

1   It might start from the Thomist vision of the *votum eucharistiae*. See J. M. R. Tillard, 'Le *Votum eucharistiae*, l'Eucharistie dans le rencontre des chrétiens', in *Miscellanea Liturgica in onore di Sua Eminenza il Cardinale G. Lercaro*, vol. 2, pp. 143-94, Desclée 1967.

2   The correspondence was published as *Tomos Agapes, Vatican-Phanar 1958-70*, Rome 1971. It is a pity that it has been so little studied.

3* Emmanuel Lanne, 'Jusqu'à quel point une primauté romaine est-elle inacceptable pour les églises orientales?', in *Concilium* 64, pp. 53-7 (53), 1971.

4   Stylianos Harkianakis, 'Un ministère pétrinien dans l'Église peut-il avoir un sens? Une réponse grecque orthodoxe', ibid., pp. 103-8 (107-8).

5   *Tomos Agapes*, pp. 81-3.

6   So Athenagoras to Paul VI in 1964, ibid., p. 131.

7   ibid., p. 173.

8   Undoubtedly one of the most important documents in the history of Catholic ecumenism.

9   ibid., p. 378.

10 ibid., p. 413.

11 ibid., p. 619.

12 So Lancelot Andrewes, *Responsio ad Apologiam cardinalis Bellarmini*, pp. 327, 386-88, 404, in Library of Anglo-Catholic Theology; Richard Hooker, *Sermo* 3.4 in *Works* 3, p. 634; Joseph Mede, *Clavis Apocalyptica*, in *Works*, pp. 419-605; Richard Field, *Of the Church*, Bk 3, ch. 46 (vol. 1, p. 358); Bk 5, ch. 46 (vol. 3, p. 547). These authors are Anglicans (but this view was not enshrined in formal teaching. For a selection of seventeenth-century Anglican views, see P. E. More and F. L. Cross (ed.), *Anglicanism* (SPCK 1935), pp. 53-72—E.Tr.). For Antichrist in Reformed thought, see J. J. von Allmen, *La Primauté de l'Église de Pierre et de Paul* (Paris 1977), pp. 32-4.

13 *Lutherans and Catholics in Dialogue V*, Minneapolis 1974. (Hereafter LCD.)

14 This is repeated almost literally at no. 30.

15 This passage is from the American edition. It is not translated into French in *DC* 71.

16 *Teaching Authority and Infallibility in the Church*, *LCD* VI (1980): 'Lutheran Reflections' 18.

17 The Lutherans themselves in a tortuous explanation show why they distance themselves from this traditional position, *LCD* V (1974), pp. 37-8.

18 ibid., no. 32.

19 For John XXIII see *AAS* 54, p. 786; for Paul VI, see *DC* 61 (1964), pp. 967 (Constance), 1154, 1218, 1221.

20 See V. Peri, *I Concili e le Chiesi*, Rome 1965; id. 'Il numero dei concili ecumenici nella tradizione cattolica moderna' in *Aevum* 37 (1963), pp. 430-501.

21 See L. Bouyer, *l'Église de Dieu, Corps du Christ et Temple de l'Esprit*, (Paris 1970), pp. 678-9; Y. Congar, '1274-1974, Structures ecclésiales et Conciles dans les relations entre Orient et Occident' in *RSPT* 58 (1974), pp. 355-90.

22 Text in *DC* 72 (1975), pp. 63-5.

23* On the notion of sister churches and its implications for ecclesiology, see E. Lanne, 'Églises-soeurs: implications ecclésiologiques du *Tomos Agapes*' in *Istina* 48 (1975), pp. 47-74.

24 So G. Thils, *La Primauté pontificale* (Gembloux 1972), p. 161, taken up by R. Minnerath, *Le Pape évêque ou premier des évêques?* (Paris 1978), p. 5.

25 Text in *DC* 64 (1967), p. 870. Eng. trans. is from E. Yarnold SJ, *They are in Earnest* (Slough 1982), p. 66.

26 Commission scolaire régionale de l'Outaouais, *Programme officiel. Enseignement religieux catholique* 521, May 1980, PPO, 480-521-80, Module 2 unit 4, *L'Organization de l'Église*, sub-unit 1: *Les Fonctions*, p. 49. It occurs in the 'correct version' column. The offices listed are: pope, bishop, clergy, deacon, layman (the order is in itself revealing). The item on the pope reads: '*Pope*: successor to God, shepherd of all the faithful and sent to secure the general good of the universal Church and the good of each of the churches. *Bishop*: each bishop has the care of a particular church, he feeds his sheep in the Lord's name, under the authority of the pope, he is charged with teaching, sanctifying and governing them.'

27 As that of A. B. Hasler, *Pius IX* (1977); id. *How the Pope became Infallible*, New York 1981.

28 See the very detailed work of R. Aubert, *Le Pontificat de Pie IX*, coll. Histoire de l'Église 21, Paris 1952. See also brief article by C. Gerest, 'Le pape au XIXe Siècle; histoire d'une inflation' in *Lumière et Vie* (1977), 26, pp. 70-86. A fundamental work is C. Butler, *The Vatican Council 1869-70, based on Bishop Ullathorne's Letters*, London 1930.

See also J. Derek Holmes, *The Triumph of the Holy See*, London 1978.

29 See Aubert, op. cit., pp. 290-2. Pius IX's emotional temperament was often emphasized.

30 Cardinal Sterckx, an unsentimental Fleming, was sufficiently carried away by the charm to confess, 'I shall begin to wonder if the pope is not an angel from heaven', ibid., p. 293. R. Aubert notes, 'To understand the spell which Pius IX cast over those who only knew him at a distance, we should add the universal sympathy which his misfortunes brought him from the Catholic world, from his exile at Gaeta to the brutal aggression and constant threat of the Piedmontese government. His was a "noble attitude, patient and firm, the disarmed sovereign facing the insolent Revolution". To many of the faithful the good pontiff, his virtues idealized by distance, was literally a martyr and a saint', ibid., p. 294.

31 C. Gerest, loc. cit., p. 81.

32 Émile Ollivier, quoted in R. Aubert, op. cit., wrote: 'Feeling full of life and always good for a ready answer, persuasive words and winning movements, he liked, without too much care for etiquette, to show the papacy as likeable in the public square as it had hitherto been in the privacy of the Vatican.' He began the custom of mass audiences and of charming gestures towards children and simple people. ibid., p. 294.

33 ibid., p. 292.

34 So P. de Quirielle in R. Aubert, op. cit., p. 294.

35 The view of Veuillot's friend E. Lafond, ibid., p. 294.

36 On all this see G. Thils, op. cit., pp. 25-38 and Mgr Baunard, *Histoire du Cardinal Pie*, vol. 2, pp. 392-3, 3rd edn, Paris 1887. The latter is of great importance.

37 *Correspondance*, IV, p. 428. This passage is often cited, e.g. by C. Gerest, op. cit., p. 73; Y. M. J. Congar, 'Affirmation de l'autorité' in *L'Ecclésiologie au XIXe Siècle*, p. 82, coll. *Unam Sanctam* 34, Paris 1960.

38 Cited among others by Y. Congar, ibid., p. 82. See also the article dated 22 December 1830 in Lamennais, *Les Meilleures Pages*, pp. 187-91, Tourcoing 1921.

39 R. Aubert, op. cit., p. 277.

40 Witness this passage from the *Cours d'Instruction religieuse ou exposition complète de la doctrine catholique* by the director of catechism at Saint-Sulpice parish, vol. 2, pp. 94-5, 2nd edn, Paris 1859 (cited by R. Aubert, 'La Géographie ecclésiologique au XIXe Siècle' in *L'Ecclésiologie au XIXe Siècle*, p. 47n. 'The disciplinary decrees which the popes make for the universal Church claim no less obedience than the dogmatic definitions, for the authority from which they derive is the same. Failure of any province to put into effect these decrees, or if they have been allowed to fall into disuse, should not be attributed to

any right on the part of the particular churches concerned to maintain their own discipline or to keep local customs independently of the Holy See. No church, however great its reputation, has such rights, for they would be incompatible with Catholic unity; the hierarchy of powers divinely constituted within Christianity would be confused and misunderstood on the very day when the dioceses, the provinces, even the nations, claimed to keep their customs or to depart from the law which binds them all, contrary to the prescriptions of that Church which is the mother and mistress of all other Churches. The true reason, the principle which justifies the general discipline of the Catholic Church, should not be sought elsewhere than in the approval of the Sovereign Pontiff. It follows from that that if the Sovereign Pontiff, for reasons of which he is the sole judge, believes that he has a duty to suppress some particular use which his predecessor had allowed, the Churches must conform with filial obedience to what is prescribed for them. That which might earlier have been legitimate ceases to be so when the supreme authority of Peter has ordered its discontinuance.'

41 On this whole problem see the interesting article by Henri de Lavalette, 'Qu'est-ce que la théologie romaine?' in *Lumière et Vie* 26, no. 133, pp. 98-106. See also Mgr Baunard, op. cit., vol. 2, pp. 578-601 (a typical situation recorded at the time).

42 R. Aubert, *Le Pontificat* . . ., p. 273, cites among the condemned works, Canon Bernier, *Humble Remontrance au R. P. Dom Prosper Guéranger*; Abbé Guettée, *Histoire de l'Église de France*, published with the approval of forty-two bishops; Abbé Lequeux, *Traité de droit canon*; Abbé Bailly, *Théologie*. For the link joining the definition of the Immaculate Conception with the insistence on infallibility, we quote the revealing lines of Mgr Baunard: 'This news [the designation of Mgr Pie as Reporter for introducing the schema on infallibility] will bring great joy to the French friends of Mgr Pie. Mgr de Ségur, returned from Lourdes, sent him some enthusiastic words expressing his most ardent devotion to Mary and the Church. Pius IX had said to Mary: "You are immaculate." Mary went on to answer the pope, "You are infallible".' op. cit., vol. 2, p. 399.

43 G. Thils, op. cit., pp. 67, 72.

44 R. Aubert, *Le Pontificat* . . . , p. 320. I have not been able to trace the quotation, but study of various texts of Manning convinces me that it gives the true sense of his 'apart from the bishops'. See the following note.

45 The publication in 1869 of Mgr Maret's *Du Concile générale et de la Paix religieuse* increased those suspicions. Dom Guéranger replied with his *Monarchie pontificale*. The ultramontanes used the expression 'separated infallibility' to oppose the link with the consent of the bishops affirmed by Mgr Maret among others (cf. Mgr Baunard, op. cit., vol. 2, pp. 352-3 and note 44 above). We cite in support this passage from Baunard on Cardinal Pie's 'profession of faith': 'Speaking

against the alleged need to submit papal decisions in matters of doctrine to the agreement, at least tacit, of the bishops, he declared himself in this fine profession of faith: "No, I will never outrage the promise of Jesus Christ, nor the help of the Holy Spirit, nor my reason or good sense, by believing that when your lips, O Peter, speak an oracle of doctrine, that oracle will gain from my silence and that of my brethren a quality of infallibility underived from the promise and the divine help!" Yet at the same time as he professed this belief in separated infallibility . . .' op. cit., p. 353.

46 Well emphasized in C. Gerest, art. cit., pp. 73-4.

47 R. Aubert, Le Pontificat . . ., p. 301.

48 C. Butler, op. cit., vol. 1, pp. 76-7, cf. Aubert, ibid., pp. 302-3, repeated almost verbatim, without references. 'Rerum PIUS tenax vigor, Immortus in te permanens . . .'; 'Pontifex sanctus, innocens, impollutus, segregatus a peccatoribus et excelsior coelis factus'; and this hymn to the pontiff-king: 'Pater pauperum, dator munerum, lumen cordium, emitte coelitus lucis tuae radium.'

49 Often cited, e.g., R. Aubert, Le Pontificat . . . , pp. 302-3. We have not been able to check the reference.

50 See note 48.

51 Baunard, op. cit., vol. 2, p. 182. This was pronounced before the Council. Y. M. J. Congar, 'Le Développement historique de l'autorité dans l'Église' in Problèmes de l'Autorité, pp. 145-81 (174), coll. Unam Sanctum 38 (1962), states: 'More than one spoke of a real presence of Christ under the pontifical species.' We have rarely found identifications as sharp as that, but similar expressions are common. Thus in 1872 Cardinal Pie could say, 'Peter is on this earth the vicar and continuing person of Christ.' (Baunard, op. cit., vol. 2, p. 471). But Congar, Je Crois en l'Esprit Saint, vol. 1, pp. 218-26 (Cerf, Paris 1979), assembles texts showing how far this uncritical view of the papacy could go.

52 An expression of E. Lafond, Veuillot's friend, cited in Aubert, Le Pontificat . . . , p. 302. Others speak of 'the vicar of God'; e.g., M. l'Abbé Besson, Panégyriques et Oraisons funèbres, vol. 1, p. 314, Paris 1870.

53 See Henry Marc-Bonnet, Les Papes de la Renaissance (Paris 1969), p. 75.

54 See J. Lecler, Le Pape ou le Concile?, pp. 40-6, Lyons 1974; Y. Congar, 'Infaillibilité et indéfectibilité', in RSPT 54, pp. 601-18 (606), 1970. For Vatican I, see Zinelli's intervention, Mansi 52, 1109.

55 Reported in E. Veuillot, Louis Veuillot, p. 360, no date, 6th edn, Paris.

56 ibid., p. 319.

57 Jean Carrère, Le Pape, p. 99, Paris 1924.

58 It was said of the illustrious Döllinger, well before the Council, that his

Considerations were schismatic (cf. Baunard, op. cit., vol. 2, p. 352); of Father Gratry that he was more high-flown than solid, his conscience honest but spoiled (ibid., p. 385); that Montalembert, who had dared call Pius IX 'the idol of the Vatican', was classed as 'the victim of a moment's lapse and suffering', ibid., pp. 385-6. Great contempt fills the title 'misled scholar' (*érudit fourvoyé*) who 'hurls himself along the ways of error and perdition' - used after the Council to speak of Döllinger.

59 G. Thils, op. cit., p. 67. On the context of Vatican I, see especially F. J. Cwiekowski, *The English Bishops and the First Vatican Council*, coll. *Bibliothèque de la revue d'histoire ecclésiastique*, Louvain 1971; J. R. Palanque, *Catholiques libéraux et Gallicans en France face au Concile du Vatican*, published by the Faculty of Aix-en-Provence, 1962; L. Veuillot, *Oeuvres complètes*, series II, vol. 10, Paris 1932. The 'Vota' of the consultants of Vatican I may be found in *Divinitas* 6, 1962. They are illuminated by R. Derre, *Lamennais et ses amis: le mouvement des idées à l'époque romantique*, Paris 1962; C. Butler, *The Vatican Council* . . . (key work); U. Betti, *La Constituzione dommatica Pastor Aeternus*, Rome 1961; F. Mourret, *Le Concile du Vatican* Paris 1919 (a precious book); H. Rondet, *Vatican I*, Paris 1962 (easy and interesting).

60 Mgr Baunard, op. cit., vol. 2, p. 411. On Mgr Pie's view of Gallicanism, an enemy to be defeated, see ibid., pp. 386-7: ' "A poison had slipped unnoticed into the veins of the Christian society. Undetected it would infect the whole body. But the Council came and, drawing off the virus, brought about and began the cure of the illness of which it is the remedy." So speaks [Mgr Pie] of renascent Gallicanism.'

61 ibid., p. 411.

62 Lamennais, *Les Meilleures Pages*, p. 188.

63 Baunard, op. cit., vol. 2, pp. 656-7.

64* See J. M. R. Tillard, 'L'Horizon de la *primauté* de l'évêque de Rome' in *POC* 25, pp. 217-44, 1975; id., 'La Primauté romaine: jamais pour éroder les structures des églises locales', in *Irénikon* 51, pp. 291-325, 1977.

65 So Mansi 52, 1140. On this formula, see J. M. R. Tillard, 'L'Horizon . . .' p. 221.

66 Mansi 52, 1108-1109A.

67 Thus Mgr de Ségur to Mgr Pie: 'I want most emphatically to add my little *Vivat* to all the cries of joy, gratitude, love and admiration which rise from so many hearts. What splendour of greatness and of doctrine this conciliar Constitution does shed on the papacy! I can think of nothing so grand, so powerful or so catholic in the annals of the Church! . . . My best respects to your mother, who must be as proud of you as if she was the definition itself, or even Infallibility!' Baunard, op. cit., p. 102.

68 Henri de Lavalette, art. cit., p. 102.

69 Mgr Cauly, *Cours d'instruction religieuse à l'usage des catéchismes de persévérance, des maisons d'éducation et des personnes du monde*, pp. 82-3, Paris, 1900.

70 Abbé Ollagnier, *Catéchisme. Livre du Maître*, p. 139, Paris 1924.

71 *La Foi Catholique*, L.III, p. 81, Paris 1941.

72 ed. Lasfargues, *Explication littérale et sommaire du Catéchisme*, pp. 66-7, Quebec 1946.

73 Regional schools commission of the Outaouais, 49, edn May 1980.

74 Victor Germain, docteur en théologie, *Catéchisme*, pp. 130-2, Quebec 1941.

75 F. Spirago, *Catéchisme catholique populaire*, pp. 605-6 (Paris 1903), reissued for the proclamation of the dogma of the Assumption, 1950.

76 Mgr Alfred Baudrillart, *Benoît XV*, p. 69, Paris 1926.

77 *Irénikon* 29, pp. 128-9, note 2 (1956) reproduces J. Beyer's paper 'Le Souverain Pontife, centre vital et unité de l'Église' in *Ut Regnet . . . , Vivre avec l'Église*, lectures given to directors of the eucharistic crusade in August 1955 at Nivelles. Special number of the monthly bulletin for directors of the crusade, 24th year, no. 2, p. 38, Nov. 1955. We have not been able to consult the bulletin itself.

78 Quoted in G. Thils, op. cit., p. 157.

79 See 'Über das Episkopat', in *Das Amt der Einheit*, pp. 245-311 (291-2), Stuttgart 1964.

80 For 'ordinary magisterium' see A. Vacant, *Le Magistère ordinaire de l'Église et ses organes*, Paris 1899; M. Caudron, 'Magistère ordinaire et Infaillibilité pontificale d'après la constitution *Dei Filius*', *ETL* 36, pp. 393-431, 1960; P. Nau, 'Le Magistère pontifical ordinaire au premier Concile du Vatican', in *RT* 62, pp. 341-97, 1962; A. L. Descamps, 'Théologie et Magistère' in *ETL* 52, pp. 82-133, 1976; Y. M. J. Congar, 'Pour une histoire sémantique du terme *magisterium*' in *RSPT* 60, 85-98, 1976; id., 'Bref Historique des formes du *magistère* et de ses relations avec les docteurs' in *RSPT* 60, pp. 99-112, 1976.

81 Baunard, op. cit., vol. 2, pp. 675-6.

82 The French Dominican centre Istina and its periodical of that name were especially important, as was the Benedictine priory of Amay-sur-Meuse (later Chevetogne) and its periodical *Irénikon*, to name only French-speaking places.

83 See D. T. Strottmann's interesting article 'Primauté et céphalisation' in *Irénikon* 37 (1964), pp. 187-97.

84 For the story behind the Vatican II texts, see Umberto Betti, *La Dottrina sull'episcopato nel Vaticano II* (Rome 1968), and, less explicit on the history of the *Lumen Gentium* schemas, G. Philips, *L'Église et son mystère au IIe Concile du Vatican* (Desclée 1967); see also *L'Église de Vatican II*, coll. *Unam Sanctam* 51, 1966.

85 (Unless otherwise stated, all Vatican II texts quoted in English will be in the translation ed. Austin Flannery, *Vatican Council II: Conciliar and Post-Conciliar Documents* (Dominican Publications, Dublin, and Costello Publishing, New York 1975), hereafter cited as Flannery. This extract is from p. 564—E.Tr.)

To avoid confusion from the outset it should be realized that here as in all Vatican II texts, the expression 'the churches' refers not to 'the other churches' (Orthodox, Anglican, etc), but to what are known judicially as dioceses. 'A church' is a Christian community gathered by the Eucharist which she (that church) celebrates under the presidency of a minister in communion with the bishop of the locality, himself in communion with the other bishops and with the apostolic community. *Christus Dominus* asserts strongly the pope's 'ordinary power' over these churches.

86 To which Karl Rahner's article cited above (note 79) tended.

87 Thus Mgr Pie applied Gregory the Great's phrase to the work of Vatican I: 'As the end of the world grows close, so the heavenly science develops and grows with the time', Baunard, op. cit., vol. 2, p. 382.

88 See the interesting book by A. Acerbi, *Due Ecclesiologie: ecclesiologia juridica ed ecclesiologia di communione nella Lumen Gentium*, Bologna 1975.

89 See the excellent tool for study, G. Alberigo and F. Magistretti, *Constitutionis Dogmaticae Synopsis Historica*, Bologna 1975 (here especially x, 22, 192-5).

90 ibid., 456. See also U. Betti, op. cit., pp. 207-8. Compare Zinelli's reply at Vatican I, note 66 above.

91 On this formula see Tillard, 'L'Horizon . . .', p. 221, n. 7.

92 See Tillard, 'La Primauté romaine . . .', pp. 302-4.

93 See the illuminating study by O. Rousseau, 'Collégialité et Communion' in *Irénikon* 42, pp. 457-74, 1969.

94 See J. Hamer on 'Les Conférences épiscopales, exercice de la collégialité', in *NRT* 85, pp. 966-9, 1963.

95 Mgr Onclin, *La Charge pastorale des évêques*, p. 94, coll. *Unam Sanctam* 74, Paris 1969.

96 Text in *DC* 66, p. 957, 1969. On the problem of synods, see H. Legrand, 'Synodes et Conseils de l'après-concile', in *NRT* 98 pp. 193-216, 1076; O. Rousseau, 'Collégialité et Communion'; P. Haubtmann, 'Le Point sur le synode (de 1969)', a rapid survey, in *Présence et Dialogue*, 25-32, November 1969; R. Laurentin, *Le Synode permanent. Naissance et Avenir*, Paris 1960; J. Grootaers, 'I Sinodi dei vescovi del 1969 e del 1974' in *Cristianisimo nella storia*, 2,271-4, 1981. On the latest synod, see *Synode des évêques 1980, 26 septembre-25 octobre*, Preface by Pascal Gaudet, Paris 1980.

97 See Tillard, 'La Primauté romaine . . .', pp. 304–20, for numerous references.

98 Thils, op. cit., p. 185.

99 ibid., p. 186.

100 Text in *DC* 61, pp. 9–14, 1964.

101 Following the exegesis of Mgr Philips, secretary of the commission. See his *L'Église et son Mystère au deuxième Concile du Vatican*, vol. 1, pp. 284–305, Desclée 1967.

102 op. cit., p. 202.

103 For the invitation of the Orthodox, see R. Aubert, *Le Pontificat . . .*, pp. 313–14. Protestants and Anglicans were also considered; see Gerard Francis Cobb, *A Few Words on Reunion and the Coming Council of Rome*, London 1869; F. Mourret, *Le Concile du Vatican*, pp. 124–6, Paris 1919. Easterns, Lutherans and Anglicans refused the invitation. The Anglicans, however, hesitated. Negotiations were even considered.

104* See M. J. Le Guillou, 'L'Expérience orientale de la collégialité épiscopale et ses requêtes', in *Istina* 10, pp. 111–24, 1964; P. Batiffol, *Cathedra Petri*, pp. 41–79, Paris 1938 (vital); Hilaire Marot, 'Décentralisation structurelle et Primauté dans l'Église ancienne' in *Concilium* 7, pp. 19–28, 1965; id., 'Note sur la Pentarchie', in *Irénikon* 32, pp. 436–42, 1959; E. Lanne, 'Églises locales et Patriarcats a l'époque des grands conciles' in *Irénikon* 34, pp. 292–321, 1961.

105 See P. Duprey, 'Brief Reflections on the title *Primus inter pares*' in *One in Christ* 10, pp. 7–12, 1974 (more complete than the original French); Jean-Simon Rocher, *Bossuet et l'Ecclésiologie gallicane au XVIIe siècle*, pp. 84–93, Paris 1979.

106 J. Ratzinger, *Le Nouveau Peuple de Dieu*, p. 54, Paris 1971.

107* Marot, ibid., p. 20.

108* As well as Marot, loc. cit., see J. F. McCue, 'La Primauté romaine aux trois premiers siècles' in *Concilium* 64, pp. 31–8, 1971; W. de Vries, 'L'Évolution postérieure à l'ère constantinienne', ibid., pp. 39–46; 'Du Haut Moyen Âge à la réforme grégorienne', ibid., pp. 47–52.

109 Le Guillou, loc. cit., p. 117.

110 Besides Le Guillou see Y. Congar, *L'Église de saint Augustin à la période moderne*, in coll. *Histoire des dogmes* III/3, pp. 269–77, Paris 1970; W. de Vries, 'La S. Sede e i Patriarcati cattolici d'Oriente' in *Or. Christ. Per.*, 27, pp. 313–61, 1961.

111 'Indicare quoque vestra beatitudo studuit, jam se quibusdam non scribere superba vocabula, quae ex vanitatis radice prodierunt, et mihi loquitur, dicens, sicut jussistis. Quod verbum jussionis peto a meo auditu removete, quia scio qui sum, qui estis. Loco enim mihi fratres estis, moribus patres. Non ergo jussi, sed quae utilia visa sunt, indicari curavi. Non tamen invenio vestram beatitudinem hoc ipsum quod

memoriae vestrae intuli, perfecte retinere voluisse. Nam dixi, nec mihi vos, nec cuiquam alteri tale aliquid scribere debere; et ecce (*Grat. dist.* 99, c. 5) in praefatione epistolae quam ad me ipsum qui prohibui direxistis, superbae appellationis verbum universalem me papam dicentes, imprimere curastis. Quod peto dulcissima mihi sanctitas vestra ultra non faciat, quia vobis subtrahitur quod alteri plus quam ratio exigit praebetur. Ego enim non verbis quaero prosperari, sed moribus. Nec honorem esse deputo, in quo fratres meos honorem suum perdere cognosco. Meus namque honor est honor universalis Ecclesiae. Meus honor est fratrum meorum solidus vigor. Tunc ego vero honoratus sum, cum singulis quibusque honor debitus non negatur. Si enim universalem me papam vestra sanctitas dicit, negat se hoc esse quod me fatetur universum. Sed absit hoc. Recedant verba quae vanitatem inflant, et charitatem vulnerant' (*Epist.* VIII, 30; *PL* 77, 933 C).

112 See Brian Tierney, 'Modèles historiques de la papauté' in *Concilium* 108, pp. 65-74 (68-9), 1975; Y. M. J. Congar, 'Le Développement historique de l'autorité dans l'Église', in *Problèmes de l'autorité*, coll. *Unam Sanctam* 38, pp. 159-61, Paris 1962; G. Hocquard, 'L'Idéal du pasteur des âmes selon Grégoire le Grand', in *La Tradition sacerdotale*, pp. 143-67, Le Puy 1959.

113 See M. Pacaut, *Histoire de la Papauté*, pp. 138-47, Paris 1976; X. H. Arquillière, *Saint Grégoire VII, Essai sur sa conception du pouvoir pontificale*, Paris 1934 (important); B. Carra de Vaux, 'Les Images de la papauté au cours des siècles' in *Lumière et Vie* 133, pp. 37-69 (56-8), 1977 (brief). A. Fliche, *La Querelle des investitures*, Paris 1946, shows that it is important not to blacken Gregory VII too much.

114 *PL* 148, pp. 407-8 (*Reg.* II, 55; in E. Caspar, *Das Register Gregors VII*, 202, Berlin 1930). An interesting study of the juridical context is William D. McCready, 'Papal *Plenitudo Potestatis* and the source of temporal authority in late Medieval Papal Hierocratic Theory' in *Speculum* 48, pp. 654-74 (1973); Charles E. Shrader, 'The Historical Development of the Papal Monarchy' in *Catholic Historical Review* 22, pp. 259-82 (1936); H. X. Arquillière, 'Origines de la théorie des deux glaives' in *Studi Gregoriani* 1, pp. 501-21 (1947). For a general view of its development, see Jan Gaudemet, 'Collections canoniques et Primauté pontificale', in *Revue de Droit canonique* 16, pp. 102-17 (1936). A brief but interesting ecumenical study is that of Georges H. Tavard, in *Papal Primacy and the Universal Church*, coll. *Lutherans and Catholics in Dialogue*, 98-104, 105-18, Minneapolis 1974.

115 A. Fliche, *La Réforme grégorienne et la reconquête chrétienne*, Paris 1944, p. 79, n. 1, writes: 'According to K. Hoffman, *Der Dictatus papae Gregor VII*, pp. 34ff. and *passim*, we should not look for the origin of the reassertion of papal power which the *Dictatus papae* represents in the difficulties encountered in the West, but in events at Constanti-

nople. The Eastern schism was a revolt against the prerogatives of the Roman Church, and Gregory VII, very upset by the separation, was concerned to emphasize both the origins and the character of the claims which justified the Roman pontiff in establishing absolute authority over the universal Church. There is evidently a great deal of truth in this thesis. The letter already mentioned as being sent to Hugh of Cluny (*Reg.*, II, 49) bears witness to Gregory VII's sadness at the check to the negotiations with the emperor Michael VII, and some of the *Dictatus papae* express clearly, as M. Hoffmann shows, the pope's desire to underline the themes of the Church of Rome's superiority to that of Constantinople. It is therefore very likely that in 1075 Gregory VII felt the need to affirm the privileges of the Holy See against countries in revolt against his authority, but this was not his only preoccupation. Resistance from among the Western clergy led him to prepare a series of propositions which would pave the way to that centralization which he was to accomplish over the following years. He took precautions against possible trouble from the Western sovereigns also by proclaiming the pope's right to release their subjects from their oath of loyalty.'

116 Hence the significance of Paul VI's gesture in selling the tiara.

117 See B. Jacqueline, *Épiscopat et Primauté chez saint Bernard de Clairvaux*, Saint-Lô 1975: very enlightening on the many factors involved in his staking of the papal claims.

118 *De Consideratione* IV, 3.6; *Opera* III, 453.

119 English translation of *Unam Sanctam* is from H. Bettenson, *Documents of the Christian Church* (London 1943), pp. 159-61, with additions—E.Tr. On *plenitudo* see the (incomplete) references in Jacqueline, op. cit., pp. 205, 306; J. Lecler, *Le Pape ou le Concile*, pp. 35, 49, 77, 80, 101, 152, 158, Lyons 1973; T. G. Jalland, *The Church and the Papacy*, pp. 18, 301-4, London 1944; M. Maccarrone, *Vicarius Christi*, Rome 1952. See also above, note 114.

120 See excellent articles by J. Rivière, 'Une première Somme du pouvoir pontifical: le Pape chez Augustin d'Ancone' in *Rev. des Sci. Rel.* 18, pp. 149-183 (1938); id., 'Augustin d'Ancone', in *Dict. de Droit can.* I, pp. 1416-22; id., 'Trionfo' in *DTC* 15, pp. 1855-60; id., *Le Problème de l'Église et de l'État au temps de Philippe le Bel*, Louvain-Paris 1926 (still valuable).

121 id., 'Trionfo' in *DTC* 15, pp. 1858-9.

122 id., 'Sur l'expression Pape-Deus au Moyen Âge', in *Miscellanea Francesco Ehrle: Scritti di Storia e Paleographia*, vol. 2, pp. 276-89 (285), Rome 1924; id., 'Le pape est-il un Dieu pour Innocent III?' in *Rev. des. Sci. Rel.* 2, pp. 447-51 (1922).

123 See Y. M. Congar, 'Titres donnés au pape', in *Concilium* 108, p. 61 (1975). On Torquemada see J. Lecler, op. cit., pp. 156-9.

124 Text in J. Rivière, 'Le pape est-il . . .', p. 450.

125 Text in id., 'Sur l'expression . . .', p. 284.

126 Texts ibid., pp. 285-7.

127 He acts *tamquam Deus* (ibid., p. 283).

128 *Non puri hominis sed vicem Dei gerit in terris*, ibid., p. 285.

129 See J. Lecler, op. cit., pp. 152-4.

130 Text in Rivière, 'Sur l'expression . . .', p. 285.

131 See note 26 above.

132 *Sermo 5, PL* 54, p. 153. So also Gregory VII and Pascal II. See texts in A. Fliche, *La Querelle des investitures*, pp. 73-4, 87, 92-3, 147, 164.

133 As E. Giles shows in *Documents illustrating Papal Authority, AD 96-454*, London 1952, text 142, p. 282. See also the brief but enlightening study by M. Maccarrone, 'Il titolo papale di vicarius Petri nella liturgia', in *Notitiae*, pp. 177-82 (1979).

134 Y. M. J. Congar, 'Titres donnés au pape', p. 60.

135 On *Vicarius Petri* read especially G. Corti, *Il Papa Vicario di Pietro, contributo alla storia dell'Idea papale*, Brescia 1966; M. Maccarrone, *Vicarius Christi*, Rome 1952; id., *Apostolicità, Episcopato e Primato di Pietro; Ricerche e Testimonianze dal II al V secolo*, Rome 1976. For Gregory VII (and Pascal II), see above, note 132.

136 See W. Bertrams, *Vicarius Christi, vicarii Christi; de significatione potestatis episcopalis et primatialis*, Rome 1964; Congar, art. cit., pp. 59-61; Maccarrone, *Apostolicità* . . . , pp. 316-22; B. Carra de Vaux, art. cit., pp. 58-60.

137 *Quamvis simus apostolorum principis successores, non tamen ejus aut alicujus apostoli vel hominis sed ipsius sumus Vicarii Jesu Christi* (*Reg.* 1, p. 326; *PL pp. 214, 292*).

138 Congar, art. cit., p. 61.

139 For this expression see H. Marot, 'La Collégialité et le Vocabulaire episcopal du Ve au VIIe siècle', in *La Collégialité épiscopale*, coll. *Unam Sanctam* 52, 59-98, Paris 1965.

140 A. Amann and A. Dumas, *L'Église au pouvoir des laïques*, p. 146, Paris 1949. For Cardinal Humbert see 'Cardinal Humbert of Silva-Candida (d. 1061)', *Duquesne Studies* in *Annuale Mediaevale III*, pp. 29-42 (1962).

141 See *Tomos Agapes*, pp. 250-303; and important article by M. Maccarrone, 'L'atto di fraternità del 7 dicembre 1965' in *Unitas* 21, pp. 20-50 (1966).

142 On this title see H. Marot, loc. cit., pp. 75-94. It is known that *Pontifex maximus* from the fifth century describes any bishop, particularly a metropolitan. From the ninth century it was reserved as a privilege of the pope: sovereign pontiff. The Code of 1917 and Vatican II used especially *Pontifex romanus*.

143 Pope is here used in the popular, affectionate sense. We know that in

the East it is applied to others than the bishop of Rome (so *Service d'information du Secr. pour l'Unité des chrétiens*, 7, Vatican 1980; *Le Monde*, 8 September 1981, 3; *The Daily Telegraph*, 8 September 1981, 5). The *Dictatus Papae* of Gregory VII tended to claim it as a personal title ('his name is unique in the world' XI). The word *papatus* appeared then. See Y. M. J. Congar, 'Note sur le destin de l'idée de collégialité épiscopale en Occident au Moyen Âge', in *La Collégialité épiscopale*, coll. *Unam Sanctam* 52, 99-129 (118), Paris 1965. On the word *papa*, see R. Bellarmine, *Tertia Controversia generalis De Summo Pontifici*, IIb. II, cap. 31, 1, pp. 420-1 ed. *Opera*, Naples 1836; H. Burn-Murdoch, 'Titles of the Roman See', in *CQR* 159, pp. 257-364 (1958); id., *The Development of the Papacy* (London 1954), pp. 73-9; P. Batiffol, 'Papa, Sedes apostolica, apostolatus' in *Riv. di Archeol. crist.*, I, pp. 99-116 (1924); H. Leclercq, 'Papa' in *DACL* XIII, pp. 1097-1111; P. de Labriolle, 'Papa', in *Bull. Du Cange* 4 pp. 65-75 (1928); Congar, art. cit. above, note 123.

144 Eng. trans. is from N. C. News Service Documentary, quoted in Raymond E. Brown, *Biblical Reflections on Crises Facing the Church* (Darton, Longman & Todd, London, 1975), pp. 116ff: (French version *DC* 19 (1973), pp. 666-7). Latin original *AAS*, LXV (1973), pp. 396-408. This whole page is important, though rarely cited. For irreformability see Mgr Philips, *L'Église et son Mystère au Deuxième Concile du Vatican* (Desclée 1977), p. 330. To fill out the detail of our rapid sketch, see: Jalland, op. cit. (fundamental); Y. M. J. Congar, *L'Ecclésiologie du Haut Moyen Âge, de saint Grégoire le Grand à la désunion entre Byzance et Rome*, Paris 1968; id., *L'Église de saint Augustin à l'époque moderne*, Paris 1970; W. Ullmann, *The Growth of Papal Government in the Middle Ages*, London 1955; M. Pacaut, *Histoire de la Papauté, de l'Origine au concile de Trente*, Paris 1976; Geoffrey Richards, *The Popes and the Papacy in the Early Middle Ages (476-752)*, Boston 1979 (important but often needs checking); M. Wilks, *The Problem of Sovereignty in the Later Middle Ages (Ecclesia in Papa, Papa in Ecclesia)*, Cambridge 1963; Brian Tierney, *Foundations of the Conciliar Theory*, Cambridge 1955; id., *The Origins of Papal Infallibility (1150-1350)*, Cambridge 1972; Yves Renouard, *La Papauté à Avignon*, Paris 1969 (easy and stimulating); Henry Marc-Bonnet, *Les Papes de la Renaissance*, coll. *Que sais-je?*, Paris 1969; id., *La Papauté contemporaine*, coll. *Que sais-je?*, Paris 1971 (excellent summary, easy to read, by a good specialist).

Part 2 The Pope, bishop of Rome

1 See J. M. R. Tillard, 'Une seule Église de Dieu: l'Église brisée' in *POC* 30, pp. 3-13 (1980).

2 The Latin text is very clear: 'Ad hanc historicam condicionem quod attinet, initio observandum est sensum, quem enuntiationes fidei continent, partim pendere e linguae adhibitae vi significandi certo

quodam tempore certisque rerum adjunctis. Praeterea, nonnumquam contingit, ut veritas aliqua dogmatica primum modo incompleto, non falso tamen, exprimatur, ac postea, in ampliore contextu fidei aut humanarum cognitionum considerata, plenius et perfectius significetur. Deinde, Ecclesia novis suis enuntiationibus, ea quae in Sacra Scriptura aut in praeteritis Traditionis expressionibus iam aliquomodo continentur, confirmare aut dilucidare intendit, sed simul de certis questionibus solvendis erroribusve removendis cogitare solet; quarum omnium rerum ratio habenda est, ut illae enuntiationes recte explanentur. Denique, etsi veritates, quas Ecclesia suis formulis dogmaticis reapse docere intendit, a mutabilibus alicuius temporis cogitationibus distinguuntur et sine iis exprimi possunt, nihilominus interdum fieri potest, ut illae veritates etiam a Sacro Magisterio proferantur verbis, quae huiusmodi cogitationum vestigia secumferant.

His consideratis, dicendum est formulas dogmaticas Magisterii Ecclesiae veritatem revelatam ab initio apte communicasse et, manentes easdem, eam in perpetuum communicaturas esse recte interpretantibus ipsas. Exinde tamen non consequitur singulas earum pari ratione ad id efficiendum aptas fuisse aut aptas mansuras esse. Qua de causa, theologi accurate circumscribere satagunt intentionem docendi, quam diversae illae formulae reapse continent, atque hac opera sua vivo Magisterio Ecclesiae, cui subduntur, conspicuum praestant auxilium. Eadem insuper de causa fieri solet, ut antiqua formulae dogmaticae et aliae iis veluti proximae, in consueto Ecclesiae usu, vivae et frugiferae permaneant, ita tamen ut iis opportune novae expositiones enuntiationesque adjungantur, quae congenitum illarum sensum custodiant et illustrent. Porro aliquando etiam factum est, ut inconsueto illo Ecclesiae usu, quaedam ex illis formulis cederent novis dicendi modis qui, a Sacro Magisterio propositi vel approbati, eundem sensum clarius pleniusve exhibebant.'

3 The importance for our subject of this reference to limitations due to the particular time will become apparent.

4 On this normative period see *Vers une profession de foi commune* in *DC* 77, pp. 653-7 (1980) (Doc. *Foi et Constitution* 100).

5 See Pierre Batiffol's fundamental study *Cathedra Petri*, coll. *Unam Sanctam 4*, Paris 1938 (posthumously published; Mgr Batiffol died in January 1929); id., *Le Siège apostolique*, Paris 1924; M. Maccarrone, 'La Cathedra Petri e lo svillupo dell'idea del primato papale dal II al III secolo' in *Misc. Piolanti*, pp. 37-56, Rome 1964; id., *Apostolicità, episcopato e primato di Pietro*, pp. 64-123, Rome 1976; C. Pietri *Roma Christiana, Recherches sur l'Église de Rome, son organisation, sa politique, son idéologie, de Miltiade à Sixte III (311-440)*, vol. 1, pp. 301-401, Rome 1976 (the interpretation of the historical evidence is never maximizing).

6 Shown in the election of the bishop whether by the local church as a whole, the chapter or (in the case of Rome) the college of cardinals. See

R. Gryson, 'Les élections ecclésiastiques au IIIe siècle' in *RHE* 68, pp. 353-402 (1973); id., 'Les élections épiscopales en Orient au IVe siècle', ibid., 74, pp. 301-45 (1979); J. Gaudemet, *Les Élections dans l'Église latine des origines au XVIe siècle*, Paris 1979. For the cardinalate, see G. Alberigo, *Cardinalato e Collegialità*, esp. pp. 14-49, Florence 1969.

7 *Epist.* 14, 5 (*PL* 54, 673): 'Cum ergo de summi sacerdotis electione tractabitur, ille omnibus praeponatur quem cleri plebisque consensus concorditer postularit: ita ut si in aliam forte personam partium se vota diviserint, metropolitani judicio is alteri praeferatur qui majoribus et studiis juvatur et meritis: tantum ut nullus invitis et non petentibus ordinetur; ne civitas episcopum non optatum aut contemnat, aut oderit; et fiat minus religiosa quam convenit, cui non licuerit habere quem voluit.' On the permanence of Leo's vision, A. Fliche writes in *La Querelle des Investitures* (Paris 1946), pp. 8-9, 'In a letter written in 445, Saint Leo the Great stated as a principle that "whoever commands everyone must have been elected by everyone"; in an episcopal vacancy the faithful are called on to make a proposal (*postulare*) after which the clergy proceed to the election (*electio*). In accordance with this pontifical decree, the Council of Clermont (635) took up a formula which the second Council of Orleans (533) had reserved for metropolitans only, stipulating that "the bishop must be elected by the clergy and the people, with the metropolitan's agreement". The Third Council of Orleans (538) made this rule its own, and from then on canon law kept it from falling into disuse. Five hundred years later Burchard of Worms issued a decree based on concilar canons as well as on the constitutions of Saint Celestine I (422-32) and Saint Gregory the Great (590-604). It did not differ from the Merovingian councils and in its turn insisted that no one should be regarded as a bishop who had not been elected by the clergy, requested by the people, and consecrated by the bishops of his own province with the approval of the metropolitan.

'The canonical tradition was thus maintained at least in point of law. In practice it was observed under many different circumstances; chroniclers and hagiographers describe many episcopal elections, giving evidence of the major part played by clergy and people. The procedure was not rigidly fixed and in different instances the lay element might be more or less influential, while the actual number of those taking part in elections varied considerably. At Rheims in 989, for example, Archbishop Arnoul was designated by the whole assembly of the clergy, while in several French and German dioceses at the same period the right to elect was restricted to the canons only. The voice of the laity was sometimes confined to the *primores civitatis* or the *milites ecclesiae*, but in other cases there was no limit to the number of *cives* who acclaimed the clergy's choice. Thus the composition of the electoral college varied, but the canonical rule stood firm.'

8 R. Gryson, 'Les Elections épiscopales . . .', p. 342.
9 ibid., p. 344.

10 See G. Bardy, 'L'autorité du siège romain et les controverses du IIIe siècle', in *Rec. de Sci. Rel.* 14, pp. 255-72, 385-410 (1924).

11 ibid., p. 261.

12 A. Harnack, 'Die Briefe des romischen Klerus aus der Zeit des Sedisvacans im Jahre 250', in *Theologische Abhandlungen Carl von Weissacker gewidmet*, 36, Freiburg 1892, translated from the French of G. Bardy, art. cit., p. 265.

13 *De Praescriptione* 36 pp 1-6. Eng. trans. is by S. L. Greenslade in *LCC* 5, p. 57. See also E. Giles, op. cit., pp. 22-3. Latin text and French trans. by P. de Labriolle, coll. *SC* 46, p. 137, Paris 1957; coll. Hemmer-Lejay, vol. 4, p. 79, Paris 1907.

14 'The "papacy" of the first centuries is the authority which the Roman Church has with the other Churches, an authority which consists in being concerned with their conformity to the authentic tradition of the faith, an authority which controls communion in the unity of the universal Church, an authority claimed by no other church than the Roman Church', Batiffol, *Cathedra Petri*, p. 28.

15 Ignatius of Antioch, *To the Romans*, int. Eng. trans. with notes in Giles, op. cit., pp. 4-5. See P. Camelot's note in his edn, *SC* 10, p. 125: 'The expression must not be taken rigidly, as if Ignatius believed the church of Rome to hold a "primacy" in the sense of later tradition.'

16 Text in *Conciliorum Oecumenicorum Decreta*, Bologna 1973, pp. 8-9. Eng. trans. is from Giles, op. cit., p. 93. Commentaries by C. Pietri, op. cit., vol. 1, pp. 182-7, and P. Duprey, 'Brèves réflexions sur l'adage *Primus inter Pares*' in *DC* 70 (1973), 29-31 (30), repeated with some variation in id., 'La structure synodale de l'Église dans la théologie orientale', in *POC* 20, pp. 123-45 (1970).

17 See C. Pietri, op. cit., who perhaps understates the bearing of this reference on the Roman see.

18 On these interpretations, see ibid., pp. 184-6 with the notes.

19 ibid., p. 186.

20 E. Lanne, 'Églises locales et Patriarcats à l'époque des grands conciles', in *Irénikon* 34, pp. 292-321 (300), (1961).

21 On the development and fate of the notion of apostolic churches, see Lanne, ibid., esp. pp. 296-8. The following passages from Tertullian's *De Praescriptione* are noteworthy: '. . .they set out through Judaea first, bearing witness to their faith in Jesus Christ and founding churches, and then out into the world, proclaiming the same doctrine of the same faith to the nations. Again they set up churches in every city, from which the other churches afterwards borrowed the transmission of the faith and the seeds of doctrine and continue to borrow them every day, in order to become churches. By this they are themselves reckoned apostolic as being the offspring of apostolic churches. Things of every kind must be classed according to their origin. These

churches then, numerous as they are, are identical with that one primitive apostolic Church from which they all come. All are primitive and all are apostolic. Their common unity is proved by fellowship in communion, by the name of brother and the mutual pledge of hospitality - rights which are governed by no other principle than the single tradition of a common creed (20, pp. 4-9).' 'If this be so, it follows that all doctrine which is in agreement with those apostolic churches, the wombs and sources of the faith, is to be deemed true on the ground that it indubitably preserves what the churches received from the apostles, the apostles from Christ, and Christ from God. It follows, on the other hand, that all doctrine which smacks of anything contrary to the truth of all the churches and apostles of Christ and God must be condemned out of hand as originating in falsehood. (21, pp. 4-5)'; Eng. trans. is by L. Greenslade, *LCC* 5, pp. 43-4. Latin text and French trans. by P. de Labriolle, *SC* 46, pp. 112-5; Hemmer-Lejay, pp. 41-3.

22 C. Pietri's phrase, op. cit., vol. 2, p. 1393.

23 W. de Vries, *Orient et Occident, les structures ecclésiales vues dans l'Histoire des sept premiers conciles oecuméniques* (Paris, 1974), pp. 138-9.

24 ibid., pp. 126-7.

25 ibid., p. 211.

26 Mansi 11, 340 A.

27 Following the text given in Mansi 11, 681 D-684 A.

28 Mansi 11, 731 D.

29 The same link is found in the famous axiom *Prima sedes a nemine judicatur*, whose origins go back to the affair of Pope Symmachus (died 514), if we are to believe A. M. Koeniger, 'Romanus Pontifex a nemine judicatur', in *Festgabe Ehrhard*, pp. 273-300, Bonn 1922. See Joseph Lecler, *Le Pape ou le Concile?*, pp. 41-4, Lyons 1973. The formula occurs in canon 1556 of the CJC of 1917.

30 See W. de Vries, op. cit., pp. 126-36, and especially W. Ullmann, 'Leo I and the Theme of Papal Primacy', in *JTS* 11, pp. 25-51 (1960); G. Medico, 'La Collégialité épiscopale dans les lettres des pontifes romains du Ve siècle', in *RSPT* 49, pp. 379-402 (380-92) (1965); Y. Congar, *L'Église de saint Augustin à l'époque moderne*, pp. 28-31 (cf. note 110 above).

31 On the meaning of *principalitas*, see P. Batiffol, 'Les *Principales Cathedrae* du concile de Carthage de 397' in *Rec. de Sci. Rel.* 14, pp. 287-92 (1924); C. Pietri, op. cit., vol. 1, pp. 300-1. What was the Greek original rendered *principalitas* in the extant text of Irenaeus? See R. P. C. Hanson, '*Potentiorem principalitatem* in Irenaeus *Adversus Haereses* III, 3. 1' in *Studia Patristica*, 3, pp. 366-9, Berlin 1961. The Latin word should be considered with *principatus* and the expres-

sion *princeps apostolorum* used of Peter. See Batiffol, *Cathedra Petri*, pp. 83-4. But it would distort its meaning to interpret it in categories of power. We follow the suggestion of Jalland, op. cit., pp. 112-13 that the notion is that of authenticity, of origin. See ibid., p. 112, n. 2. The see's privileged title is that of being marked with the seal of apostolic authenticity.

32 Text in *Conciliorum Oecumenicorum Decreta* (1973), p. 8. Here is a literal translation: 'Since it is an established custom and an ancient tradition that the bishop of Aelia (Capitolina) should be honoured, let him have the consequent honour, so long as the metropolitan (Caesarea) keeps the dignity which belongs to him.'

33 ibid., p. 28.

34 See Lanne, art. cit., and H. Marot, 'Note sur la Pentarchie', in *Irénikon* 32, pp. 436-42 (1959).

35 *Novella* 123, *cap. 3*, in *Corpus Juris civilis, volumen tertium, Novellae, recognovit Rudolfus* SCHOELL, *opus Schoellii morte interceptum absolvit Guilelmus* KROLL, p. 597, Zurich 1972.

36 A point well stressed by E. Lanne, art. cit., pp. 314-21.

37 *Adv. Haer.* III, 3, 1-2. Eng. trans. is by F. R. M. Hitchcock (SPCK, London 1916), vol. 1, pp. 84-6, slightly altered, cf. Giles op. cit., pp. 9-10. See excellent study by E. Lanne, 'L'Église de Rome, *a gloriosissimis duobus apostolis Petro et Paulo Romae fundatae et constitutae Ecclesiae*', in *Irénikon* 49, pp. 275-322 (1976). See also J. J. von Allmen, *La Primauté de l'Église de Pierre et de Paul*, Paris 1977; C. Hofstetter, 'La Primauté dans l'Église, dans la perspective de l'Histoire du Salut', in *Istina* 8, pp. 333-58 (1961-2).

38 On this expression, see above, note 31.

39 As E. Lanne establishes in 'L'Église de Rome . . .', pp. 281-94.

40 See id., ibid., pp. 302-3.

41 1 Clem. 5, 4-7; Eng. trans. is by C. C. Richardson in *LCC* 1, p. 46; French trans. is by A. Jaubert in *SC* 167, p. 109.

42 1 Clem. 6, 1; ibid.

43 *Rom.* 4, 1-3. Eng. trans. is by C. C. Richardson in *LCC* 1, p. 104.

44 E. Lanne, 'L'Église de Rome . . .', p. 313.

45 Eusebius, *Ecclesiastical History*; Eng. trans. is by H. J. Lawlor and J. E. L. Oulton (SPCK, London 1927) (1954), vol. 1, p. 60.

46 *De Praescriptione* 36, 1-6. But Tertullian also mentions the apostle John.

47 *Epist.* 75, 2; Eng. trans. is from Giles, op. cit., p. 76. Cf. Bayard, *Saint Cyprien, Correspondence*, t.2, 293 (1925).

48 '*Quoniam redecere a partibus illis minime potuisti, in quibus et apostoli quotidie sedent et cruor ipsorum sine intermissione Dei gloriam testatur*' (Mansi 2, 469).

49 M. Maccarrone, *Apostolicità* . . . , pp. 157-8.

50 On the history of the Feast of the Apostles see J. Ruysschaert, 'La Double Tradition romaine des tombes apostoliques', in *RHE* 52 (1957), pp. 791-831; C. Pietri, op. cit., vol. 1, pp. 365-76; Dom G. Oury, 'La Fête du 29 juin' in *L'Ami du Clergé* 72, pp. 385-9 (1963).

51 See D. T. Strotmann, 'Les Coryphées Pierre et Paul et les autres apôtres', in *Irénikon* 36, pp. 164-76 (168), (1963).

52 But not the distinctions made in ibid., p. 168, n. 3.

53 ibid., p. 166.

54 See Y. M. J. Congar, 'Saint Paul et l'autorité de l'Église romaine d'après la Tradition', in *Studiorum Paulinorum Congressus Internationalis Catholicus 1961*, coll. *Analecta Biblica* 17-18, pp. 491-516, Rome 1963. For Catherine of Siena, see R. Fawtier and L. Canet, *La Double Experience de Catherine Benincasa*, 54, Paris 1948.

55 *DC* 64 (1967), pp. 482, 488.

56 *DC* 74 (1977), p. 101. See also ibid., p. 105; *DC* 66 (1969), pp. 625-6, 653. The medal commemorating the coronation bore the images of Peter and Paul. John XXIII was less careful in this respect, but note *DC* 56 (1959), 194, 329 and his declaration '(I am) the humble successor of Peter and Paul' in *DC* 59 (1962), p. 1222.

57 Congar, 'Saint Paul et l'autorité . . .', p. 513.

58 Mansi 4, 1288 D. See C. Pietri, op. cit., vol. 2, p. 1382; W. de Vries, op. cit., p. 74.

59 See important study by Dom J. Dupont, 'Le Logion des douze trônes', in *Biblica* 45, pp. 355-92 (1964).

60 *Rom.* 4, 1-6, 2.

61 The theme of imitating the Passion is important, not because it adds anything to the Passion, but because it means communion with what makes the Passion salvific.

62 E. Lanne, 'L'Église de Rome . . .', p. 293.

63 See Raymond E. Brown, Karl P. Donfried and John Reumann (ed.), *Peter in the New Testament* (London 1974), pp. 155-6.

64 See *TWNT*, vol. 3, p. 64.

65 As C. Hofstetter also thinks, art. cit., p. 342.

66 *Hist. Eccles.*, II, 25, 6-8, Eng. trans. is from Lawlor and Oulton, vol. 1, p. 60.

67 See especially D. W. O'Connor, *Peter in Rome*, New York 1969.

68 As Raymond Brown shows, 'Episkopè and episcopos' in *Theol. Stud.* 41, pp. 322-38 (325), (1980).

69 See B. Carra de Vaux, 'Les Images de la papauté au cours des siècles' in *Lumière et Vie* 133, pp. 37-69 (43), (1977). C. Pietri, op. cit., vol. 2,

p. 1394, writes: 'The pope's prestige is especially valuable in very stormy times.'

70 It is interesting to follow this slow development in the thorough account of W. de Vries, op. cit.

71 B. Carra de Vaux, art. cit., pp. 48-9.

72 All that we have just written has been finely and simply said by R. Beaupère, 'Fragments du journal du pape Paul VII', in *Lumière et Vie* 133, pp. 112-16 (1977). Here are some extracts. 'The priority is not my personal primacy as pope but the primacy of the Church whose pastor I am. But why does Rome have this primacy? Let it not be said that it is a purely 'political' matter by which the civil order has instructed the ecclesiastical order, that the hierarchy of Christian sees has been traced from the hierarchy of metropolitanates in the Roman Empire. That in any case is very ancient history and since then much water has flowed under the bridges of the Tiber; a second Rome has risen on the shores of the Bosphorus and even a third in the borders of Muscovy. *Stat crux dum volvitur orbis* . . .

'There are other reasons for the choice of Rome. True, Rome was the capital, which was why Peter and Paul came there to follow through their apostolic course. The fact that the two apostles were martyred there gives a far more solid foundation to her primacy. I like the way St Irenaeus, the great bishop of Lyons, puts it. He says the Church of Rome was founded and established by the two very glorious apostles Peter and Paul, and that it is by virtue of this "more excellent origin" that all the other Churches must of necessity agree with her (*Adv. Haer.* III, 3, 2). The glory which Irenaeus attributes to Peter and Paul is evidently that of martyrdom. Our first brothers were not performing a meaningless gesture when they celebrated the Eucharist on the tomb of the martyrs. They were thereby affirming their conviction, which is still ours, that the giving of life up to the shedding of blood, for Christ and to some extent in conformity with him, is the full perfection of a Christian and that the Church is edified, in the strong sense of the word.

'Peter and Paul. The two together. Peter, the bearer of the word and coryphaeus of the twelve, the chief of the apostles. But also Paul, the outsider, the little runt whom Christ had caught up on the road to Damascus, had chosen from outside the tried paths, the 'charismatic' apostle.

'I have the impression that, for all the ancient and irrefutable witness to Paul's presence in Rome, Peter's personality has to some extent eclipsed him. It is most regrettable.

'They call me "successor to Peter", thereby making Peter the first bishop of Rome. But I am not sure that we ought not to go back to the view of Saint Irenaeus, for whom the first bishop of Rome was Linus, after the founders: Peter and Paul.

'The two apostles are in fact inseparable. Early iconography shows it.

You may see in the catacombs of St Sebastian and on the Appian Way invocations addressed to them both together. Think how, right up to the present, we have kept 29 June as the unique feast of the two apostles. If we have taken the next day, 30 June, to commemorate St Paul, it is, I believe, to make sure that Peter's personality does not eclipse that of the apostle to the Gentiles.'

73 For the terms *sedes, cathedra, thronos,* see Maccarrone, *Apostolicità* . . . , pp. 64-155.

74 *Episkope* is not synonymous with episcopate as a degree in the hierarchy brought about by the sacrament of Order. It indicates the duty of watching over the Christian community as a shepherd. The episcopate is one form of *episkope.*

75 Ignatius of Antioch, *Romans,* intro. See the note in T. Camelot (ed.), *SC* 10, p. 125.

76 P. Duprey, 'Brèves reflexions . . .', in *DC* 70, p. 30 (1973).

77 C. Hofstetter, art. cit., pp. 353-4.

78 G. Dix, *Jurisdiction in the Early Church, Episcopal and Papal* (London, reissued 1975), shows this very well.

79 See G. Bardy, 'L'Autorité du siège romain et les controverses . . .', p. 268. This is true even of Leo: 'Leo, Bishop, together with the Holy Synod gathered at Rome,' runs his letter to Theodosius condemning the Robber-synod of Ephesus (Ep. 44; *PL* 54, 827; see also Ep. 69; *PL* 54, 892).

80 French trans. is in *DC* 72, 1975, pp. 1001-11. See commentary by R. Tucci, ibid., pp. 1011-12.

81 Tucci, ibid., p. 1012. This raises the difficult problem of the cardinalate when those who hold the 'titles' of Roman parishes are bishops from other continents.

82 E. Lanne, 'Jusqu'à quel point . . .', p. 56. Also id., 'L'Église locale: sa catholicité et son apostolicité' in *Istina* 14, pp. 46-66 (53), (1969).

83 Nos. 88-91; *DC* 72, 1011 (1975).

84 Dix, op. cit., pp. 23-46.

85 id., ibid., pp. 41-6.

86 In Cyprian, *Epist.* VIII, 3; Hartel, p. 488. See G. Bardy, 'L'Autorité du Siège romain et les controverses . . .', p. 260. For Leo, *Epist.* 4.1, *PL* 54, 610B; also *Epist.* 167, pref., *PL* 54, 1201A-B.

87 Dix, op. cit., p. 42.

88 On this title see H. Leclerc, in *DACL* 15 (1950), pp. 1360-3.

89 See Y. Renouard, *La Papauté à Avignon,* p. 52, Paris 1969; Congar, 'Saint Paul et l'Autorite' . . .', p. 495. (*Coryphaei* are leaders of the chorus in ancient Greek comedy, and the word is applied by several of the Church Fathers to Peter and Paul—E.Tr.)

90 Deusdedit, Coll. Canon., Prol., ed. V. Wolf von Glanvell, 2.

91 John XXIII, *DC* 59, p. 1222 (1962).

92 *Hist. Eccles.* III, 2; III, 21 (Paul precedes Peter); IV, 1.

93 ibid., V, 28, 3.

94 *Epist.* 53, 1; *CSEL* 34/2, 153.

95 So 22, 23; see also 15, 18, 24, 25. For the history of the formula, see P. Batiffol, 'Petrus initium episcopatus' in *RSR* 4, pp. 440-53 (1924); P. Conte, *Chiesa e Primato*, Milan 1971; Y. M. J. Congar, 'Saint Paul et l'Autorité . . .'

96 *Sermo* 82, 7; *PL* 54, 428.

97 See Strotmann, art. cit., pp. 165-6.

98 See P. Batiffol, *L'Église naissante et le Catholicisme*, pp. 420-39, Paris 1911; id., *Cathedra Petri*, pp. 140-41, Paris 1938; G. Bardy, *La Théologie de l'Église de saint Irénée au concile de Nicée*, coll. *Unam Sanctam* 14, pp. 200-8, Paris 1947; M. Maccarrone, *Apostolicità, Episcopato* . . . , pp. 129-34.

99 See Batiffol's interpretation in *L'Église naissante* . . . , p. 435; id., *Cathedra Petri*, 140-41; compare that of P. de Labriolle, *Saint Cyprien, de l'Unité de l'Église catholique*, coll. *Unam Sanctam* 9, XVIII-XXX, Paris 1942.

100* See especially Dom J. Chapman, *Studies on the Early Papacy*, pp. 33-50, London 1928; M. Bevenot, *St Cyprian's de Unitate, chapter 4, in the light of the manuscripts*, Analecta Gregoriana 11, Rome 1937; Jalland, op. cit., pp. 161-9; P. de Labriolle, loc. cit. (Quotations which follow are taken from M. Bevenot's translation in ACW 25, London 1957. Cf. S. Greenslade in LCC 5—E.Tr.)

101 The text continues: 'The authority of the bishops forms a unity, of which each holds his part in its totality' (trans. Bevenot, loc. cit. Cf. trans. Greenslade, loc. cit., 'The episcopate is a single whole, in which each bishop's share gives him a right to, and a responsibility for, the whole.')

102 See J. Dupont, 'Le Logion . . .'; B. Rigaux, 'Die Zwölf in Geschichte und Kerygma' in *Der historische Jesus und der kerygmatische Christus*, pp. 468-86, Berlin 1960; J. Dupont, 'Le Nom d'Apôtres a-t-il été donné aux douze par Jésus?' in *L'Orient Syrien* 1, pp. 267-90, 425-44 (1956); L. Cerfaux, 'La Mission apostolique des douze et sa portée eschatologique' in *Mélanges E. Tisserand* I, pp. 43-66 (1964); id., 'Pour l'histoire du titre APOSTOLOS dans le Nouveau Testament' in *RSR* 48, pp. 78-92 (1960); R. Schnackenburg, 'L'Apostolicité: état de la recherche' in *Istina* 14, pp. 5-32 (1969); K. Rengstorff, 'Dodeka' in *TWNT* vol. 2, pp. 321-8 (1935); D. Muller and C. Brown, 'Apostle' in *New Testament Theology* I, pp. 126-37, Grand Rapids 1969.

103 See Y. M. J. Congar, 'Composantes et idée de la Succession apostolique' in *Oecumenica*, pp. 61-80 (62), (1966).

104 A point well stressed by J. Dupont, 'Le Logion . . .', and J. Zizioulas, 'La

continuité avec les origines apostoliques dans la conscience théologique des églises orthodoxes' in *Istina* 19, pp. 65–94 (1974).

105   J. Dupont, 'Le Logion . . .', p. 390. Conciliar statements about bishops as 'successors to the apostles' must therefore be interpreted to allow for many shades of meaning.

106   Dupont, loc. cit., p. 390, n. 2. See also the very concentrated pages in J. J. von Allmen, op. cit., pp. 74–9, who, despite keeping the vocabulary of succession, sees things in the same way as the author. He draws a most enlightening parallel between the Jesus–apostles link and the apostles–successors link. 'If for example someone entrusted with a mandate is unable because of death to complete that mandate, what becomes of the mandate? Should not the *shaliach*, the apostle, then hand over his mandate to someone in whom he has confidence; or is he to allow death, itself defeated at Easter, to interrupt, indeed to end his mandate? To put it more crudely, is the proclamation of the gospel, the gathering by baptism of the believers into the Church, the celebation of the Lord's Supper – to cease because those entrusted with them have died? Certainly not! On the contrary, the mandate must be continued right up to the parousia, that is to the moment when it will be handed back to Christ who gave it . . . Therefore I say that the messianic mandate, excluding what is unique in it (the substitutionary and victorious struggle with the devil, death and the world) is capable of transmission to the apostles, and that the mandate to the apostles – excluding what is unique (having been one of the authorized witnesses, chosen in advance, to Christ's resurrection) may be transmitted to the successors of the apostles. Indeed it must be so transmitted, for history goes on, for the parousia has not arrived.'

107   This has been well studied by G. Corti, *Il papa vicario di Pietro, contributi alla storia dell'idea papale*, Brescia 1966. See also M. Maccarrone, 'La Dottrina del Primato papale dal IV all' VIII secolo nelle relazioni con le Chiese occidentali' in *Le Chiese nei regni dell'Europa occidentale*, vol. 2, Spoleto 1960; id., *Apostolicità, episcopato . . .* , pp. 167–9; V. Monachino, 'La perennità del primato di Pietro in uno studio recente', in *Archivum historiae pontificiae* 5, pp. 325–39 (1967).

108   For Damasus, see Maccarrone, *Apostolicità, episcopato . . .* , p. 168: 'For Damasus as for Julius before him (337–52), it is the authority of Peter, stable and always at work in the Roman see, which puts the holder of that see in such a relationship with the apostle, that the steps which the bishop of Rome takes in ruling from the *cathedra Petri* may be attributed to the apostle.' For Siricius, text in *PL* 13, 1132; see E. Giles, op. cit., p. 142.

109   *Epist.* 12, 1; *PL* 20, 676.

110   Declaration of the legate Philip, Mansi 4, 1296.

111   *PL* 54, 743. See Giles, op. cit., p. 282 and note.

112   *Sermo* 5, 4; *PL* 54, 153–5.

113 *Sermo* 3, 2-3; *PL* 54, 145-6. We will return to the interpretation of P. A. McShane, *La Romanitas et le Pape Léon le Grand*, pp. 143-7, Desclée 1979.

114 Pietro Conte, *Chiesa e Primato nelle lettere dei Papi del Secolo VII*, esp. pp. 192-201, Milan 1971.

115 ibid., p. 193, note 192. The expression *successor Petri* occurs only once, from the pen of Eulogius of Alexandria.

116 ibid., p. 200. But Leo II has *successores apostolorum, scilicet Petro et Pauli*. An appendix lists references in the papal letters studied.

117 ibid., p. 359.

118 Mansi 11, 340 A, B.

119 Mansi 12, 1074 C: 'Per eundem Apostolum, cuius vel immeriti vices gerimus, sancta catholica et apostolica Romana Ecclesia usque hactenus et in aevum tenet principatum ac potestatis auctoritatem.'

120 *Registrum* III, 5-10 a; *PL* 148, 790; French trans. is from A. Fliche, *La Querelle des investitures*, pp. 73-4.

121 *PL* 148, 710. Attacks on the Church are attacks 'on the apostle Peter' (ibid., p. 708). Other examples in A. Fliche, *La Réforme Grégorienne*, vol. 2, coll. *Spicilegium sacrum Lovaniense* 9, pp. 194-5, note (1926).

122 Mansi 6, 972.

123 Mansi 11, 683-4 C, 711-12 B. See Y. M. J. Congar, 'Conscience ecclésiologique en Orient et en Occident du VIe au XIe siècle', in *Istina* 9, pp. 187-236 (220, note 128), (1965).

124 *PL* 214, 292 A. On this matter see esp. M. Maccarrone, *Vicarius Christi, storia del titolo papale*, Rome 1952.

125 *Controversia*, V, c. 4.

126 *Prima Controversia generalis* Liber III, *De Ecclesia militante*, caput 2.

127 For the liturgy since Vatican II, see M. Maccarrone, 'Il titolo papale di "vicarius Petri" nella Liturgia', in *Notitiae* 15, pp. 177-82 (1979). It is to be regretted that the new pontifical has changed *vicarius Petri* to *successor Petri*. See *De Ordinatione Diaconi, Presbyteri et Episcopi*, pp. 66, 108, Vatican 1968.

128 So *DC* 55 (1958), p. 1410; *DC* 60 (1963), p. 930.

129 J. J. von Allmen, op. cit., p. 79.

130 *Sermo* 295, 2-8; *PL* 38, 1349-52.

131 See J. Ludwig, *Die Primatworte Mt XVI, 18-19 in der altkirkliche Exegese*, coll. *Neutestamentliche Abhandlungen* XIX/4, Münster 1952; see also enlightening presentation of the evidence in A. Rimoldi, *L'Apostolo San Pietro*, coll. *Analecta Gregoriana* 96, Rome 1958.

132* Underlined by G. Dix, op. cit., pp. 117-22. On the scriptural evidence see R. E. Brown, K. P. Donfried and J. Reumann (ed.), *Peter in the New Testament*, London 1974, with extensive bibliography. See also O. Cullmann, *Peter: Disciple - Apostle - Martyr*, Eng. trans., SCM Press,

London 1953, a key work which provoked fruitful study even if its conclusions have been revised; id., 'L'Apôtre Pierre, instrument du diable et instrument de Dieu', in *New Testament Essays*, ed. A. J. B. Higgins, *Festschrift T. W. Manson*, pp. 98-103, Manchester 1959; B. Rigaux, 'Saint Pierre et l'exégèse contemporaine', in *Concilium* 27, pp. 129-52 (1967); J. J. von Allmen, *'La primauté de l'Église* . . . , pp. 61-91; R. Schnackenburg, 'Das Petrusamt; die Stellung des Petrus zu den anderen Aposteln', in *Wort und Wahrheit, Zeitschrift für Religion und Kultur*, 26, pp. 110-33 (1971); A. Brandenburg and H. J. Urban, *Petrus und Papst*, Münster 1977.

133 Translations are from E. Giles, op. cit., with notes.

134 See the evidence assembled by A. Rimoldi, op. cit.

135 *Peter in the New Testament*, p. 158.

136 ibid., p. 159. Cf. J. J. von Allmen, op. cit., p. 63.

137 *Peter in the New Testament*, p. 161.

138 J. J. von Allmen, op. cit., p. 69; see also pp. 73, 96.

139 Well expressed by von Allmen, ibid., p. 67.

140 See Raymond E. Brown, *The Community of the Beloved Disciple*, New York 1979, for the different understanding of the ministry in those communities which looked to the Johannine Gospel.

141 On the priority of Mark to Matthew, see especially *Peter in the New Testament*, pp. 83-101.

142 ibid., p. 160.

143 See esp. R. H. Fuller, *The Formation of the Resurrection Narratives*, p. 166, London 1972; *Peter in the New Testament*, pp. 86-8, 91.

144 *Peter in the New Testament*, pp. 88-9. The issue has been very carefully discussed by C. Kahler, 'Zur Form und Traditiongeschichte von Matth. XVI. 17-19', in *NTS* 23, pp. 36-58 (1976).

145 On this pericope see esp., for the Fathers, J. Ludwig, op. cit. and A. Rimoldi, op. cit. For exegesis, we pick out from the immense literature O. J. F. Seitz, 'Upon this Rock. A critical examination of Matt. 16, 16-19' in *JBL* 69, pp. 329-40 (1950); J. Kahmann, 'Die Verheissung an Petrus: Matt. 16, 18-19 im Zusammenhang des Matthäusevangeliums' in *L'Évangile selon Matthieu*, coll. *Bibliotheca Ephemeridum Theologicarum Lovaniensium* 29, pp. 261-80 (1972); C. Kahler, art. cit., very illuminating; A. Vögtle, 'Zum Problem der Herkunft von Matt. 16, 17-19' in *Orientierung an Jesus, Festschrift J. Schmid*, pp. 372-93, Freiburg 1973; P. Hoffman, 'Der Petrus Primat im Matthäusevangelium' in *Neuen Testament und Kirche, Festschrift R. Schnackenburg*, pp. 94-114, Freiburg 1974; J. Sell, 'Simon Peter's Confession and the Acts of Peter and the Twelve Apostles' in *Nov. Test.* 21, pp. 344-56 (1979); P. Lampe, 'Das Spiel mit dem Petrusnamen Matt. XVI. 18' in *NTS* 25, pp. 227-45 (1979). P. Benoît's study, 'La Primauté de Pierre dans le Nouveau Testament' in *Exégèse et Théologie*, vol. 2, pp.

250-84, Paris 1961, is important for its subtlety in handling the evidence. See also id., 'Saint Pierre d'après O. Cullmann', ibid., pp. 285-308.

146 *Retractationum* Book I, XXI, 1. Eng. trans. is from E. Giles, op. cit., p. 177.

147 As A. Rimaldi shows, op. cit., pp. 138-9.

148 *In Joh.* 124, 5; *PL* 35, 1973-4; *CC* 36, 685. Eng. trans. is from Marcus Dodds, *Works of Aurelius Augustine*, vol. XI, 2 (Edinburgh 1874), pp. 553-4.

149 *Tract. Mysteriorum* I, 10 (*CSEL* 65, 11-12) and *De Trinitate* 6, 21 (*PL* 10, 172). See also *Tract. in Ps.* 131 (*CSEL* 22, 663).

150 So *Epist.* 41, 2: 1 (*CSEL* 54, 312), 15, 2: 1 (ibid., 64); *Adv. Jovinianum* I, 26 (*PL* 23, 247); *In Matt.* 1,7: 26-8 (*PL* 26, 50-1), 16:18 (*PL* 26, 117).

151 *Sermo* IV, 2 (*PL* 54, 150). Also *Sermo* III, 2-3 (*PL* 54, 145-6); note emphasis placed on Peter's faith; also in this sense see *Epist.* 5, 2 (*PL* 54, 615).

152 *In Matt.* 54, 2 and 82, 3 (*PG* 58, 534, 741).

153 *Epist.* 77 (*PG* 83, 1249).

154 Thus *In transfiguratione Domini* (*PG* 96, 556).

155 *Les Homélies catéchétiques de Théodore de Mopsueste*, Homélie X, 16-18; French trans. is from R. Tonneau and R. Devreesse, coll. *Studi e Testi* 145, p. 271, Vatican 1949.

156 So *Adv. Eunomium* II, 4 (*PG* 29, 580) and *De Paenitentia* 4 (*PG* 31, 1481-4).

157 VI, 97-8; French trans. is from G. Tissot, in Ambrose of Milan, *Traité sur l'Évangile de saint Luc*, I, books I-VI, *SC* 45, pp. 264-5, Paris 1956.

158 *De Trinitate* II, 23 (*PL* 10, 66); VI, 36 (*PL* 10, 187).

159 Following the position established by R. H. Fuller, art. cit., and confirmed by the writers of *Peter in the New Testament*.

160 *Peter in the New Testament*, pp. 165-6.

161 Which underlines the note on the *TOB* on 22, 32.

162 See Gerald O'Collins, 'Peter as Easter Witness' in the *Heythrop Journal*, 22, pp. 1-18 (1981).

163 See U. Wilckens, *Resurrection*, pp. 112-13, Edinburgh 1977.

164 See J. Jeremias, article 'kleis' in *TWNT*, vol. 3, pp. 744-53; O. Cullman, *Peter* . . . pp. 201-6; S. Gero, 'The Gates or the Bars of Hades? A Note on Matthew 16, 18' in *NTS* 27, pp. 414-15 (1981); G. Bornkamm, 'Die Binde und Lösegewalt in der Kirche der Matthaeus' in *Die Zeit Jesu, Festschrift H. Schlier*, pp. 93-107, Freiburg 1970.

165 J. Jeremias, loc. cit., p. 750.

166 See O. Cullmann, op. cit., p. 203.

167 J. J. von Allmen, op. cit., p. 96.

168 See C. H. Dodd, *Historical Tradition in the Fourth Gospel*, pp. 347-9, Cambridge 1963, for the connection between the two traditions.

169 See esp. A. L. Deschamps, 'Paul, Apôtre de Jésus Christ' in *Paul de Tarse, apôtre de nos temps*, pp. 25-60, Rome 1979; R. Pesch, 'Peter in the mirror of Paul's letters', ibid., pp. 231-309; Salvatore Alberto Panimolle, 'L'Autorité de Pierre en Ga 1-2 et Ac 15', ibid., pp. 269-89; P. Bonnard, *L'Épître de saint Paul aux Galates*, pp. 37-43, Neuchâtel-Paris 1972; J. Dupont, 'Saint Paul, témoin de la collégialité apostolique et de la primauté de saint Pierre', in *La Collégialité épiscopale*, coll. *Unam Sanctam* 52, pp. 11-40 (17-35), Paris 1965.

170 See J. Dupont, 'Saint Paul, témoin de . . .', p. 32.

171 R. Pesch, art. cit., p. 309.

172 To use the expression of Philip A. McShane, op. cit., pp. 143, 146. The writer here follows W. Ullmann, 'Leo I and the theme of Papal Primacy' in *JTS* 11, pp. 25-51 (1960), who takes up the idea of K. D. Schmidt, 'Papa, Petrus ipse' in *Zeitschrift fur Kirchengeschichte* 54, pp. 267-75 (1935).

173 Expressions of P. A. McShane, op. cit., pp. 146-7. We do not follow the author in this explanation of Leo's thought, which fails to do him justice by making his outlook more rigid. Seen properly in the mainstream of tradition, Leo's notion of 'succession' is still essentially that of a 'vicariate'. If Peter still occupies his see, it is not because he has been 'reincarnated' in Leo. It is because Leo can only echo what has been established in Peter. He is no more than his 'vicar'.

174 *De Incarn.* IV, 32 (*PL* 16 826c).

Part 3   The Servant of Communion

1 *Epist.* 28, *PL* 54, 757; *Sermo* 89, 5, *PL* 54, 446.

2 The title of patriarch was found from AD 440 and was used at Chalcedon.

3 So *Epist.* 106, 5, *PL* 54, 1007; *Epist.* 119, *PL* 54, 1042; *Epist.* 129, *PL* 54, 1075-7.

4 *Epist.* 106, 2, *PL* 54, 1003; Epist. 104, 3, *PL* 54, 995.

5 *Epist.* 43, *PL* 54, 821.

6 Underlined by W. de Vries, *Orient et Occident, les structures ecclésiales vues dans l'histoire des sept premiers conciles oecuméniques*, pp. 136-49, Paris 1974. 'In one way we may say that the Council of Chalcedon marks a high point in the East's disposition to recognize the primacy of Rome'; 'The primacy of Rome was certainly affirmed more strongly at Chalcedon than at the other councils, but Rome was once again unable to enforce her claim to the absolute government of the Church. The other bishops had too strong a sense of collegiality for that', pp. 136, 139.

7   *Epist.* 114, *PL* 54, 852. It was a question of the letter confirming the Council of Chalcedon.

8   W. de Vries, op. cit., p. 136. The author shows no tendency to exaggerate the positive elements in Leo's government.

9   See ibid., pp. 156-60. Leo writes to Anastasius of Thessalonica: 'The care of the universal Church must centre on the unique chair of Peter, and nothing should be in disagreement with his direction' (*Epist.* 14, 11, *PL* 54, 676).

10 Philip A. McShane, *La Romanitas et le pape* . . . , pp. 301-3. This is clear in, for example, the story of Hilary of Narbonne. Leo wrote to the Gaulish bishops, 'We do not claim the right to ordain in your provinces . . . Indeed, our concern is to claim it for you . . . Let no one allow any presumptuous person the possibility of destroying your privileges' (*Epist.* 10, 9, PL 54, 636).

11 So *Epist.* 6, 5, *PL* 54, 619; *Epist.* 12, 9, *PL* 54, 662; *Epist.* 15, 17, *PL* 54, 690; *Epist.* 108, 1, *PL* 54, 1011.

12 See *Peter in the New Testament*, pp. 49-56.

13 For the meaning and origin of this expression, see P. Batiffol, 'Papa, sedes apostolica, apostolatus' in *Rivista di archeologia cristiana* 2, pp. 99-116 (1925); id., *Le Siège apostolique*, pp. 359-451, Paris 1924; id., *Cathedra Petri*, pp. 151-68; M. Maccarrone, *Apostolicità, episcopato* . . . , pp. 156-85.

14 Mansi 52, 338, for the intervention of Mgr de las Cases.

15 G. Sweeney, 'The Primacy: the Small Print of Vatican I' in *The Clergy Review* 59, pp. 96-121 (110), 1974.

16 As we have heard it publicly stated, since Vatican II, to justify current Catholic practice in naming the pope before the local bishop in the canon of the mass.

17 Mansi 52, 338.

18 Mansi 52, 678. See also Mgr Haynald (52, 668) and Cardinal Schwarzenberg (52, 95: 'How can we speak of a centre and a head while setting aside the rest of the hierarchy?').

19 As in Mgr Dinkel's intervention (Mansi 51, 734) or that of Cardinal Schwarzenberg (51, 733).

20 Mansi 52, 204.

21 Mansi 52, 135, 673-5.

22 Mansi, 52, 601-4.

23 Mansi 52, 385, 691-2.

24 Mansi 52, 678.

25 Mansi 52, 302-4.

26 Mansi 51, 930.

27 Mansi 51, 969, no. 71.

28 To adopt the expression of Mgr Gollmayr, bishop of Goritz (Mansi 51, 957).

29 See G. Thils, op. cit., summarized in G. Thils, 'Potestas ordinaria' in Y. M. J. Congar and B. D. Dupuy, *L'Épiscopat et l'Église universelle*, pp. 689–707. See also Umberto Betti, 'Natura e portata del primato del Romano Pontefice secundo il Concilio Vaticano' in *Antonianum* 34 (1959), pp. 161–244, 369–408.

30 Mansi 52, 1096 (see Mansi 53, 272 C) for Mgr Youssef and Mansi 52, 1114 D for Mgr Zinelli.

31 'To say that the exercise of the pope's universal jurisdiction cannot destroy the episcopate, etc., is in fact to lay down some form of limitation, of boundaries, whether or not such words are used': G. Thils, 'Potestas ordinaria', p. 703.

32 Text in *Constitutionis Lumen Gentium synopsis historica*, pp. 432, 456, Bologna 1975.

33 G. Thils, 'Potestas ordinaria', p. 693.

34 Mansi 52, 593 D–594 A. For the same Mgr David see Mansi 51, 955, no. 37. The same distinction was to be made by Mgr Dupanloup, 10 June 1870 (Mansi 52, 574) and by other Fathers.

35 Mansi 52, 541 A.

36 Mansi 52, 1105 B.

37 G. Thils, 'Potestas ordinaria', p. 702.

38 Mansi 52, 1105 C, D. The phrase '*non ad aedificationem sed ad destructionem*' is of great importance. It was used in full conciliar debate and came from the lips of Mgr Zinelli as he spoke in the name of the Deputation of the Faith itself before the final vote: 'Certe si summus pontifex . . . se ut ita dicam multiplicaret et quotidie, nulla habita ratione episcopi, ea quae ab hoc sapienter determinarentur destrueret: uteretur non in aedificationem sed in destructionem sua potestate' (Mansi 52, 1105 C, D). Its roots are very ancient: 'As John of Paris and Nicholas of Cusa wrote on several occasions, the papal power should be, in St Paul's phrase, *ad aedificationem non ad destructionem Ecclesiae*; Christendom must be watchful that it remains so', J. Lecler, *Le Pape ou le Concile? Une interrogation de l'Église mediévale*, p. 177, Paris 1973. We limit ourselves to two passages from the Dominican John of Paris (*c.* 1302): 'Papa non potest ad libitum detrahere bona ecclesiastica ita quod quidquid ordinet de ipsis teneat. Hoc enim verum esset si esset dominus, sed cum sit dispensator bonorum communitatis in quo requiritur bona fides, non habet sibi collatum potestatem super bonis ipsi nisi ad necessitatem vel utilitatem ecclesiae communis. Propter quod dicitur II ad Corinthos 13, 10 quod Deus dedit potestatem praelatis ad aedificationem non ad destructionem' (Tractatus de potestate regia et papali, ed. J. Lecler; *Jean de Paris et l'Ecclésiologie du XIIIe siècle*, p. 188, Paris 1942; 'Deus non dedit potestatem Petro

vel ministris ecclesiasticis ad ordinandum pro libito sed bona fide ad aedificationem et non ad destructionem' (ibid., p. 240).

39 Compare the bishop of Saint Augustine, Augustin Verot's intervention with Cardinal Capalti's reply, Mansi 52, 585-91: '*Non sumus in theatro ad audiendas scurras, sed sumus in ecclesia Dei viventis ad tractanda gravia ecclesiae negotia*'; see also Zinelli's replies to amendments proposed (ibid., pp. 1100-19, esp. 1103 C, 1105 D).

40 On this, see G. Thils, *La Primauté pontificale*, pp. 94-100, 131-7.

41 Mansi 52, 541 C.

42 See Mgr Smiciklas, Mansi 51, 969 A B.

43 Mansi 52, 668 D.

44 Mgr Gollmayr, Mansi 51, 957 B.

45 Mansi 52, 1105 B.

46 ibid., C-D.

47 There is good reason to believe that without it several men would not have assented. See the attitude of Mgr Dupanloup (Mansi 51, 956) from the time of the first 'observations', or of Mgr Krementz (51, 948). But Mgr Zinelli did not take up the suggestion, made by several participants, to speak of *utilitas* or *necessitas* for declaring legitimate the interventions of the bishop of Rome.

48 'Vani et futiles (parcant verbo) illi clamores, qui difficillime ut serii considerari possunt, ne si papae tribuatur perplena et suprema potestas, ipse possuit destruere episcopatum, qui jure divino est in ecclesia, possit omnes canonicas sanctiones sapienter et sancte ab apostolis et ecclesia emanatas susque deque evertere, quasi omnis theologia moralis non clamitet legislatorem ipsum subici quoad vim directivam, non quoad coactivam, suis legibus, quasi praecepta evidenter injusta, nulla et damnosa possent inducere obligationem nisi ad scandalum vitandum' (Mansi 52, 1109). It was in reply to Mgr Papp-Szilagyi and Mgr Guilbert (Mansi 52, 1091, 1092). He returned to the theme later in answering an amendment put by the Melchite patriarch Gregory Youssef: 'No sane person could suggest that the pope or a council could destroy (*destruere*) the episcopate or any other rights divinely determined in the Church' (Mansi 52, 1114 D).

49 The *modus* may be seen in Mansi 52, 1271-2.

50 Mansi 52, 1310.

51 Mansi 52, 338. See above, note 17.

52 To return to Mgr de las Cases's example.

53 These very important texts were published with noteworthy comments by Dom O. Rousseau, 'La vraie valeur de l'épiscopat dans l'Église, d'après d'importants documents de 1875', both in *Irénikon* 29 (1956), pp. 121-42, 143-50, and in Y. M. J. Congar and B. D. Dupuy, *L'Épiscopat et l'Église Universelle*, pp. 709-36. They are summarized

in J. M. R. Tillard, 'L'Horizon de la primauté de l'évêque de Rome' in *POC* 25 (1975), pp. 217-44. (Here they are translated from the French of Dom O. Rousseau—E.Tr.)

54 So Canon P. Cossa, cited in G. Thils, *La Primauté pontificale*, p. 20 (Latin text in a note).

55 Mansi 52, 5.

56 On this point see W. Dewan, 'Potestas vere episcopabilis' in *L'Épiscopat et l'Église universelle*, 661-87 (667-9), clarified further in id., 'Preparation of the Vatican Council's schema on the Power and Nature of Primacy' in *ETL* 36 (1960), pp. 30-7. Text in Mansi 53, 246.

57 So Mgr Haynald, bishop of Kalocsa (Mansi 52, 668), or Mgr de las Cases (52, 338), or Mgr Sola, bishop of Nice (52, 584).

58 See W. Dewan, 'Potestas vere episcopalis', pp. 661-5.

59 'Episcopis datum est tantum pascere qui in eis est gregem, scilicet determinatas partes gregis illis commissas.'

60 Mansi 52, 1104.

61 Mansi 53, 244.

62 So Zinelli in Mansi 52, 1109-10.

63 Mgr Ketteler of Mainz (Mansi 51, 934), Mgr Melchers of Cologne (51, 937), Mgr Krementz of Ermland (51, 948), Mgr Dupanloup of Orléans (51, 936).

64 Mansi 52, 598.

65 Mansi 52, 600; 52, 1082.

66 Mansi 52, 1102.

67 Mansi 52, 668.

68 Mansi 52, 1081; 52, 658-61.

69 Mansi 52, 1101.

70 Mansi 52, 627.

71 Several texts in G. Thils, *La Primauté pontificale*, pp. 228-9.

72 Mansi 52, 638-9 C.

73 See G. Alberigo's fine article 'La Juridiction' in *Irénikon* 49 (1976), pp. 167-80 (168, note 1).

74 This comes from the Council of Florence (*DS* 1307).

75 See G. Alberigo, art. cit., and id., *Lo Sviluppo della dottrina sui poteri nella Chiesa universale*, esp. pp. 69-101, Rome 1964.

76 A. Schmemann, 'The Idea of Primacy in Orthodox Ecclesiology' in *The Primacy of Peter* (Eng. trans. London 1963; 2nd edn 1973), p. 48, expresses well the desires of the other Churches: '. . . an objective study of the canonical tradition cannot fail to establish beyond any doubt that, along with local 'centres of agreement' or primacies, the Church had also known a universal primacy. The ecclesiological error of Rome lies not in the affirmation of her universal

primacy. Rather, the error lies in the identification of this primacy with 'supreme power' . . .' - from an Orthodox viewpoint. F. Heiler, cited by O. Karrer, 'La succession apostolique et la Primauté' in *Questions théologiques d'aujourd'hui*, takes up a similar position.

77* J. Hamer, *L'Église est une communion*, coll. *Unam Sanctam* 40, p. 38, Paris 1962. See also E. Lanne, 'L'Église locale: sa catholicité et son apostolicité' in *Istina* 14, pp. 46-66 (1969); J. M. R. Tillard, 'L'Église de Dieu est une communion' in *Irénikon* 53, pp. 451-68 (1980).

78 J. Zizioulas, 'La communauté eucharistique et la Catholicité de l'Église' in *Istina* 14, pp. 67-688 (78), (1969).

79 A. Schmemann, art. cit., here translated from the original French text, *La Primauté de Pierre dans L'Église Orthodoxe* (Neuchâtel-Paris 1960), p. 132. Cf. Eng. trans. in *The Primacy of Peter* (note 76 above), p. 40.

80 For Vatican II's well-known emphasis on eucharistic presidency see esp. *LG* 26, with further explanation in the Instruction *Eucharisticum Mysterium* of 25 May 1967 (Flannery, pp. 100-36), which explains the Constitution on the Liturgy.

81 This is attested by the *Apostolic Tradition* of Hippolytus, chapter 3. See also canon 4 of Nicaea (*Conciliorum Oecumenicorum Decreta*, 6). As J. Zizioulas writes, 'the fact that at least two or three bishops of neighbouring churches must take part in an episcopal ordination show at how deep a level the bishop's charge, and with it the eucharistic community in which his ordination takes place, is bound together with all the other eucharistic communities throughout the world' (art. cit., pp. 76-7).

82 J. Zizioulas, art. cit., p. 85.

83 ibid., p. 87.

84 On this problem see Mgr Leahy at Vatican I (Mansi 52, 638-9): 'Principle and centre of unity, are not these one and the same? Certainly. The Lord Christ is not only the principle of unity, he is also its centre; in him they are one and the same. However, the word principle does not convey the same notion or the same relations as *centrum unitatis*. For principle means properly principle of unity, that which is given in the very constitution of the Church, the relation of the sovereign pontiff to the members of the Church, while *centrum unitatis* signifies the relation of the members of the Church to the pontiff.' This reasoning is hardly convincing . . .

85 See T. I. Jimenez Urresti, *El Binomio Primado-Episcopado*, Bilbao 1962, esp. pp. 79-105 (we would qualify his arguments).

86 On this problem read G. Ghirlanda, *Hierarchica communio*, Rome 1980; id., 'De hierarchica communione ut elemento constitutivo officii episcopalis juxta Lumen Gentium' in *Periodica*, pp. 31-57 (1980); id., 'De notione communionis hierarchicae juxta Vaticanum secundum', in

ibid., pp. 41–68 (1981). Also G. Philips, *L'Église et son Mystère au IIe Concile du Vatican*, vol. 1 (Desclée 1967), pp. 277–90; Umberto Betti, *La Dottrina sull'episcopato nel Vaticano II*, pp. 290–96, Rome 1968. An English trans. of the Note is in Flannery, pp. 423–6.

87 G. Philips, op. cit., p. 289.

88 Mansi 51, 934, 936, 939, 941, 949, 957, 958, 960, 968, 969.

89 Mansi 52, 1109 C–1110.

90 See H. Wheeler Robinson, 'The Hebrew Conception of Corporate Personality' in *Zeitschrift für die alttestamentliche Wissenschaft* 66, pp. 49–61 (1936); R. Aubrey Johnson, *The One and the Many in the Israelite Conception of God*, Cardiff 1942; id., *The Vitality of the Individual in the Thought of Ancient Israel*, Cardiff 1949; J. de Fraine, *Adam et son lignage, études sur la notion de 'personnalité corporative' dans la Bible*, Desclée 1959.

91 H. H. Rowley, *The Rediscovery of the Old Testament*, p. 152, London 1945.

92 J. de Fraine, op. cit., p. 220.

93 Fully presented, with bibliography, in J. de Fraine, op. cit.

94 J. de Fraine, op. cit., p. 224, summarizes these positions. It is the insight behind René Girard's work.

95 Compare J. de Fraine, op. cit., pp. 202–17, with the well-known views of Augustine.

96 J. Zizioulas, op. cit., sets his eucharistic ecclesiology within this perspective from the start (esp. pp. 69–76).

97 Mansi 52, 1110, 1314.

98 See J. Zizioulas, 'Cristologia, pneumatologia e istituzioni ecclesiali: un punto di vista ortodosso', in *Cristianesimo nella storia*, 2, pp. 111–28 (1981).

99 Mansi 7, 9.

100 W. de Vries, op. cit., pp. 118–19.

101 Mansi 6, 972.

102 P. T. Camelot, 'Les Conciles oecuméniques des IV et V siècles' in *Le Concile et les Conciles*, pp. 45–73 (62, note 69), Paris 1960; also W. de Vries, op. cit., pp. 128–9, 140–3.

103 Mansi 7, 9.

104 P. T. Camelot, *Ephèse et Chalcédoine*, coll. *Histoire des Conciles oecuméniques*, 2, p. 146, Paris 1961. On the problem generally, see Y. M. J. Congar, 'La Primauté des quatre premiers conciles oecuméniques' in *Le Concile et les Conciles*, pp. 75–109.

105 *Epist.* 120, *PL* 54, 1046–7 (to Theodoret).

106 *Sermo* 24, 6, *PL* 54, 207; *Sermo* 46, 3, *PL* 54, 294; *Sermo* 72, 7, *PL* 54, 394; *Epist.* 59, 2, *PL* 54, 868; *Epist.* 124, 8, *PL* 54, 1068.

107 *Epist.* 104, 3, *PL* 54, 995; *Epist.* 105, 3, *PL* 54, 1000; *Epist.* 106, 2, *PL* 54, 1005; *Epist.* 165, 3, *PL* 54, 1159.

108 *Epist.* 104, 5, *PL* 54, 977; *Epist.* 106, 2, *PL* 54, 1003; *Epist.* 119, 2, 4, 5, *PL* 54, 1042, 1043, 1045; *Epist.* 127, 3, *PL* 54, 1075.

109 Mansi 11, 711-12 B.

110 W. de Vries, op. cit., p. 214 (citing Mansi 11, 636 D E).

111 See esp. V. Peri, 'Leone III e il Filioque' in *Rivista di Storia delle Chiesa in Italia* 25, pp. 3-58, (1971); id., 'Leone III e il Filioque, ancora un falso e l'autentico simbolo romano', in *Rivista di Storia e Letteratura Religiosa*, 6, pp. 245-74, with bibliography; id., 'Pro amore e cautela orthodoxae fidei; note sul ministero ecclesiale del Vescovo di Roma nella dottrina comune tra l'VIII et il IX secolo' in *Rivista di Storia e Letteratura Religiosa*, 12, pp. 341-63, (1976); B. Capelle, 'Le Pape Léon III et le Filioque' in *1054-1954, L'Église et les Églises; études et travaux offerts à dom Lambert Beauduin*, vol. 1, pp. 309-22, Chevetogne 1954.

112 *Mysterium Ecclesiae.*

113 See Philip A. McShane, op. cit., pp. 146-7 (but he reads the writings of Leo in the light of his own position concerning *succession*).

114 Paul VI, to the Secretariat for the Unity of Christians, 28 April 1967. Eng. trans. in E. J. Yarnold, op. cit., p. 66.

115 J. J. von Allmen, op. cit., p. 24.

116 F. Kramer, 'A Lutheran Understanding of Papal Primacy' in *Papal Primacy and the Universal Church*, Lutherans and Catholics in Dialogue V, pp. 127-33, Minneapolis 1974.

117 A. Schmemann, op. cit., p. 48.

118 J. Meyendorff, 'Il regionalismo ecclesiastico: per la communione o per il separatismo?' in *Cristianesimo nella storia* 2, pp. 295-310 (309), (1981).

119 *Epist.* 16, 2, *PL* 54, 698.

120 V. Peri, 'Pro amore . . .', 363, brings out the point well.

121 Thus *Epist.* 23, *PL* 54, 731; *Epist.* 24, *PL* 54, 736; *Epist.* 43, *PL* 54, 821.

122 V. Peri, 'Pro amore . . .', p. 363.

123 See A. Liégé, 'Encyclique' in *Catholicisme*, 3, pp. 114-17.

124 id., ibid., p. 115.

125 See esp. A. Vacant, *Le Magistère ordinaire de l'Église et ses organes*, Paris 1899; M. Caudron, 'Magistère ordinaire et Infaillibilité pontificale d'après le constitution *Dei Filius*' in ETL 36 (1960), pp. 393-431; P. Nau, 'Le Magistère pontificale ordinaire au premier Concile du Vatican' in RT 62 (1962), pp. 341-7; G. Thils, *L'Infaillibilité pontificale, source, conditions, limites*, pp. 176-86, Gembloux 1968. The question must be considered within the ample evidence assembled by

Y. M. J. Congar, 'Pour une histoire sémantique du terme *magisterium*', in *RSPT* 60 (1976), pp. 85-98; id., 'Bref historique des formes du *magistère* et de ses relations avec les docteurs', ibid., pp. 99-112.

126   Pius XII, *Humani Generis* AAS 46 (1954), pp. 314-15. Eng. trans., *False Trends in Modern Teaching*, CTS (rev. edn 1959), no. 20, p. 11.

127   And by more reliable means than the *Osservatore Romano*, especially since its translations into other languages often fail to do justice to the finer shades of meaning in the original.

128   Dating from 1929, this saying appeared in French in *Le Messager orthodoxe*, 1959 and 1960. See esp. no. 8 (1959), pp. 16-17.

129*   Treatments of infallibility from the present point of view are: G. Thils, *L'Infaillibilité pontificale*...; *Église infaillible ou intemporelle?*, coll. *Recherches et Débats* 79, Paris 1973; E. Schillebeeckx, 'Le Problème de l'infaillibilité ministérielle' in *Concilium* 83 (1973), pp. 83-102; Y. M. J. Congar, 'Après *Infaillible?* de Hans Küng: bilans et discussions' in *RSPT* 58 (1974), pp. 243-52; H. Küng: *Infallible?*, Eng. trans., Collins, London 1971.

130   Mansi 6, 972; Mansi 7, 117, 169.

131   *Mysterium Ecclesiae*, cited above, is sensitive to these limits.

132   Mansi 52, 1213-14. See comments by G. Thils, *L'Infaillibilité*..., pp. 176-9, 186-221.

133   M. Maccarrone, *Apostolicità, episcopato*..., p. 165.

134   See esp. H. Fries, 'Ex sese, non ex consensu Ecclesiae', in *Volk Gottes, Festgabe J. Hofer*, pp. 480-500, Munich 1967.

135   Text in *DTC* 4, p. 197.

136   Mansi 52, 1215.

137   ibid.

138   In his encyclical letter of 1849, *Ubi Primum*, Pius IX felt that the moment had come to intervene and asked the bishops to inform him about the devotion of the clergy and the faithful as well as about their wish for the promulgation of a decree on 'the Immaculate Conception of Mary'. The bull *Ineffabilis* of 8 December 1854, following long discussions, set the *perpetuus Ecclesiae sensus* well to the fore. It began with a 'tradition of practice' - that which had been shown by the faithful and their pastors - and went on to show how this rested on a 'tradition of doctrine' to which the Fathers and other ecclesiastical writers bore witness. The same proceedings were put in hand, though more explicitly, for the definition of the Assumption. In his letter *Deiparae Virginis* of 1 May 1946, Pius XII asked the bishops to let him know 'what devotion to the Assumption of the most blessed Virgin Mary the clergy and the people committed to their government, each in measure to his faith and piety, bring'; and what, in union with their clergy and people, the bishops themselves thought about a dogmatic definition of this point. He later justified the action he took by the

demands of the Christian people. The Allocution to the Consistory on 30 October 1950 is even clearer. 'We have addressed letters to all the bishops asking them to reveal to Us not only their own opinions but also the opinions and the wishes of their clergy and people. In splendid and almost unanimous chorus, the voices of pastors and faithful throughout the entire world reached Us, professing the same faith and requesting the same thing as sovereignly desired by all . . . As the entire Catholic Church can neither make a mistake nor be deceived since her divine Founder, who is Truth himself, said to his apostles, "Behold, I am with you always, even to the end of the world", it must follow that the truth of the Assumption firmly believed by pastors and people is divinely revealed and may be defined by Our supreme authority.' The bull *Munificentissimus Deus* of 1 November 1950 often appealed to this conviction shared by pastors and faithful: 'This remarkable agreement of bishops and the catholic faithful (*haec singularis catholicorum Antistitum et fidelium conspiratio*) who consider that the bodily Assumption to heaven of the Mother of God may be defined as a dogma of faith, since it offers Us the agreement between the teaching of the ordinary magisterium of the Church and the responding faith of the Christian people upheld and guided by the same magisterium (*cum concordem Nobis praebeat ordinarii Ecclesiae Magisterii doctrinam concordemque christiani populi fidem*), thus shows itself in a manner quite certain and free from every error that this privilege is a truth revealed from God and contained in the divine deposit which Christ committed to his Bride, so that she should guard it faithfully and make it known in an infallible manner.'

139 Y. M. J. Congar, *Sainte Église*, coll. *Unam Sanctam* 41, p. 311, Paris 1963.

140 ibid.

141 See J. Ratzinger, *Das zweite Vatikanische Konzil*, I in *LTK*, pp. 348-57 (356-7).

142* See J. M. R. Tillard, 'Le *Sensus Fidelium*, réflexion théologique' in *Foi populaire et foi savante*, coll. *Cogitatio fidei* 87, Paris 1976, pp. 9-40; M. Seckler, 'Glaubenssin', in *LTK*, vol. 4, pp. 945-8 (biblio), Freiburg 1960; B. van Leeuwen, 'La Participation universelle à la fonction prophétique du Christ', in *L'Église de Vatican II*, coll. *Unam Sanctam* 51b, vol. 2, pp. 425-55 (445-9), Paris 1965.

143 See *DC* 78, 198, 537-50.

144 On 'reception' see especially two articles by Y. M. J. Congar, 'La Réception comme réalité ecclésiologique' in *RSPT* 56, pp. 369-403 (1972); id., 'Quod omnes tangit ab omnibus tractari et approbari debet' in *Rev. hist. du droit français et étr.*, 36, pp. 210-59 (1958). One should read also, on the precise problem of the 'reception' of councils, P. Fransen, 'L'autorité des conciles', in *Problèmes de l'autorité*, coll. *Unam Sanctam* 38, pp. 59-100, Paris 1962, and the interesting

collection in German and English, *Councils and the Ecumenical Movement*, World Council Studies 5, Geneva 1968. Also A. Grillmeier, '*Konzil und Reception, methodische Bemer Kungen zu einem Thema der ökumenischen Diskussion*' in *Theol. u. Phil.* 45, pp. 321-52 (1970). For Chalcedon, see the report 'Le Concile de Chalcédon, son histoire, sa réception par les Églises et son actualité' in *Irénikon* 44, pp. 349-66 (1971), together with *The Ecumenical Review* 22, pp. 348-423 (1970). All this may be considered in terms of the infallibility of the Church as such, very well presented by G. Thils, '*L'Infaillibilité du peuple chrétien "in credendo"*, *Notes de théologie post-tridentine*', Paris-Louvain 1963.

145 To quote P. Camelot's phrase, 'Les Conciles oecuméniques des . . .', p. 63.

146 *Epist.* 119, 4, *PL* 54, 1043-5.

147 *Epist.* 104, 3, *PL* 54, 995.

148 *Epist.* 106, 5, *PL* 54, 1007.

149 *Epist.* 119, 4, *PL* 54, 1044.

150 *Epist.* 10, 2, *PL* 54, 629-30.

151 On this expression, see H. Leclercq, in *DACL.*, 15 (1950), pp. 1360-3.

152 Underlined by T. I. Jimenez Urresti, op. cit., p. 95.

153 On these points see J. M. R. Tillard, 'La Primauté romaine . . .', pp. 304-20.

154 *Ordo Missae cum populo*, nos. 19, 20, 21.

155 *Ritus servandus in concelebratione Missae*, pp. 62, 69.

156 See T. I. Jimenez Urresti, op. cit., p. 92.

157 See especially J. Ratzinger in Herbert Vorgrimler, *Commentary on the Documents of Vatican II* (Herder & Herder 1966), pp. 297-305.

158 See G. Thils, *La Primauté pontificale*, pp. 196-8.

159 Thus *Epist.* 4, 1-5, *PL* 54, 611-14; *Epist.* 12, 1, *PL* 54, 645-6.

160 So *Epist.* 14, 5, *PL* 54, 673.

161 F. X. Wernz, *Jus canonicum*, vol. 2, no. 578 (edn 1943), p. 725, cited by G. Thils, op. cit., p. 197.

162 On the notion of subsidiarity see above all W. Bertrams, 'De principio subsidiaritatis in jure canonico' in *Periodica* 46, pp. 3-65 (1957); id., *Quaestiones fundamentales Juris Canonici*, pp. 545-62, Rome 1969; O. Karrer, 'Le Principe de subsidiarité dans l'Église' in *L'Église de Vatican II*, vol. 1, coll. *Unam Sanctam* 51b, Paris 1966, pp. 575-606; R. Metz, 'La Subsidiarité, Principe régulateur des tensions dans l'Église' in *Rev. de Droit Canon*, 22 (1972), pp. 155-76; G. Thils, *La Primauté pontificale*, pp. 239-45.

163 *Epist.* 124, *PL* 54, 1062-8.

164 *Epist.* 12, 7, *PL* 54, 653; *Epist.* 15, 17, *PL* 54, 690-2.

165 See Philip A. McShane, op. cit., p. 305.

166 ibid., p. 306.

167 See V. Peri, '*Pro amore* . . . (see note 111 above), taking up an intervention made during the important colloquy at Gazzada on 'the meaning of the Roman primacy for the Eastern Churches between Chalcedon and Photius'); V. Grumel, 'Quelques témoignages byzantins sur la primauté romaine' in *Échos d'Orient*, pp. 34, 322-30 (1931), esp. pp. 432-7; see also P. O'Connell, *The Ecclesiology of St Nicephorus I, 758-828, Patriarch of Constantinople, Pentarchy and Primacy*, coll. *Orientalia Christiana Analecta* 194, Rome 1972; on the pentarchy, see esp. Dom H. Marot's study, 'Note sur la Pentarchie' in *Irénikon* 32, pp. 436-42 (1959); C. Vogel, 'Unité de l'Église et Pluralité des formes historiques d'organisation ecclésiastique du IIe au Ve siècle', in *Épiscopat et Église Universelle*, coll. *Unam Sanctam* pp. 39, 591-638, Paris 1962.

168 J. Meyendorff, *L'Église orthodoxe hier et aujourd'hui*, pp. 171-2, Paris 1969.

169 See V. Peri, 'Pro amore . . .', p. 342.

170 John of Jerusalem, *PG* 95, 332 CD; V. Peri, 'Pro amore . . .', p. 343.

171 *PG* 100, 597 C; V. Peri, 'Pro amore . . .', pp. 342-3.

172 V. Peri, 'Pro amore . . .', p. 344. See also id., *I Concili e le Chiese*, pp. 44-8, Rome 1965.

173 See esp. V. Peri, *I Concili e le Chiese*, pp. 21-4; id., 'Pro amore . . .', pp. 345-6; text in Mansi 13, 208-9.

174 V. Peri, 'Pro amore . . .', pp. 346-7. Compare with W. de Vries, op. cit., pp. 231-2, 237-9.

175 *PG* 100, 1144 B C; V. Peri, 'Pro amore . . .', p. 348. See also the passages of Theodore the Studite cited by S. Salaville, 'La Primauté de saint Pierre et du pape' in *Échos d'Orient*, pp. 17, 23-42 (1914-15) (a tendentious article, it must be said).

176 *PG* 100, 597 A B; V. Peri, 'Pro amore . . .', p. 349.

177 W. de Vries, op. cit., pp. 238-9.

178 V. Peri, 'Pro amore . . .', p. 351.

179 Well emphasized in V. Peri's analysis, ibid., p. 352.

180 Mansi 51, 934 C.

181 *PL* 77, 933.

NOTES - ADDENDA

The following is a list of English versions of articles already cited in French versions in the asterisked notes above.

Part 1

3   Emmanuel Lanne, 'To what extent is Roman primacy unacceptable to the Eastern Churches?', in *Concilium* VII, 4, pp. 62-7, 1971.

23   See E. Lanne, 'United Churches or Sister Churches? A Choice to be Faced', in *One in Christ* XII, 2, pp. 106-23, 1976, translated for *Irenikon* 3 (1975), pp. 322-42.

64   See J. M. R. Tillard, 'The Horizon of the "Primacy" of the Bishop of Rome', in *One in Christ* XII, 1, pp. 5-33, 1976.

104 See . . . Hilaire Marot, 'The Primacy and the Decentralization of the Early Church', in *Concilium* 1, pp. 9-16, September 1965.

107 Marot, art. cit.

108 See J. F. McCue, 'Roman Primacy in the First Three Centuries', in *Concilium* VII, 4, pp. 36-44, 1971; W. de Vries, 'Theoretical and Practical Renewals of the Primacy of Rome: I The Development after Constantine', ibid., pp. 45-53; 'II From the Middle Ages to the Gregorian Reform', ibid., pp. 54-61.

Part 2

100 . . . P. de Labriolle, loc. cit. (See also G. S. M. Walker, *The Churchmanship of St Cyprian*, London 1968, pp. 19-32. Quotations . . .)

132 . . . B. Rigaux, 'St Peter in Contemporary Exegesis', in *Concilium* III, 7 (3), pp. 72-86, September 1967 . . .

Part 3

77   J. Hamer, *The Church is a Communion*, London 1964 (Eng. tr.); J. M. R. Tillard, in *One in Christ* XVII, 2, pp. 77-94, 1981 (Eng. tr.).

129 . . . E. Schillebeeckx, 'The Problem of the Infallibility of the Church's Office: a theological reflection', in *Concilium* IX, 3, pp. 77-94, 1973.

142 See also J. M. R. Tillard, 'Sensus Fidelium', in *One in Christ* X, 1, pp. 2-29, 1975.

Index